South Asia Economic and Policy Studies

The Series aims to address evolving and new challenges and policy actions that may be needed in the South Asian Region in the 21st century. It ventures niche and makes critical assessment to evolve a coherent understanding of the nature of challenges and allow/facilitate dialogue among scholars and policymakers from the region working with the common purpose of exploring and strengthening new ways to implement regional cooperation. The series is multidisciplinary in its orientation and invites contributions from academicians, policy makers, practitioners, consultants working in the broad fields of regional cooperation; trade and investment; finance; economic growth and development; industry and technology; agriculture; services; environment, resources and climate change; demography and migration; disaster management, globalization and institutions among others.

Arindam Banik • Sahana Roy Chowdhury
Dona Ghosh

Extraordinary Health Hazards and their Socio-Economic Effects in South Asia

What have we Learnt from COVID-19

Springer

Arindam Banik
ICCR's Chair Professor of Indian Studies (Economics)
Samarkand State University, named after Sharof Rashidov
Samarkand, Uzbekistan

Sahana Roy Chowdhury
IMI Kolkata
Kolkata, West Bengal, India

Dona Ghosh
Management
Thiagarajar School of Management
Madurai, Tamil Nadu, India

ISSN 2522-5502 ISSN 2522-5510 (electronic)
South Asia Economic and Policy Studies
ISBN 978-981-95-5728-8 ISBN 978-981-95-5729-5 (eBook)
https://doi.org/10.1007/978-981-95-5729-5

This Springer imprint is published by the registered company Springer Nature Singapore Pte Ltd.
The registered company address is: 152 Beach Road, #21-01/04 Gateway East, Singapore 189721, Singapore

To Amitayus, Ahana, Aum
We believe the world is on the brink of change, and South Asia will experience a profound transformation with it. We have faith in your ability to be the guiding light for this region's future. Your dedication and vision inspire hope, and we are excited to see the positive impact you will make.

Preface and Acknowledgments

The COVID-19 pandemic has heralded a transformative era, unveiling a cascade of profound and lasting effects that have echoed across the globe, fundamentally reshaping socio-economic landscapes in ways never previously witnessed. These alterations have manifested uniquely in different countries and regions, underscoring stark contrasts in their responses and the resulting outcomes. Particularly striking is the variation in fatality rates linked to COVID-19, which have illustrated significant disparities between nations burdened by high levels of poverty and inequality. This variation can be attributed to a multitude of factors, including the inadequacies of healthcare infrastructure, demographic characteristics of populations, and the relative success of vaccination campaigns, with emphasis on the implementation of the BCG vaccine. Given the intricate web of circumstances that have unfolded, it becomes imperative to conduct a thorough and nuanced analysis of the diverse scenarios that emerged during the pandemic. This analysis should encompass a detailed examination of the range of interventions that were deployed and their varying degrees of effectiveness, particularly within the framework of South Asian economies. Such an investigation will delve into the demand and supply dynamics of the healthcare systems currently in place across South Asia, offering a clearer understanding of the challenges encountered and the strategies employed to mitigate the pandemic's impact. To achieve this, a comprehensive evaluation of health sector interventions is essential, focusing on critical elements such as vaccine-related policies and the enhancement of health infrastructure. Moreover, it is crucial to assess how effectively these interventions were executed during the pandemic, considering the nuances of their implementation, administration, and monitoring. This careful scrutiny is vital for ensuring that these policies yield significant and enduring impacts. Four overarching pillars or objectives warrant meticulous examination. First, it is essential to explore the pre-pandemic economic and socio-economic structures of South Asian economies that laid the groundwork for their performance during the crisis. Second, we should evaluate the quality and scale of the interventions undertaken in response to the pandemic. Third, understanding performance from various perspectives across the multiple waves of the COVID-19 crisis is necessary for drawing informed conclusions. Lastly, attention must be paid to the preparations for adaptive mitigation strategies, including the development of effective health insurance schemes. Such initiatives are crucial for safeguarding these economies against the devastating economic fallout associated with health crisis-induced poverty, fostering greater resilience to confront future challenges.

Numerous international agencies, including the United Nations, have highlighted in their report titled (United Nations, 2021) that the pandemic has dramatically transformed South Asia from a growth leader to the most poorly performing region. This stark change is evidenced by a decline in economic growth from 3.1% in 2019 to a staggering −8.6% in 2020. The setbacks extend beyond mere economic figures, with the region experiencing sluggish progress on various Sustainable Development Goals (SDGs), particularly in education (SDG-4), access to clean drinking water and sanitation (SDG-6), and energy availability (SDG-7). The existing deficiencies in health infrastructure further exacerbated the situation, marking the region as a hotspot for pandemic-related crises.

In response to these immense challenges, many South Asian economies employed a range of unconventional strategies to address the urgent consequences of the pandemic in both the short and medium term. Countries in this region implemented containment strategies and lockdown measures with a level of control and timeliness that stood out globally. According to the World Bank's report (World Bank 2021*)*, the average stringency of these measures was notably high at 71 out of 100, compared to a global average of 66. While some nations saw effective outcomes from these initiatives, others struggled to manage the toll of COVID-19 fatalities. This disparity is often attributed to the variations in health infrastructure, existing policies, and administrative capabilities before the pandemic.

It is essential to highlight that a substantial percentage of COVID-19 cases recorded in developing Asia can be traced back to South Asia. The consequences of the pandemic reached far beyond mere health concerns; they ignited a sweeping economic crisis characterised by plummeting consumer demand and significant disruptions within supply chains. This upheaval contributed to an alarming nearly 30 per cent reduction in global output linked to the challenges faced by developing Asia. Countries heavily reliant on tourism in South Asia saw a dramatic decline in service sectors' role in their economic landscapes and international trade. Nonetheless, amidst this turbulent and challenging period, a select few nations stood out as exceptions, showcasing resilience and adaptability in the face of adversity.

In response to the unprecedented challenges posed by the COVID-19 pandemic, many countries adopted expansionary monetary policies, significantly increasing government expenditures, particularly within the health sector. This surge in spending, however, led to a rise in national debts, creating a complicated financial landscape. In contrast, countries that implemented well-calibrated fiscal consolidation measures found a way to navigate the turmoil effectively. They achieved their essential targets during the pandemic while maintaining a sense of budgetary discipline, demonstrating the importance of strategic financial planning in crises. Amid these economic trials, some noteworthy similarities emerged across different performance indicators. For example, the agricultural sector displayed remarkable resilience, continuing to thrive despite the widespread disruptions caused by the pandemic. However, the development implications of these economic outcomes were stark, as they highlighted the deepening issues of poverty, significant job losses, and the alarming rise in the number of working poor, all exacerbated by the crisis. Within this context, exploring synergistic opportunities by integrating healthcare frameworks across South Asian regions proved pivotal. Numerous studies have been conducted to analyse COVID-19 performance on global and regional scales, examining various country interventions and the economic aftershocks resulting from the pandemic. Nonetheless, this crisis has revealed not only shared experiences but also many unique challenges across different regions, complicating the ability of policymakers to learn from one another and craft effective, customised interventions. A significant barrier to meaningful international comparisons has been the scarcity of quality data, which hampers the ability to draw robust conclusions. From a developmental perspective, the South Asian region has made weak progress toward achieving several Sustainable Development Goals (SDGs), particularly in areas such as education (SDG-4), access to drinking water and sanitation (SDG-6), and energy (SDG-7). This deficit in quality and accessible health infrastructure rendered the region particularly vulnerable during the pandemic, turning it into a hotbed of challenges. It is crucial to recognise that evaluating a country's pandemic performance and vulnerabilities requires a holistic approach. Judging solely based on policy interventions enacted during the pandemic overlooks the significant influence of pre-existing socio-economic configurations and the prevailing conditions within those countries. These foundational factors have played a crucial role in how nations coped with the unprecedented economic shock, particularly concerning issues like poverty during the COVID-19 crisis.

The concept of the Demand Side within the health care system emerged as a crucial response to the pressing need in developing countries to enhance access to and utilisation of health services, particularly for low-income individuals. In South Asia, the economic impacts of the COVID-19 pandemic led to widespread job losses, leaving many people without employer-sponsored health benefits that previously served as their safety net. To address this gap, some governments have implemented universal health insurance schemes. However, these initiatives have fallen short of achieving their intended outcomes. They have struggled to adequately address the critical shortages on the supply side of health care, especially concerning the availability of doctors and hospital facilities. Furthermore, a significant portion of the population remains uninsured, unable to afford health insurance products available in the market, leaving them vulnerable and without coverage throughout their lives. This highlights the urgent need to shift our focus towards innovative demand-side solutions in South Asian economies. Emphasising critical areas such as regulation, accessible transportation, sustainable insurance models, and compelling price controls is essential for creating a more equitable healthcare landscape. It is equally important to acknowledge that doctors and support staff in government hospitals often bear the brunt of criticism for systemic lapses. These instances of alleged negligence are frequently sensationalised by politicians, diverting attention from the root issues of supply shortages and systemic inefficiencies. The discrepancies between healthcare demand and supply are stark and often lead to the denial of necessary care for many individuals. To address these challenges, it is vital to develop regulatory frameworks that are both sophisticated and minimalistic, ensuring they do not stifle innovation and growth in the healthcare sector under the guise of preventing malpractice. For example, while price controls seem straightforward, they often result in unintended consequences such as shortages, compromised quality, or inflated costs in other essential areas. Instead of rectifying the supply-side challenges, they may exacerbate the problems they aim to solve. A prevailing argument suggests fostering transparency and healthy competition within the healthcare market could lead to a comprehensive price reduction. This approach would not only enhance the overall quality of care. Still, it could also significantly bolster India's burgeoning medical tourism sector, promising job creation and economic growth opportunities.

There is a shortage of doctors in South Asia, and those that exist seldom venture beyond urban areas. This issue significantly contributes to the region's disproportionately high out-of-pocket healthcare expenses exceeding 80%. A primary factor behind this shortage is the underwhelming performance of the Medical Council of India (MCI), which has maintained stringent control over the licencing of doctors and their scope of practice. In recognition of this deficiency, the government has proposed a bill to disband the MCI, liberate medical education from restrictive regulations, and implement an exit exam at the undergraduate level. However, one aspect of the supply-side issue that has been overlooked is the integration of experienced nurses into roles with greater responsibility for patient care. To address supply shortages, the region must leverage its skilled nursing workforce. Additionally, the gaps in rural healthcare can only be adequately addressed by governmental action. National health policies aim to gradually increase healthcare spending from the current 3.27% of GDP, with most of the additional funding directed towards enhancing healthcare provision in rural areas and for underserved urban populations. As with many other sectors, healthcare requires a broader array of options, including increased supply and competition.

Trade-in health services have garnered significant policy interest in recent years across many developing regions, particularly in South Asia. Several factors have contributed to the growth of these services in the area. Improvements in travel, information, and communication technology enable patients to seek higher-quality treatment at lower costs, especially from India. This trend has created an opportunity for a greater demand for portable health insurance coverage, both public and private, as patients become increasingly mobile.

However, there is a notable lack of substantial research on the role and impact of trade in health services within South Asian economies. Understanding the interaction between the demand for and supply of health services in this context is essential. Various organisations and groups play significant roles in this industry. Factors such as treatment processes (including considerations of quality, safety, and risk) and the system-level implications for countries of origin and destination (financial issues, as well as the impact on providers and professionals from cross-border trade in the health sector) are essential to consider. Research indicates a considerable arbitrage opportunity for local professionals and service providers due to the existing demand and supply gaps—barriers defined by Modes 3 and 4 need to be addressed to enhance economic welfare. Establishing a regional skills council to standardise skills will be pivotal in leveraging these arbitrage opportunities. Once these barriers are identified, investments can be encouraged. This would also involve facilitating the movement of natural persons by simplifying visa processes, providing favourable work permits, and addressing dual taxation, among other issues. Such measures can create a win-win situation, leading to economic welfare gains in the region.

Several significant policy implications emerge regarding integrating the healthcare system in South Asia. Firstly, India holds a competitive advantage in the cross-border provision of health services, attributed to its extensive pool of trained and skilled professionals, mainly through modes 1 and 2. Enhancing the cross-border supply of services in these areas could strengthen regional service trade flows, benefiting member countries and their skilled populations. Secondly, to improve service trade under mode 3 (commercial presence), South Asian nations should consider liberalising Foreign Direct Investment (FDI) and establishing transparent domestic regulations for health services. Such reforms and liberalisation efforts could attract increased FDI to the region. Lastly, South Asia is a significant exporter of services through the movement of natural persons (mode 4). The healthcare sector in the area is organised into four primary levels of care: primary, secondary, tertiary, and quaternary. India demonstrates a comparative advantage in exporting services at the secondary, tertiary, and quaternary levels through mode 4. By liberalising this mode, potential imbalances may be minimised, thereby facilitating the free movement of natural persons.

There are growing concerns that the educational standards in the region are insufficient to effectively integrate new entrants into the workforce. This disparity in educational attainment presents a significant obstacle to fully exploiting the potential benefits of technology spillovers within the health sector across South Asian economies. By comprehensively analysing these educational deficiencies and their implications, stakeholders can formulate targeted strategies aimed at enhancing skill development initiatives. These efforts could significantly elevate the overall performance of the labour force, which, in turn, would facilitate a more dynamic environment for technology transfer and foster innovation within healthcare systems.

The authors wish to express their heartfelt gratitude to Springer Nature for their steadfast trust and support throughout the challenges encountered during this endeavour. The first author also extends appreciation to ICCR, the Ministry of External Affairs, the Government of India, and Ms. Smita Pant, the ambassador of the Indian Embassy in Tashkent, for her encouragement and assistance in writing this book. Special thanks are owed to Professor Alimdjan Rakhimovich Khalmukhamedov, Rector of Samarkand State University; Professor Akhatov Akmal Rustamovich, Vice Rector of International Cooperation; and Dr Ibodilla Ximmatov of Samarkand State University in Uzbekistan for their invaluable support at various stages of the project. The second author would like to thank Dr. Aishwarya Harichandan, Faculty of Economics, IIM Sirmaur, for her research assistance in writing part of the chapters of this book.

The authors are also grateful to their families, as this book project has been an extensive and transformative journey, filled with both triumphs and obstacles, during which the authors' families have also encountered their share of challenges. The authors would like to convey their heartfelt appreciation to Mousumi (the first author's loving wife), Arijit (the second author's supportive husband), Chandril Bhattacharyya (the third author's encouraging husband), Amitayus (the first author's spirited son), Ahana (the second author's inspiring daughter), and Aum Bhattacharyya (the third author's supportive son) for their steadfast encouragement and remarkable patience throughout the emotional fluctuations and creative process of writing.

Samarkand, Uzbekistan — Arindam Banik
Kolkata, India — Sahana Roy Chowdhury
Madurai, India — Dona Ghosh

Contents

About the Authors

Arindam Banik is an Indian economist. He is the ICCR's Chair of Indian Studies (Economics) at Samarkand State University, named after Sharof Rashidov, Samarkand, Uzbekistan, appointed by the Indian Council for Cultural Relations, Ministry of External Affairs, Government of India. He earned his PhD at the Delhi School of Economics, University of Delhi, in 1994 and pursued post-doctoral research at Alliance Manchester Business School, the University of Manchester, United Kingdom. He was a distinguished professor and the Associated Cement Companies Chair in International Finance and Business at the International Management Institute, New Delhi. He teaches Digital Economy, Development Economics, and International Finance and Business at Samarkand State University. Taught Macroeconomics, International Finance and Business, Micro and Managerial Economics, Project Appraisal, Social Cost and Benefit Analysis, and Development Economics at the Department of Economics at the University of the West Indies, Cave Hill Campus, Barbados (West Indies, period 2000-2005) and at the International Management Institute, New Delhi, Kolkata, and Bhubaneswar, India. He was also a visiting professor at various universities, such as the Rajiv Gandhi Institute of Petroleum Technology, IIM-Shillong, Tezpur University, Sichuan Academy of Social Sciences, Chengdu, China, Centrum Graduate Business School, Pontificia Universidad Cato'lica del Peru, and Rio de Janeiro, Brazil, and UERJ, Brazil. He was a recipient of numerous awards and positions, including the prestigious Shastri Indo-Canada Collaborative Research Grant 2020–22, ICSSR Research Grant, SANEI Research Award (South Asia Network of Economic Institutions by World Bank and Global Development Network), Campus Research Award in 2 consecutive years (May 2002 and 2003), University of the West Indies, Cave Hill Campus, Barbados, and so on. He is among the founders of IMI Delhi, IMI Kolkata, and IMI Bhubaneswar. He was a director of IMI Kolkata from 2014 to 2020. Worked as a consultant for various governmental and multilateral agencies, including the World Bank, Asian Development Bank, FICCI-New Delhi, International Development Research Centre (IDRC), Associated Cement Companies, Mumbai, UNIDO, ILO, Indo-Canadian Cooperation Unit, GTZ, and the Government of India (Ministry of Rural Development, Ministry of Corporate Affairs, Ministry of Finance), the

Caribbean Development Bank, and the Government of Barbados. Author of more than 150 scientific articles on International Economics and Business, International Finance, Macroeconomics, Corporate Governance, and Economic Development. He wrote several books published by Palgrave Macmillan, Springer, and University Press Limited. Authored articles for various magazines and newspapers. Founding editor of a reputed management journal, *Global Business Review*, published by Sage Publications, New Delhi, India

Sahana Roy Chowdhury is a professor of economics at the International Management Institute in Kolkata. She earned her Master's (M.S. in Quantitative Economics) and Ph.D. from the Indian Statistical Institute. She is the *Editor-in-Chief* of the journal *Studies in Microeconomics* (Sage Publications). Dr. Roy Chowdhury has several publications in international journals of repute, such as Economic Modelling, Journal of Economics, Metroeconomica, Indian Growth and Development Review, Journal of International Trade and Economic Development, etc. She has worked with several national and international organisations, such as NIPFP, ICRIER, Delhi, and ICRA limited, and the Monetary Policy Research Division. She was awarded the prestigious Raghuram Rajan Young Scholar Grant and visited the NBER Summer Institute at Cambridge, Massachusetts, USA. She was a visiting scientist at Cornell University, USA. She delivered several invited lectures at the University of Paris-Est Marne-la-Vallée, Paris, France, on Indian macro-developmental and fiscal issues, and labour market issues. She worked with several commissions under the Ministry of Finance, Department of Economic Affairs, such as the Expenditure Management Commission, to provide key research inputs. She also served as an expert panellist several times to offer opinions and comments on employability and education-related issues. She contributed to an invited chapter in the India Higher Education Report 2020 (Centre for Policy Research in Higher Education, Department of Educational Finance, MHRD, GOI).

Dona Ghosh possesses 9 years of experience in research, teaching, and corporate consultancy. She currently serves as a senior faculty member in Economics at the Thiagarajar School of Management and also works as a Securities Market Trainer for the Securities and Exchange Board of India. Dr. Ghosh is the author of two books and numerous book chapters and articles published in international journals, magazines, and newspapers. Her research interests encompass Demography, Behavioural Finance, Health Economics, and Artificial Intelligence adoption. She has provided consultancy services to multiple corporate and research entities. In recognition of her contributions, she was awarded the Honorary Rosalind Membership from London Journals Press in 2020 and jointly received the Faculty Scholarship from the Reserve Bank of India in 2023.

List of Figures

List of Tables

Chapter 1
Unveiling the Health Care Crisis in South Asia: A Call for Transformation Amplified by COVID-19

Abstract The COVID-19 pandemic has revealed numerous lasting effects globally, particularly in South Asia, where the intensity of economic impacts and recessionary shocks varies across countries and regions. It is observed that the case fatality ratio of COVID-19 differs among nations, influenced by factors such as inadequate health infrastructure, substandard quality of services, demographic differences, and vaccination rates. This study investigates the various elements that contribute to these differing circumstances, interventions, and the efficacy of responses to the COVID-19 pandemic, with a particular focus on South Asian economies. It explores both demand and supply side aspects of the healthcare system in South Asia, noting that nearly all initiatives relied on information technology to enhance their scale and reach. The analysis critically assesses health sector interventions, encompassing vaccine-related policies, support for health infrastructure, and overall effectiveness during the pandemic. Our discussion is organised around four key pillars: first, the pre-pandemic economic and socio-economic structures of South Asian economies that influenced their performance; second, the quality and scope of interventions undertaken; third, the outcomes from various perspectives during the multiple waves of the pandemic; and finally, preparations for adaptive mitigation. This includes the design of appropriate health insurance schemes aimed at safeguarding these economies from the poverty-inducing shocks associated with catastrophic health crises. Throughout the study, we present regional snapshots from diverse perspectives, employing a well-balanced mix of methodologies that draws on rigorous empirical research, qualitative analysis, and anecdotal evidence.

Keywords South Asia · COVID-19 · Inadequate health infrastructure · Demographic compositions · Vaccination profiles · The pre-pandemic economic and socio-economic structures · Quality interventions · Multiple waves · The preparations under adaptive mitigation

A. Banik et al., *Extraordinary Health Hazards and their Socio-Economic Effects in South Asia*, South Asia Economic and Policy Studies,
https://doi.org/10.1007/978-981-95-5729-5_1

1.1 Introduction

The COVID-19 pandemic is widely recognised as one of the most significant global threats since World War II and is the greatest health crisis of the twenty-first century. The origins of the COVID-19 disease remain unclear. However, the crisis began in late December 2019 when a previously unrecognised virus, known as the severe acute respiratory syndrome coronavirus 2 (SARS-CoV-2), was first identified in Wuhan City, Hubei Province, China. This outbreak stemmed from residents infected by this novel virus, leading to widespread transmission that soon spread to other countries and continents. As the pandemic unfolded, it rapidly moved beyond Asia, entering Europe and the United States. In response to the escalating crisis, developed nations embarked on extensive vaccination campaigns to mitigate the impact of the virus and gradually emerge from the turmoil caused by COVID-19. The pandemic has profoundly impacted global well-being on multiple fronts, including significant increases in mortality rates, escalating poverty levels, and disruptions to educational systems. A comprehensive understanding of these multifaceted effects is essential for informing policy decisions and enhancing preparedness for future public health emergencies.

The World Health Organization (WHO) officially designated the illness caused by this novel coronavirus as Coronavirus Disease 2019 (COVID-19). The virus's rapid spread resulted in a global cascade of health, economic, and social challenges. Notably, the pandemic set off a global financial crisis, prompting nations to adopt stringent lockdown measures—either fully or partially—to curtail the virus's transmission. These lockdowns led to severe disruptions in economic activity, compelling countless businesses to either scale down their operations or cease them entirely, which triggered substantial job losses across various sectors. The pandemic's ramifications did not spare any sector; in addition to service industries, areas including manufacturing, agriculture, the food industry, education, sports, and entertainment faced significant setbacks. These economic disruptions revealed deep-seated vulnerabilities within global systems, underscoring the need for a resilient infrastructure to respond to health crises.

The fatality rates associated with COVID-19 vary significantly across countries. They are influenced by various factors deeply embedded in health inequalities, including inadequate health infrastructure, unequal access to public health services, the prevalence of BCG (Bacillus Calmette Guerin) vaccinations in specific populations, and distinct demographic characteristics (Baniket al. 2020). Extensive evidence suggests that many developing nations and certain developed countries struggle with substandard public health conditions, leaving them ill-prepared to manage an outbreak of this magnitude (The Guardian 2016). The unequal distribution of healthcare access has led to stark disparities among different demographic groups, with ethnic minorities in both the United States and the United Kingdom experiencing disproportionately higher mortality rates compared to their white counterparts. Recent studies have highlighted this pressing issue, illustrating how these minority communities suffered significantly more during the pandemic (Barret al. 2020; O'Neal 2020). For instance, an analysis published by The Guardian (2016) reported that, among 12,593 individuals who succumbed to the virus in hospitals across England by April 19, 2020, an alarming 19% were from Black, Asian, and minority ethnic (BAME) communities. This statistic is particularly striking given that these groups represent only 15% of England's population. Similar trends were observed in the United States, where infection and death rates related to COVID-19 have been markedly higher among minority populations across all states. Taking Michigan as a case study provides a stark illustration of these disparities: the Black population, which makes up just 15% of the state's total demographic, accounted for an astounding 35% of confirmed COVID-19 cases. This alarming figure indicates that Black residents in Michigan are 133% more likely to contract the virus than their representation in the population would suggest.

The issue is further exacerbated by a report from the Brookings Institution (Reeves and Deng 2021), which indicated that Michigan's projected fatality rate was nearing 4%. Here, Black individuals disproportionately contributed to the COVID-19 mortality figures, making up 40% of all deaths associated with the virus statewide. In stark contrast, White individuals, who represent more than 75% of Michigan's population, accounted for only 25% of confirmed infections and 26% of deaths (Ray 2020). This data illustrates the significant health inequalities deeply entrenched within American and British healthcare systems.

Moreover, countries like Italy and Spain have also reported distressingly high fatality rates during the pandemic, which can be partially attributed to demographic characteristics, such as a significantly older population in these regions. Across many areas, the high mortality rates witnessed during the pandemic can be directly linked to the longstanding inadequacies in public health infrastructure that governments have failed to address over the years. In conclusion, the COVID-19 pandemic has revealed the fragility of global health systems and the urgent need for comprehensive reforms to address the inequalities that have exacerbated the crisis.

1.2 The Journey of South Asia: Shedding Light on the Challenges of Its Healthcare System

Historically, South Asian countries have faced numerous infectious disease outbreaks, with cholera standing out as one of the most notable examples (Chakrabarti 2010; Mahapatraet al. 2014). This diverse region comprises eight nations: Afghanistan, Bangladesh, Bhutan, India, the Maldives, Nepal, Pakistan, and Sri Lanka. Each confronts unique health challenges and responses to disease. In this analysis, we explore the trajectory of the COVID-19 pandemic across these eight South Asian countries.

Figure 1.1 illustrates a horizontal dashed line representing the proportion of the world's population residing in South Asia, approximately 24%. This comparison reveals two critical insights. Firstly, throughout the pandemic, the burden of

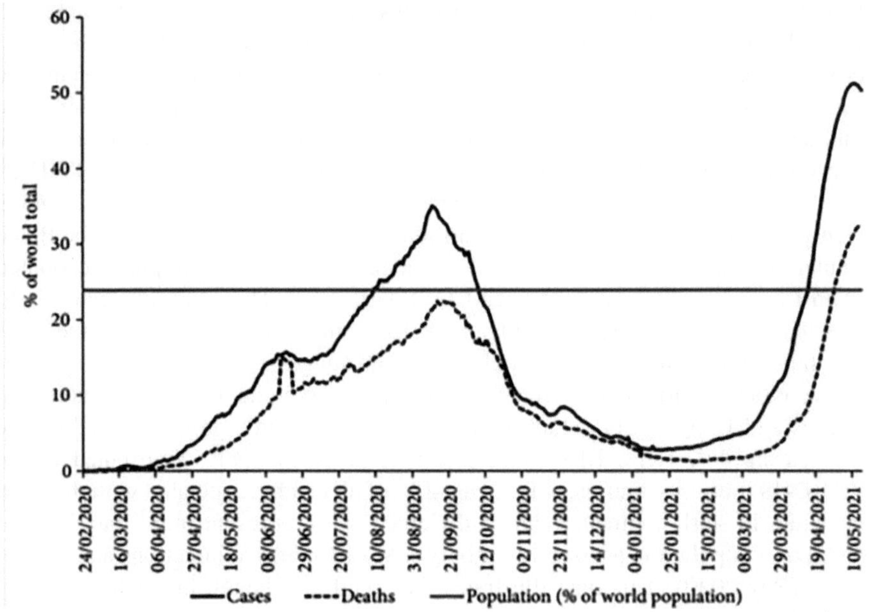

Fig. 1.1 The proportion of daily reported COVID-19 cases and deaths in South Asia as a percentage of the world's total. *Note*: The horizontal dashed line is the population share of South Asia in the World (23.9%). Data covers the period from 24th February 2020 to 15th May 2021. *Source*: https://oneworldindata.org/coronavirus

COVID-19 cases and deaths in South Asia has remained below its proportionate share of the global population. However, during the peaks of the first and second waves, the region experienced a significant surge in COVID-19 cases and deaths that exceeded its demographic share, underscoring the pandemic's severe impact in this area.

In addition, Fig. 1.1 highlights the share of reported COVID-19 cases and deaths in South Asia as a percentage of global totals. This infographic underscores the evolution of the pandemic through two major waves. The first wave of COVID-19 began in early April 2020, gaining momentum until it peaked by the end of September 2020. During this initial rise, COVID-19 cases in South Asia surged dramatically, increasing from less than 1% to over 35% of all cases reported worldwide. Concurrently, the region witnessed a stark escalation in COVID-19-related deaths, which rose from under 1% to approximately 24% of the total global deaths attributed to the virus. The decline of the first wave extended from October 2020 to January 2021, marking a period of relative reduction in both case and death counts.

As the world transitioned into 2021, a perilous second wave of COVID-19 began to sweep through South Asia, overwhelming many of its less-developed nations starting in January. This surge was alarming and significantly more destructive than previous waves. Preliminary evidence indicated that the peak of this crisis may have occurred around mid-May 2021. During this intense period, COVID-19 cases in

South Asia escalated dramatically, rising from a mere 2% of the global total at the beginning of January to over 50% by mid-May 2021. By that same point, South Asia accounted for more than 35% of all COVID-19-related deaths worldwide, highlighting the severe impact of the pandemic in this region.

Figure 1.2 illustrates the profound consequences that COVID-19 inflicted on South Asia while concurrently shedding light on the pandemic's broader global effects. The region showed a heightened vulnerability to the highly transmissible delta variant, which emerged in the second quarter of 2021 when vaccination efforts were still in their early stages and significantly hindered by global supply shortages. This emergence of the delta variant coincided with a pivotal moment in the

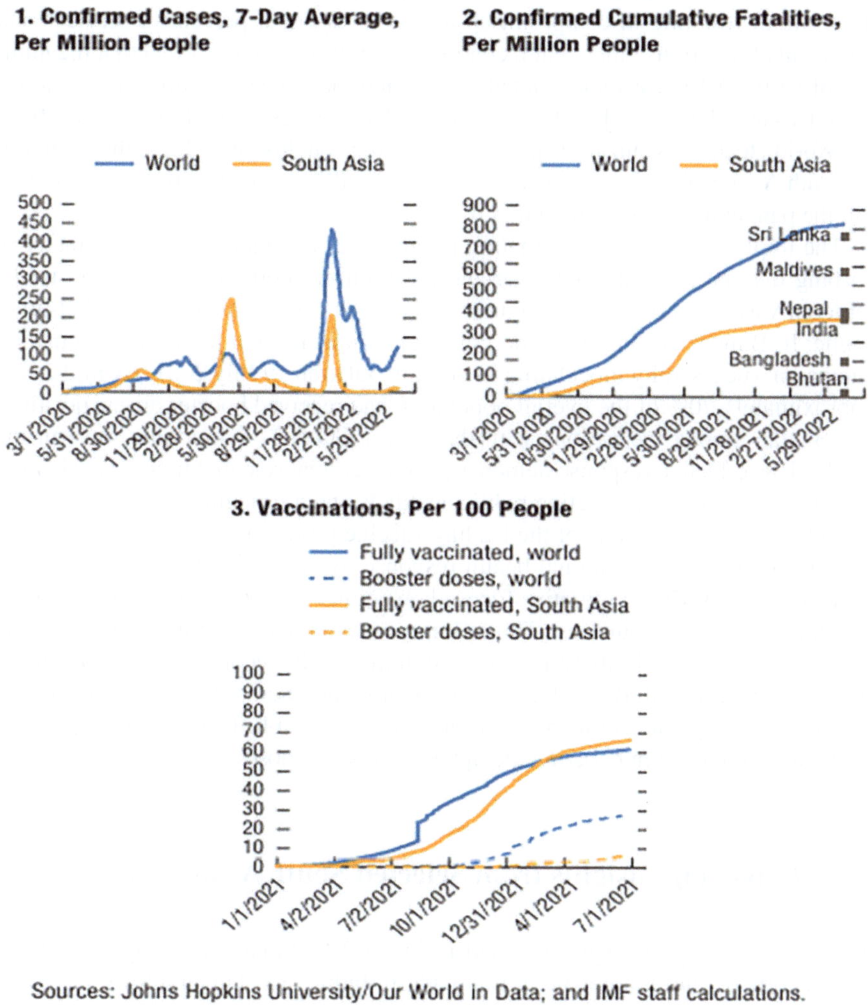

Fig. 1.2 COVID-19's health effects and vaccination in South Asia

pandemic; many countries were beginning to roll out their vaccination programmes. This challenging scenario was particularly detrimental for South Asian countries, as they were ill-prepared to manage the staggering infection surge amidst limited vaccination coverage.

By early 2022, the arrival of the omicron variant set off yet another wave of infections, with considerable impact felt in Bhutan. This tiny nation had previously managed to ward off significant outbreaks through effective public health interventions. As of mid-2022, South Asia recorded an estimated 47 million confirmed COVID-19 cases and around 584,000 deaths attributed to the virus, representing nearly 9% of the total fatalities reported globally. However, it is essential to recognise that the humanitarian ramifications of the pandemic likely went far beyond these documented statistics. Healthcare systems across the region endured tremendous strain, resulting in compromised access to essential preventive services and treatments for various other health conditions. Multiple studies reveal that the number of COVID-19 cases and related deaths may have been significantly underreported, as noted by Anand et al. (2021). Cumulative excess mortality estimates from the World Health Organization suggest that by the conclusion of 2021, the death toll in South Asia could range between 3.3 and 6.8 million, underscoring the profound toll the pandemic exacted on human life.

The implementation of vaccination programmes emerged as a critical factor in curbing the spread of the delta variant and limiting mortality rates linked to the omicron variant, even amidst a significant surge in case numbers during that timeframe. In Bhutan, for instance, the government undertook a proactive vaccination campaign, successfully inoculating its adult population by July 2021. By mid-2022, approximately 70% of the overall population had received booster doses, positioning Bhutan among the nations with the lowest COVID-19 mortality rates in the world. This effective response demonstrated the crucial role that timely vaccination initiatives can play in protecting public health during a pandemic.

India, recognised as one of the leading vaccine producers in the world, played a pivotal role in the international health response by serving as a major supplier of vaccines to COVAX, an initiative focused on equitable vaccine distribution to low- and middle-income countries. This effort was essential for strengthening public health initiatives within these nations and aiding global economic recovery in the post-pandemic period. By mid-2022, vaccination rates across South Asia surpassed the global average, indicating progress in the region's public health efforts, although challenges remained in boosting the uptake of booster doses.

1.3 Exploring Insights from Selected South Asian Nations

The 7-day moving average illustrated in Fig. 1.3 highlights the daily COVID-19 case reports per million people in Bangladesh, India, Pakistan, and Sri Lanka. The data reveals a clear pattern of fluctuating waves in the pandemic's progression across all four nations. Each wave reflects the varying intensity and impact of the

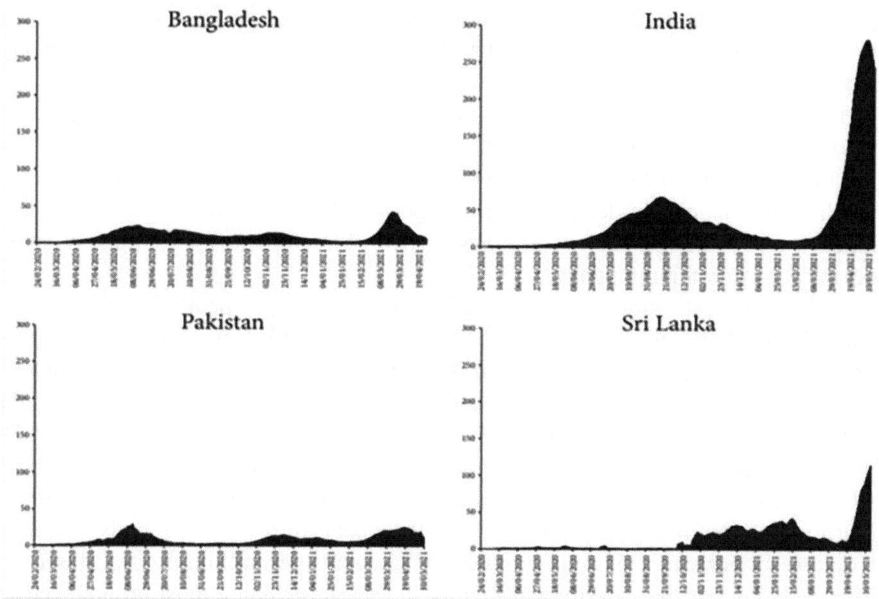

Fig. 1.3 Weekly snapshot: daily COVID-19 cases per million population in select South Asian countries (7-day moving average). *Note*: Data covers the period from 24th February 2020 to 15th May 2021. *Source*: https://oneworldindata.org/coronavirus>

virus over time, underscoring the distinct trajectories each country has experienced throughout the pandemic.

India has prominently experienced two waves of the COVID-19 pandemic. The first case was reported on 30 January 2020, but the initial wave did not gain momentum until April 2020. It peaked in late September 2020 and began to decline until March 2021. A devastating second wave struck India in April 2021, exactly 1 year after the first case was reported. During the peak of the first wave, the daily reported cases reached approximately 75 per million population. In contrast, the second wave saw this number soar to nearly 300 daily reported cases per million—an increase of four times.

Sri Lanka has exhibited a similar two-wave pattern. The first COVID-19 case was confirmed on 27 January 2020, with relatively low daily reported cases for the next 8 months. The first wave commenced in early October 2020, peaked in early March 2021, and then saw a decline before a significant second wave was hit in early April 2021. At the peak of the first wave, daily reported cases in Sri Lanka were about 50 per million population; however, the second wave surpassed 100 daily reported cases per million by the first week of May 2021.

Bangladesh and Pakistan have displayed similar patterns, with both countries encountering three relatively small waves of infections compared to India and Sri Lanka. During the peak of the latest wave, which began in early March, Bangladesh reported daily cases of just under 50 per million population, while in Pakistan, the peak was even lower. Notably, the latest wave in both countries is declining, contrasting sharply with the ongoing situations in India and Sri Lanka, where the waves have yet to peak.

Figure 1.4 presents a detailed view of the 7-day moving average of daily reported COVID-19 deaths, depicting a notable wavelike trend reminiscent of Fig. 1.3. During the height of the initial wave in India, the number of daily recorded deaths reached just under one death per million people. However, this figure saw a dramatic increase during the second wave, rising threefold to approximately three deaths per million individuals.

In Sri Lanka, the situation mirrored this trend; during the peak of the first wave, daily deaths were recorded at below 0.5 per million. This figure has since surged, approaching one death per million during the second wave. Similarly, Bangladesh experienced a stark increase, with daily deaths during the first wave significantly falling below 0.5 deaths per million. However, this number exceeded the 0.5 deaths per million threshold in the most recent third wave. Pakistan's journey through the COVID-19 pandemic has been particularly significant, marked by a troubling trend. During both the initial outbreak and the subsequent third wave, the daily fatalities from the virus have consistently exceeded 0.5 deaths per million people. Based on Figs. 1.3 and 1.4, the severity and fatality of the outbreak are most pronounced in

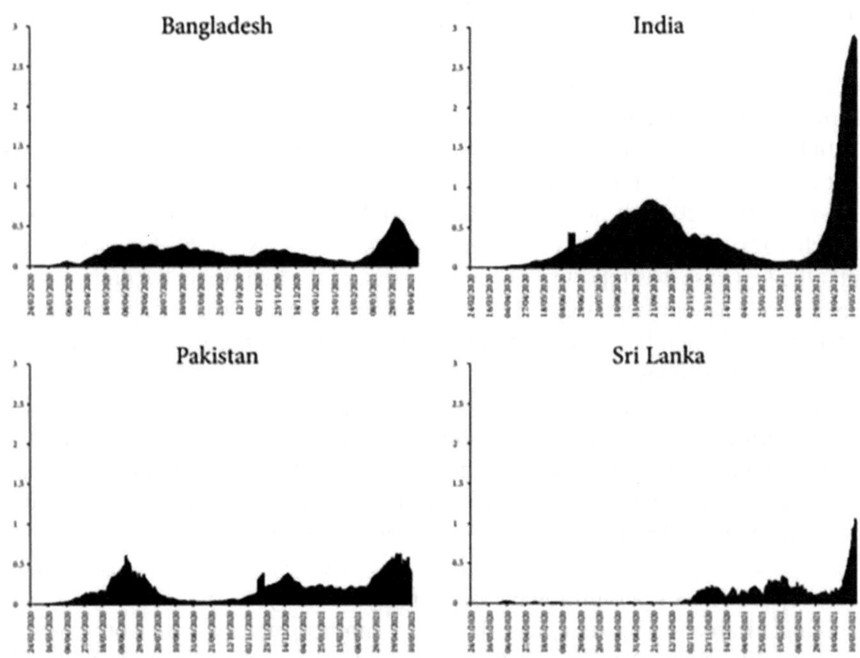

Fig. 1.4 Weekly snapshot: daily COVID-19 deaths per million population in select South Asian countries (7-day moving average). *Note*: Data covers the period from 24th February 2020 to 15th May 2021. *Source*: https://oneworldindata.org/coronavirus

India, where the second wave has been nothing short of catastrophic. Sri Lanka follows closely, grappling with its devastating second wave that began in April 2021. In contrast, Bangladesh and Pakistan have managed the situation more effectively than India and Sri Lanka thus far. This alarming statistic highlights the persistent and formidable challenges the nation has confronted at various stages of the pandemic, reflecting the broader struggles faced by the region as it navigated the complexities of this public health crisis.

Table 1.1 comprehensively examines key indicators illuminating various health sector dimensions amidst the pandemic. It focuses on the Human Development Index (HDI), health systems, and access to vital infrastructure and connectivity. These indicators serve as valuable proxies for assessing the preparedness of eight South Asian countries to tackle the challenges posed by the COVID-19 crisis. The data reveals that Sri Lanka stands out as the top performer in South Asia, with an impressive HDI of 0.782, indicating a relatively high level of development compared to its regional counterparts. Following closely behind is the Maldives, with an HDI of 0.740, reflecting its strong health and social support systems. On the other end of the spectrum, Afghanistan reported the lowest HDI at 0.511, highlighting significant challenges in its health and development sectors. The Maldives again leads the way regarding health expenditure, allocating 6.64% of its GDP to health

Table 1.1 Key indicators related to the health sector serve as a proxy for assessing the readiness of eight South Asian countries to tackle the COVID-19 pandemic

Select Indicators	Human Development	Health Systems				Access to basic infrastructure			Connectivity	
Country/ region/group	*HDI Score*	*Domestic general government health expenditure (per cent of GDP)*	*Hospital beds (per 1000 people)*	*Nurses and Midwives (per 1000 people)*	*Physicians (per 1000 people)*	*Usage of basic drinking water services (per cent of population)*	*Usage of basic sanitation services (per cent of population)*	*Open defecation (per cent of population)*	*Fixed broadband subscription (per 100 people)*	*Mobile cellular subscription (per 100 people)*
Afghanistan	0.511	0.49	0.39	0.17	0.27	67.06	43.41	12.74	0.05	59.35
Bangladesh	0.632	0.39	0.79	0.41	0.5	97.01	48.23	0.27	4.95	101.54
Bhutan	0.654	2.43	1.74	1.85	0.42	97.23	69.25	0	1.15	95.56
India	0.645	0.95	0.53	1.72	0.85	92.67	59.54	25.73	1.4	84.27
Maldives	0.740	6.64	4.3	6.42	2.57	99.25	99.37	0	9.97	155.95
Nepal	0.602	1.46	0.3	3.1	0.74	88.81	62.05	21.49	2.81	139.44
Pakistan	0.557	1.13	0.63	0.66	0.98	91.46	59.86	10.42	0.81	76.37
Sri Lanka	0.782	1.54	4.15	2.18	1	89.41	95.78	0.55	7.81	144.33
South Asia	0.641	0.95	0.59	1.40	0.83	92.3	58.72	21.01	1.7	85.09
East Asia and Pacific	0.747	4.42	4.51	3.42	1.66	92.86	84.02	2.24	25.31	128.97
Middle Income	0.631	2.82	2.37	2.67	1.38	91.15	72.67	9.6	12.61	108.61
High Income	0.898	7.65	5.04	9.61	2.92	99.42	98.2	0.21	31.84	123.53
World	0.737	5.87	2.89	3.81	1.56	89.6	73.4	9.05	15.67	109.4

Source: World Development Indicators (Accessed on 20 August 2021) — Unprepared (orange) — Prepared (green)

services. In contrast, Bangladesh lags significantly, spending only 0.39% of its GDP in this critical area, which may impact its health system's resilience. Examining health infrastructure reveals that the Maldives has a ratio of 2.57 physicians per 1000 people, showcasing its robust healthcare workforce. Afghanistan, however, faces stark challenges, with only 0.27 physicians per 1000 population, underscoring the pressing need for improvement in its healthcare delivery system. Additionally, Sri Lanka shines in terms of hospital bed availability, boasting an impressive 4.15 beds for every thousand people.

This contrasts sharply with Nepal, which has only 0.3 beds per thousand, revealing healthcare access and capacity disparities. Moreover, the Maldives also provides qualified healthcare personnel, having the highest number of midwives and nurses per thousand population during the pandemic, at a noteworthy figure of 6.42. This indicates a prioritisation of maternal and child health services. In examining basic infrastructure and connectivity, both Sri Lanka and the Maldives demonstrate commendable performance, with their figures closely aligning, suggesting a strong foundation for addressing health needs in their populations.

Let us now examine two key measures of health expenditure. A more effective approach to comparing healthcare spending is to analyse per capita figures. Regarding current healthcare expenditure per capita, adjusted for purchasing power parity (PPP) and expressed in current international dollars, there is a significant disparity among the four South Asian countries: India, Bangladesh, Pakistan, and Sri Lanka. Bangladesh ranks lowest, with an expenditure of $94.3 per person, followed by Pakistan at $160.6 per person and India at $253.3 per person. Leading the group in Sri Lanka, with a per capita expenditure of $503.6, significantly surpassing the other three countries (Basu and Srivastava 2022).

Additionally, we can assess the share of current health expenditures funded by the government and the share of out-of-pocket expenses for healthcare. The trends in these shares align closely with per capita healthcare spending. Bangladesh, which has the lowest per capita health expenditure, also records the smallest share contributed by the government at 16.7%. Conversely, Sri Lanka, which has the highest per capita health expenditure, benefits from the most considerable government contribution at 43%. India and Pakistan fall in between, with 27% and 32% government contributions, respectively. Notably, the figures for out-of-pocket healthcare expenditure are essentially the inverse of government contributions: countries with a higher proportion of government funding tend to have lower out-of-pocket expenses (Basu and Srivastava 2022, ibid).

The economic repercussions of the COVID-19 pandemic in South Asia presented a vivid and wide-reaching crisis, particularly during the initial waves when strict lockdown measures were imposed to slow the spread of the virus. In India, the region's largest economy, the impact was staggering: real GDP suffered a dramatic decline of 23.8% in the second quarter of 2020 compared to the same period in 2019. This steep contraction highlighted the extreme vulnerability of the economic landscape during the pandemic's early days.

The situation was even more critical in the Maldives, a nation heavily dependent on tourism. With the pandemic's onset, economic activity fell by over 50%, showcasing the devastating effects of a global travel halt. Other countries in the region, such as Bangladesh and Bhutan, faced similarly alarming downturns. Production indices in these nations reflected a notable decline, mirroring the broader negative economic trend that swept through South Asia.

The pandemic's detrimental impact on the economy has proven severe and enduring. By 2021, nearly all South Asian countries, except Bangladesh, recorded annual real GDP per capita figures that remained below the pre-pandemic levels established in 2019. This dynamic emphasised the region's ongoing economic hurdles as it worked towards recovery.

These economic shifts hit the contact-intensive service sectors hardest, with many businesses struggling to return to their previous levels of operation. The situation could have deteriorated further without the timely implementation of supportive policies. In response to the crisis, governments throughout the region ramped up healthcare expenditures and initiatives to support vulnerable households. These initiatives included cash transfers to those in need, distributions of essential food rations, and subsidised utility payments to alleviate financial pressures.

On the revenue side, governments took proactive measures, extending deadlines for tax filings and payments while enacting tax exemptions to relieve the financial burdens on their citizens. These fiscal stimulus packages were bolstered by monetary policies, which involved lowering policy rates and sometimes providing central bank lending to various governmental entities. The financial sector reacted by offering a range of loan moratoriums and low-interest loans, which proved vital in providing liquidity support to borrowers. Additionally, macroprudential measures were implemented to maintain stability within the financial system.

Research by Górnicka et al. (2021) indicates that government interventions significantly enhanced the liquidity conditions of corporate balance sheets across a wide range of firms in India. However, the effects of the pandemic were particularly damaging for low-income households. Workers employed in South Asia's extensive informal economy, who often relied on physical labour and lacked substantial employment protections, faced unique challenges. For instance, data from Sri Lanka showed that micro-enterprises experienced a sharper decline in sales compared to small- and medium-sized enterprises, heightening the risk of closures and job losses, especially among smaller firms. Informal workers, typically without adequate savings and limited access to financial support during unexpected job losses, found themselves especially vulnerable during this period.

Moreover, government assistance programmes in South Asia were often less comprehensive than those available in many other emerging markets, leaving numerous individuals without adequate support. The pandemic further exacerbated existing gender disparities. Research by Deshpande (2020) indicated that during the early lockdowns in India, women were 20% more likely to lose their jobs than men. Similar survey data from Bangladesh and the Maldives indicated that women were also more prone to reduce their working hours than their male counterparts.

In summary, the COVID-19 pandemic has left profound and lasting impacts across the globe, uniquely shaping economies and societies. The extent and severity of these economic impacts and recessionary shocks have varied significantly from one nation to another and across different regions. Studies reveal that fatality rates associated with COVID-19 differ amongst countries, influenced by factors such as the resilience of healthcare infrastructure, demographic compositions, and varying vaccination strategies, including the implementation of the BCG vaccine.

In South Asia and beyond, citizens increasingly look to their governments and public healthcare systems for effective measures to combat this health crisis (Banik and Bhaumik 2020). However, there remains a pervasive skepticism about the ability of these nations to successfully tackle the pandemic, mainly due to historically feeble public healthcare systems. A critical question: Does the existing healthcare framework, predominantly linked to the private sector, create barriers preventing a substantial portion of the population from accessing the health benefits that should be available to all? It has become increasingly clear that, under the current system, the primary beneficiaries are affluent households, who can easily navigate and exploit the healthcare services, leaving many others in South Asia and elsewhere disadvantaged.

The COVID-19 pandemic has created a profound and enduring set of repercussions worldwide, particularly in South Asia, with the severity of economic impacts and recessionary shocks differing markedly from one country and region to another. In particular, the rates of fatalities linked to COVID-19 have exhibited significant variation across nations. This disparity can be attributed to a myriad of factors, including the strength and resilience of health infrastructure, such as the availability of hospital beds, the number of healthcare professionals, the adequacy of essential medical supplies like oxygen, and the accessibility of intensive care unit (ICU) beds. Additionally, the demographic characteristics of populations and the effectiveness of vaccination strategies have also played critical roles in shaping these outcomes.

1.4 Organisation of the Book

This book offers a comprehensive exploration of various scenarios, interventions, and their effectiveness throughout the COVID-19 pandemic, with a particular emphasis on the economies of South Asia. It scrutinises the demand and supply side dimensions of healthcare systems in this region, revealing how nearly every initiative has relied heavily on Information Technology to improve scale and accessibility. Through a critical lens, the book analyses health sector interventions, focusing on vaccine policies and the functioning of health infrastructure amid a global crisis. The successful implementation, administration, and monitoring of these policies are essential for achieving any meaningful impact.

To structure the discussion, the book is organised around four key pillars or objectives: first, it examines the pre-pandemic economic and socio-economic frameworks of South Asian economies that set the foundation for their performance during the crisis; second, it evaluates the quality and scale of interventions made; third, it assesses performance from various perspectives throughout the multiple waves of the pandemic; and finally, it considers preparations for adaptive mitigation, which include creating suitable health insurance schemes to safeguard these economies from the poverty risks that arise due to catastrophic health shocks.

The chapters of this book unfold in a manner that authentically reflects the struggles faced by South Asia during a challenging period. Chapter 2, titled "Navigating COVID-19 in South Asia: A Challenging Journey", thoughtfully examines the complexities the region has encountered. Chapter 3 explores "The Economic Consequences of COVID-19 on South Asia", emphasising the significant impact on livelihoods and communities. Chapter 4 primarily focuses on "COVID-19 and Economic Hardship in South Asia", illuminating the difficulties experienced by many. Chapter 5 addresses the "Vaccine Initiative in South Asia", recognising both the hope and challenges associated with vaccination efforts. Chapters 6 and 7 tackle the critical demand-side and supply side challenges confronting the healthcare system, reflecting the urgent needs of the population. Chapter 8 discusses Bridging Healthcare Gaps in South Asia: A Collaborative Journey Towards Healthier Communities, emphasising the necessity of integrating healthcare systems across South Asian economies to serve all citizens better. Lastly, Chap. 9 presents final thoughts and policy insights to strengthen the region's health infrastructure and foster a resilient economic future, ensuring we are better equipped to face whatever lies ahead.

References

Anand A, Sandefur J, Subramanian A (2021) Three new estimates of India's all-cause excess mortality during the COVID-19 pandemic. Center for Global Development. https://www.jstor.org/stable/resrep33160.1?seq=1

Banik A, Bhaumik PK (2020) India: emerging as major destination of quality health care services. In: Banik A (ed) Trade in health Care Services in South Asia: an examination of the need for regional co-operation. Springer, Singapore, pp 105–126

Banik A, Nag T, Chowdhury SR, Chatterjee R (2020) Why do COVID-19 fatality rates differ across countries? An explorative cross-country study based on select indicators. Glob Bus Rev 21(3):607–625

Barr C, Komenda N, McIntyre N, Voce A (2020, April 22) Ethnic minorities are dying of COVID-19 at a higher rate, analysis shows. https://www.theguardian.com/world/2020/apr/22/racial-inequality-in-britain-found-a-risk-factor-for-covid-19

Basu D, Srivastava P (2022) COVID-19 in South Asia: Health economics, and politics https://www.scielo.org.mx/scielo.php?pid=S0185-16672022000100117&script=sci_arttext

Chakrabarti P (2010) Curing cholera: pathogens, places and poverty in South Asia. Int J South Asian Stud 3:153–168

Deshpande A (2020). The covid-19 pandemic and lockdown: first order effects on gender gaps in employment and domestic time use in India, glo discussion paper series 607, Global Labor Organization (GLO)

Górnicka, Ogawa, Xu (2021) Corporate sector resilience in india in the wake of the covid-19 shock, imf working papers 2021/278, International Monetary Fund

Mahapatra et al (2014) Vibriocidal antibody responses to a bivalent killed whole-cell oral cholera vaccine in a phase III trial in Kolkata, India. PLoS ONE. https://doi.org/10.1371/journal.pone.0096499

O'Neal L (2020, March 13) Public health expert says African Americans are at greater risk of death from coronavirus. https://theundefeated.com/features/public-health-expert-says-african-americans-are-at-greater-risk-of-death-from-coronavirus
Ray R (2020, April 9) Why are Blacks dying at higher rates from COVID-19? https://www.brookings.edu/blog/fixgov/2020/04/09/why-are-blacks-dying-at-higher-rates-from-covid-19/
Reeves RV, Deng B (2021) At least 65,000 more men than women have died from COVID-19 in the US, Commentary, Brookings, October 19
The Guardian (2016). https://www.theguardian.com/environment/2016/apr/27/uk-air-pollution-public-health-emergency-crisis-diesel-cars

Chapter 2
Confronting the Socio-Economic Challenges Stemming from the Extraordinary Health Crisis Created by COVID-19

Abstract The COVID-19 pandemic has presented significant challenges to South Asian economies, exacerbated by high poverty rates, limited social protection, and inadequate access to sanitation. Key impacts included a decline in migration, setbacks for micro, small, and medium enterprises (MSMEs), and challenges like labour shortages and demand shocks. However, the region showed resilience through extensive vaccination campaigns, a youthful workforce, and proactive recovery policies. Strict pandemic management strategies were initially implemented, but by 2021, a shift to less stringent measures occurred, unlike China's Zero COVID policy. India notably advanced in vaccine development, creating its indigenous COVISHIELD and Covaxin vaccines. Economic activity slowed significantly, resulting in job losses, especially in the informal sector, where 44% of India's workforce became unemployed in 2020. While countries like India, Bhutan, Sri Lanka, Maldives, and Nepal fared reasonably well, Bangladesh, Pakistan, and Afghanistan faced more difficulties due to political instability.

Keywords South Asia · Barbell strategy · COVID-19 deaths · Stringency Index · COVID-19 vaccination · COVAX · AstraZeneca · COVID-19-induced job losses · COVID-19-induced poverty and unemployment · Migration and remittances · Economic recovery

2.1 Introduction

The greatest threat to lives, livelihoods, and the international economy has arisen from the rapid spread of the COVID-19 virus. What began as a health crisis has escalated into a global economic catastrophe, resulting in an unprecedented recession in an increasingly interconnected world (Ozili and Arun 2020). As COVID-19 has affected virtually all economies, regardless of size, it has become a global systemic economic risk. In today's highly globalised environment, a shift in one sector or country can have ripple effects across other sectors and nations due to deep

A. Banik et al., *Extraordinary Health Hazards and their Socio-Economic Effects in South Asia*, South Asia Economic and Policy Studies,
https://doi.org/10.1007/978-981-95-5729-5_2

economic integration and interdependence. Pandemics are now recognised as global threats, akin to climate change, due to their swift and widespread impact, irrespective of their origins (Acharya and Porwal 2020).

The COVID-19 pandemic has posed significant challenges to South Asian economies, primarily due to the region's large population, high poverty rates, poor socio-economic conditions, inadequate social protection systems, and limited access to water and sanitation facilities, alongside substandard living conditions (Rasul et al. 2021). South Asia is home to one-third of the world's poorest individuals, with most residing in rural areas and relying predominantly on agriculture. Recognised as one of the poorest regions globally, South Asia had 649 million people facing moderate to severe food insecurity before the pandemic, including 271 million who experienced severe food insecurity. Additionally, 16% of children in the region suffered from severe malnutrition, and 36% were stunted in their growth (FAO 2020; FAO et al. 2020). The COVID-19 crisis has only exacerbated the overall economic conditions in the region.

This region has many megacities, including Delhi, Dhaka, Mumbai, Karachi, Colombo, and Kathmandu, with extraordinarily high population densities. People frequently lack access to necessities, including hygiene, sanitation, and clean water facilities. For instance, nearly 42% of Afghan households are forced to drink contaminated water, and more than 50% lack access to soap and water for handwashing (Rasul et al. 2020). Furthermore, it is particularly challenging to maintain social distance due to high population density, unfavourable working conditions, and insufficient dwelling space. Most people in this region have low resources and a weak capacity to deal with the risks of a pandemic shock because of challenging economic conditions. The difficulties are exacerbated because a significant portion of the population relies solely on self-employment or informal sectors for employment, with no social or health benefits.[1]

The immediate impact of the pandemic brought about profound disruptions across several key areas. There was a noticeable decline in large-scale migration, significant setbacks in micro, small, and medium enterprises (MSMEs) outputs, and

---

[1] India has introduced Ayushman Bharat PM-JAY or the "Live Long India Prime Minister's People's Health Scheme". This national public health insurance initiative, launched by the Government of India, aims to provide free health insurance coverage to low-income individuals, benefiting approximately the bottom 50% of the population. The programme was expanded to include all senior citizens aged 70 and above, irrespective of their economic status. Participants in the scheme can access primary care services through a designated family doctor. For those requiring additional care, PM-JAY provides free secondary healthcare for specialist treatments and tertiary healthcare for hospitalisation needs (GoI 2024). In addition, several state governments, including West Bengal, Karnataka, Andhra Pradesh, and Tamil Nadu, have implemented independent health programmes aimed at low-income earners. Other South Asian countries, such as Sri Lanka, the Maldives, and Nepal, have also made significant progress towards universal health coverage, though their specific models and implementation strategies differ. The World Bank's reports (World Bank 2018) highlight Sri Lanka's success in attaining pro-poor universal health coverage, while UNICEF (2021a) notes Sri Lanka's strong performance in sustaining universal access to free services. Furthermore, the Maldives has established a robust health system, and Nepal is actively working to enhance its initiatives for universal health coverage.

challenges such as supply side constraints, labour shortages, and demand shocks. Despite these hurdles, the region has demonstrated remarkable resilience in managing the fallout from the pandemic. This success can be attributed to many factors, including extensive vaccination drives to protect public health, a youthful demographic contributing to a dynamic workforce, and proactive policy measures to stimulate recovery. Taking India as a case study, the country implemented agile policy frameworks. It adopted the "barbell strategy",[2] which effectively balanced risks and opportunities, allowing for a more robust response to the ongoing challenges.

Compared to many developed nations, South Asian countries have demonstrated a noteworthy ability to contain the spread of the coronavirus and protect lives during the initial phases of the pandemic. However, this achievement has not come without significant economic repercussions. Implementing extended lockdowns has severely affected regional economic activities. Simulation studies indicate that a single month of lockdown could lead to a substantial annual GDP contraction between 1.5% and 2.0% (ESCAP 2020). To put this into perspective, it is estimated that every day of lockdown imposes a staggering economic toll on India, costing the country approximately $4.64 billion in US dollars, highlighting the stark balance between public health measures and economic sustainability (Acuite Ratings 2020).

2.2 Innovative Measures During COVID-19 Shock: World and South Asia

Figures 2.1 and 2.2 provide a striking visual representation of the daily new confirmed COVID-19 deaths per million people, both on a global scale and specifically within South Asian countries, from 1 May 2020 to 5 July 2023. In Fig. 2.1, the global data reveals a troubling trend, showcasing nearly ten peaks in the fatality rate due to COVID-19 over the 3 years. This fluctuation indicates the virus's varying intensity and the waves it has produced worldwide. In contrast, Fig. 2.2 focuses on South Asia, where the data illustrate a particularly pronounced peak in 2021. Despite this alarming spike, the region has demonstrated a notable capacity to manage the pandemic effectively. The improvement in the situation can largely be attributed to several key factors: a robust and widespread vaccination campaign that has helped shield the population, demographic advantages such as a younger population, effective government policies that have prioritised public health, and proactive measures, including lockdowns and public awareness campaigns. Together, these elements have contributed to a marked decrease in COVID-19 fatalities in South Asia compared to earlier phases of the pandemic.

[2] The barbell strategy is an investment concept that suggests the best way to balance reward and risk is to invest in the extremes of high-risk and no-risk assets while avoiding the middle-of-the-road choices. See, GoI (2021).

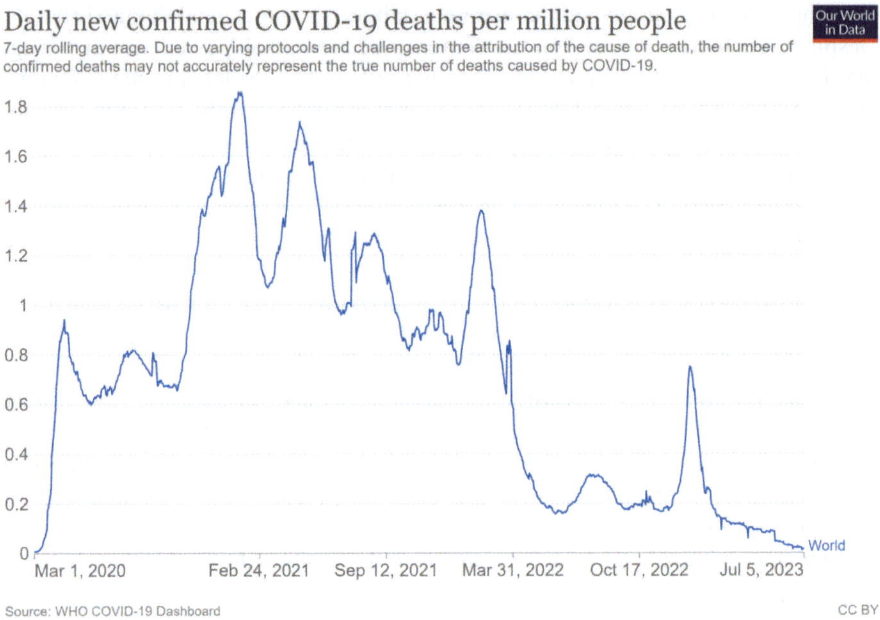

Fig. 2.1 Daily new confirmed COVID-19 deaths per million people. *Source*: WHO COVID-19 dashboard

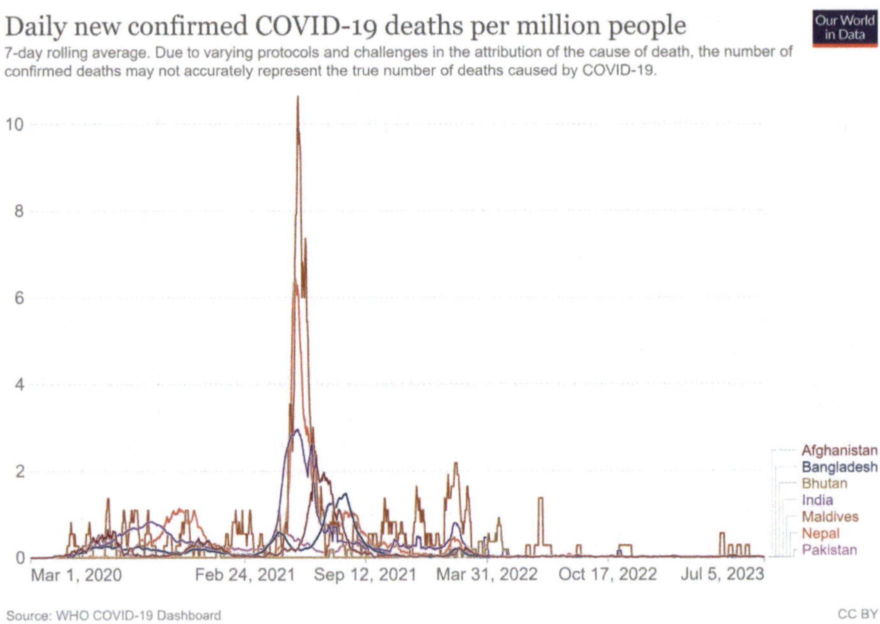

Fig. 2.2 Daily new confirmed COVID-19 deaths per million people. *Source*: WHO COVID-19 dashboard

Table 2.1 Innovative strategies employed by South Asian countries during the COVID-19 pandemic

Country	Airport screening initiated	Quarantine initiation	Lockdown initiation	Duration of lockdown
India	31 January 2020	26 January 2020	25 March 2020	75 days
Pakistan	24 January 2020	28 March 2020	No national lockdown	–
Bhutan	6 March 2020	16 March 2020	24 March 2020	21 days
The Maldives	26 January 2020	10 March 2020	16 April 2020	–
Bangladesh	22 January 2020	9 March 2020	26 March 2020	50 days
Sri Lanka	27 January 2020	13 March 2020	18 March 2020	52 days
Nepal	End of February 2020	Mid-February 2020	19 March 2020	–
Afghanistan	25 January 2020	–	28 March 2020	–

Source: Babu et al. (2021)

Different nations implemented unique strategies and encountered diverse outcomes in their attempts to control the pandemic's spread. Various notable approaches were adopted to alleviate the pandemic's effects. For instance, many countries adopted a lockdown model, whereas South Korea employed a more open model (Banik et al. 2020).

In February and March of 2020, South Asian nations began to respond to the COVID-19 pandemic by implementing various initiatives. Each country enacted measures to limit the influx of visitors from abroad. These measures included bans on international travel, the suspension of air travel, and mandatory quarantine periods for incoming travellers, with the duration of quarantine determined by individual nations. Within South Asia, various strategies were employed to execute lockdown procedures. An overview of the early responses of these countries to the coronavirus epidemic is presented in Table 2.1.

According to Table 2.1, nearly all South Asian nations opted to impose a complete emergency, except for Pakistan, which did not take this path. During this time, the lockdown measures implemented in countries such as the Maldives, Nepal, and Afghanistan were less stringent than needed. Conversely, India, Bhutan, Bangladesh, and Sri Lanka enforced lockdowns that lasted 75, 21, 50, and 52 days, respectively.

The South Asian region presents an interesting case for comparison within the broader global context, particularly when we leverage the insights provided by the Stringency Index (Figure 2.3) and the Containment and Health Index. These indices, accessed through The Oxford Coronavirus Government Response Tracker (OxCGRT)[3], offer valuable metrics that reflect the effectiveness and severity of government responses to the pandemic. By analysing these indicators, we can better

[3]The Oxford COVID-19 Government Response Tracker (OxCGRT) is a project that collected information on policy measures to tackle COVID-19 in 2020, 2021, and 2022, available at https://www.bsg.ox.ac.uk/research/covid-19-government-response-tracker.

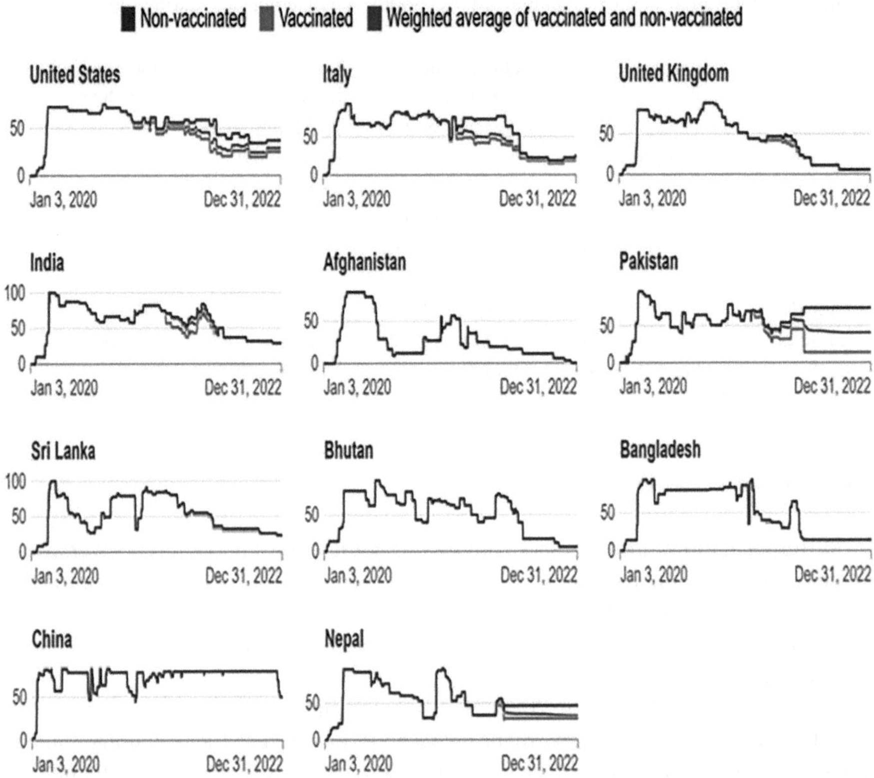

Fig. 2.3 Stringency index. *Source*: Hale et al. (2021). Note: "The nine metrics used to calculate the Stringency Index are: school closures; workplace closures; cancellation of public events; restrictions on public gatherings; closures of public transport; stay-at-home requirements; public information campaigns; restrictions on internal movements; and international travel controls. The index on any given day is calculated as the mean score of the nine metrics, each taking a value between 0 and 100", see Hale et al. (2021)

understand how the measures implemented in South Asia align with or differ from those in other parts of the world.

The Stringent Index is a composite measure encompassing nine response indicators, including school closures, workplace closures, and travel bans. Each indicator is assigned a value on a scale from 0 to 100, where 100 indicates the most stringent measures. Figure 2.3 demonstrates that South Asian countries, similar to nations around the globe, initially implemented a strict strategy for managing the pandemic. However, in the later stages, especially after 2021, these countries collectively transitioned to a relatively less stringent approach to controlling the spread of COVID-19. This shift is particularly notable compared to countries like China, which upheld a Zero COVID policy.

The Containment and Health Index is a comprehensive metric that evaluates the effectiveness of various policy responses in managing and controlling the spread of

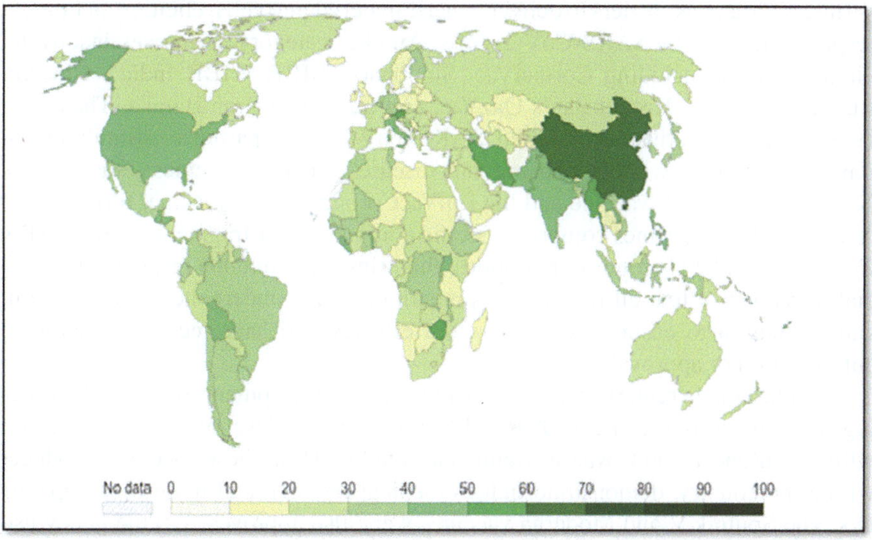

Fig. 2.4 Containment and health index. *Source*: https://ourworldindata.org/covid-stringency-index

a disease. This index considers thirteen key indicators, including school closures, workplace closures, travel bans, testing policies, contact tracing efforts, face coverings, and vaccine policies. Each indicator contributes to the overall index score, which ranges from 0 to 100. A higher score indicates a stricter, more comprehensive approach to containment and health measures. In cases where policies differ across different regions within a country, the index will display the information corresponding to the region with the most stringent policies. Based on Fig. 2.4, it can be observed that the average containment and health index tends to be more stringent in South Asian countries when compared to European, Australian, and South American nations. In contrast, the South Asian region adopts a comparatively more lenient stance towards China, Iran, select Southeast Asian nations, and the United States of America.

In the wake of the pandemic, nations adopted the strategy of immunising their populations. Vaccines became available through two primary channels: COVAX and inter-country transfers, exemplified by the Vaccine Maitri programme launched by the Government of India. Recently, notable advancements have also been achieved in the realm of vaccine development. Two prominent categories of vaccines have emerged: mRNA vaccines, such as the Pfizer-BioNTech and Moderna vaccines, and adenovirus vector vaccines, represented by the Oxford-AstraZeneca vaccine. These innovative vaccines have transformed the approach to immunisation and attracted significant global attention. The landscape of COVID-19 vaccines comprises various types designed to combat the pandemic, categorised based on their composition and mechanism of action. One category includes viral vector vaccines, including the Sputnik V and Janssen COVID-19 vaccines. These utilise harmless viruses as carriers to deliver genetic material into cells, eliciting an immune response against the SARS-CoV-2 virus. Another category comprises inactivated virus vaccines, including CoronaVac, Sinopharm BIBP, WIBP, India's Covaxin, Russia's CoviVac, Kazakhstan's QazVac, and Iran's COVIran Baraka. These vaccines contain inactivated or killed SARS-CoV-2 virus particles, stimulating an immune response without causing the disease. Subunit vaccines[4], such as the Novavax COVID-19 vaccine and the EpiVacCorona peptide vaccine, form another category. These vaccines comprise specific components or fragments of the SARS-CoV-2 virus, like F-proteins or peptides, that trigger an immune response. It is crucial to recognise that all the vaccines mentioned have undergone rigorous testing and evaluation to ensure their safety and efficacy and have received emergency authorisation or approval.

India has made remarkable progress in vaccine development, successfully creating its indigenous vaccine, COVISHIELD, which was developed in collaboration with AstraZeneca and Covaxin (Banik and Singla 2021). These vaccines, produced within the country, demonstrate India's medical research and innovation capabilities. The Sputnik V and Moderna vaccines were also approved for emergency use. Several South Asian nations, in addition to Pakistan, have begun their vaccination campaigns using India's COVISHIELD and Covaxin. The COVAX programme has further supplemented these efforts. Pakistan commenced its vaccination drive with the Sinopharm vaccine developed in China (Hayat et al. 2022).

According to Fig. 2.5, India leads the world in the total number of individuals who have received at least one dose of the COVID-19 vaccine, with an impressive total of 1.03 billion vaccinated people. In Europe, the overall figure for vaccinated individuals stands at 523.06 million, while North America reports a tally of 458.35 million. This indicates that South Asian countries have exhibited greater success in administering at least one dose of the COVID-19 vaccine to their populations compared to other regions, including North America, South America, Africa, and beyond.

Figure 2.6 depicts the proportion of individuals who have completed the full vaccination regimen outlined in the initial vaccination protocol. This proportion is measured relative to the entire population of the nation. Analysing the percentage of individuals who have successfully received the recommended complete dosage of vaccines according to the prescribed protocol reveals that certain South Asian countries, notably India, Pakistan, and Afghanistan exhibit a level of comparability with regions such as North America, Europe, and South America. In contrast, Bangladesh and Nepal have shown remarkable performance compared to other areas. Thus, it can be concluded that South Asia has achieved a relatively high degree of success in managing COVID-19 vaccinations compared to other geographical regions worldwide.

[4]A subunit vaccine is a vaccine that contains purified parts of the pathogen that are antigenic or necessary to elicit a protective immune response. A subunit vaccine can be made from dissembled viral particles in a cell culture or recombinant DNA expression, which is a recombinant subunit vaccine.

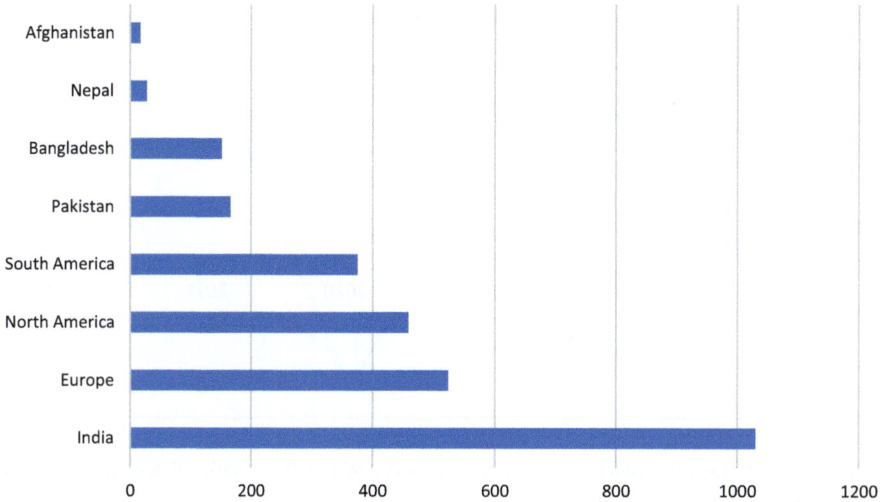

Fig. 2.5 Total number of people who received at least one dose of the COVID-19 vaccine till 28 June 2023 (in million). *Source*: Official data collated by Our World in Data https://ourworldindata.org/covid-vaccinations

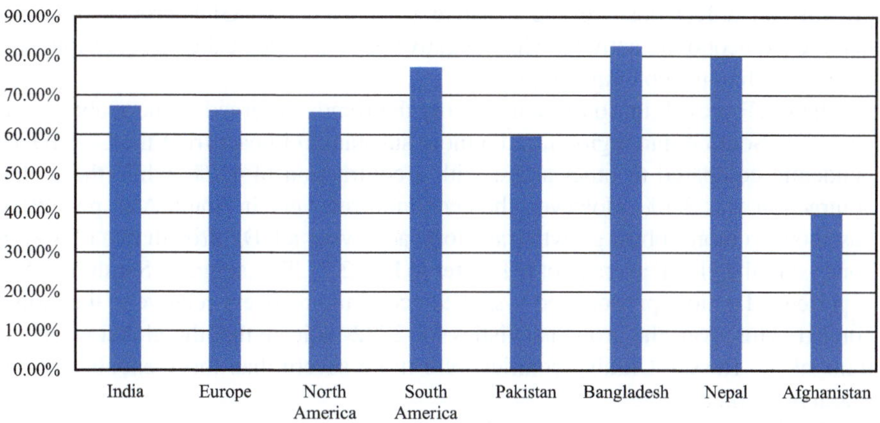

Fig. 2.6 Share of people who completed the initial COVID-19 vaccination protocol, 28 June 2023. *Source*: Official data collated by Our World in Data https://ourworldindata.org/covid-vaccinations

2.3 Exploring Major Trends in Macro and Demographic Development

Growth of Gross Domestic Product (GDP)

GDP growth refers to the increase in a nation's Gross Domestic Product (GDP) over a designated period, frequently measured annually. The assessment and evaluation

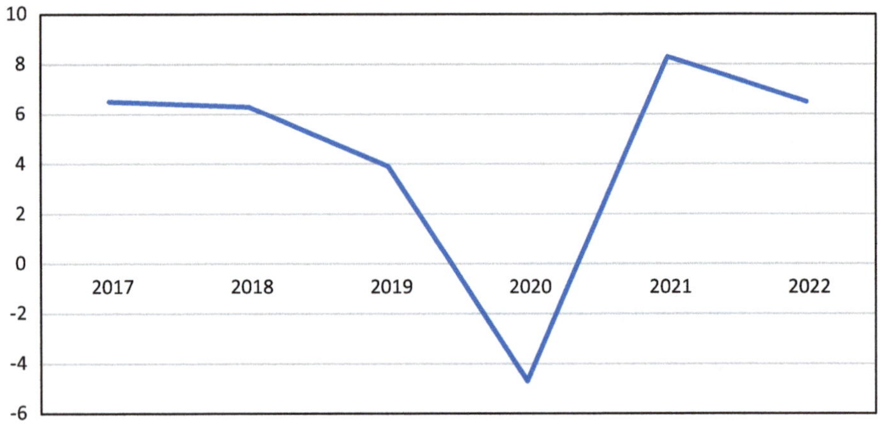

Fig. 2.7 GDP growth (annual%) South Asia. *Source***:** World Bank national accounts data and OECD National Accounts data files

of economic performance rely heavily on GDP metrics. Various factors influence this phenomenon, including investment, consumer spending, government regulations, and global economic conditions. Typically expressed as a percentage, GDP growth can reflect positive and negative values. Positive GDP growth indicates heightened economic activity, while negative growth, often called a recession, signifies a decline in economic output.

The GDP growth in South Asia mirrors the trends observed in the global economy. The South Asian region faced a more substantial impact from the COVID-19 pandemic compared to other areas, with a contraction of 4.7%, while the global contraction was 3.1%. However, the economic recovery in South Asia post-2020 has shown a more robust growth trajectory, achieving a GDP growth rate of 8%, in contrast to the global average of 6% (refer to Fig. 2.7). This suggests South Asia has experienced a more pronounced V-shaped economic recovery relative to the global context. Moreover, the growth statistics for 2022 indicate that the global ramifications of the Russia–Ukraine conflict were more severe than those encountered in South Asia, on average[5].

The tightening of financial conditions has adversely affected the growth prospects of South Asia, leading to considerable downside risks in many countries

[5] Based on the findings of the Asian Development Bank (2023), it is anticipated that South Asia's export growth will experience a range of 6.8% to 3.9%. This projection is attributed to a decrease in external demand, which is expected to endure beyond the conclusion of the lockdown phase in 2021. The projected import growth in the region is expected to range from 7.3% to 6.2%. The anticipated decrease in export revenues was expected to worsen the economic crisis in multiple areas, including employment and household income. The textile and apparel industry, which employed a considerable workforce and contributed significantly to export revenues, encountered notable difficulties due to its reliance on global markets, available at https://www.adb.org/sites/default/files/publication/896606/asian-development-outlook-july-2023.pdf.

within the region. This situation is primarily attributed to limited fiscal capacity and decreasing reserves. The current circumstances highlight the urgent need to address market distortions caused by the pandemic and to confront the significant socioeconomic disparities that hinder South Asia's growth potential. The regional growth forecast for 2023 has been revised downwards from the October 2022 projection, resulting in an average estimate of 5.6%. Following a robust recovery of 8.2% in 2021, the growth rate is expected to stabilise at a more modest level of 5.9% in 2022, as demonstrated in Fig. 2.7.

A mix of favourable and unfavourable global economic trends influence the outlook for South Asia. Declining commodity prices, a robust service sector rebound, and fewer value chain disruptions support the region's economic recovery. However, South Asian economies are grappling with challenges posed by rising interest rates and the volatility of financial markets[6].

Chapter 3 thoroughly explores GDP growth, emphasising the differing expansion rates across various economic sectors. This analysis carefully examines how each sector's contributions to GDP have evolved after the COVID-19 pandemic, comparing data from the pre-pandemic period with current statistics. Additionally, Chap. 3 highlights essential regional macroeconomic indicators, such as employment rates, consumer spending, and investment trends, revealing the geographic disparities and economic recovery patterns that have emerged since the pandemic. Through this in-depth examination, readers gain a deeper insight into the complexities and nuances of economic performance in a rapidly changing landscape.

Trade

The global pandemic of COVID-19 has profoundly impacted international trade, as illustrated by Figs. 2.8 and 2.9. The epidemic has led to supply side disruptions, resulting in a notable increase in cases since its onset. Furthermore, the ongoing conflict between Russia and Ukraine, fluctuations in commodity prices, the introduction of stringent monetary policies by central banks worldwide, and concerns about potential economic slowdowns and recessions pose significant challenges to global trade.[7] This situation is especially pertinent for the South Asian region, which heavily depends on crude oil imports. Consequently, the financial dynamics in South Asia are highly influenced by the current geopolitical landscape.

The COVID-19 pandemic significantly influenced trade and supply chains, affecting global and regional scales (Baldwin and Tomiura 2020). Many countries took various actions during the global crisis to address the situation. These measures included reducing or stopping the importation of non-essential goods, temporarily closing their borders, and cancelling import orders from other nations. The

[6] According to the UN World Economic Situation and Prospects report (United Nations, 2023), the global economy is projected to grow by 2.3% in 2023, reflecting an increase of 0.4% compared to the previous forecast in January. Furthermore, the report estimates a growth rate of 2.5% for 2024, a slight decrease of 0.2% from the earlier projection. These figures indicate a modest uptick in the global growth rate for 2023.

[7] See for the text: https://unctad.org/system/files/official-document/osg2022d1_en.pdf.

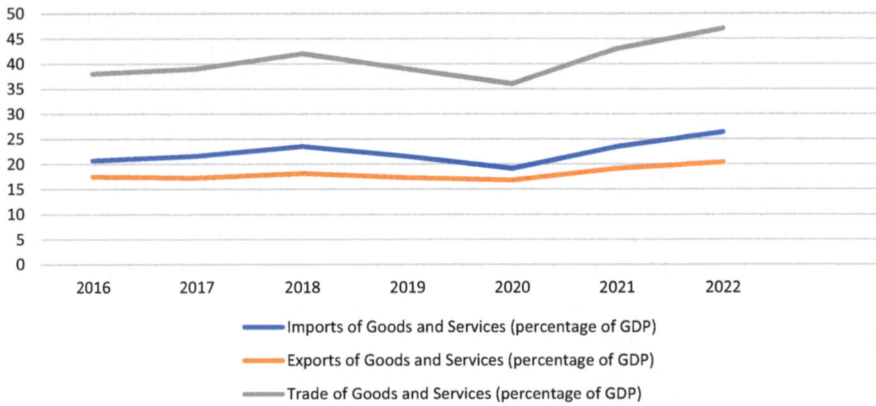

Fig. 2.8 Trade in South Asia (2016–2022). *Source*: World Bank national accounts data and OECD National Accounts data files. https://data.worldbank.org/indicator/NE.TRD.GNFS.ZS?locations=8S

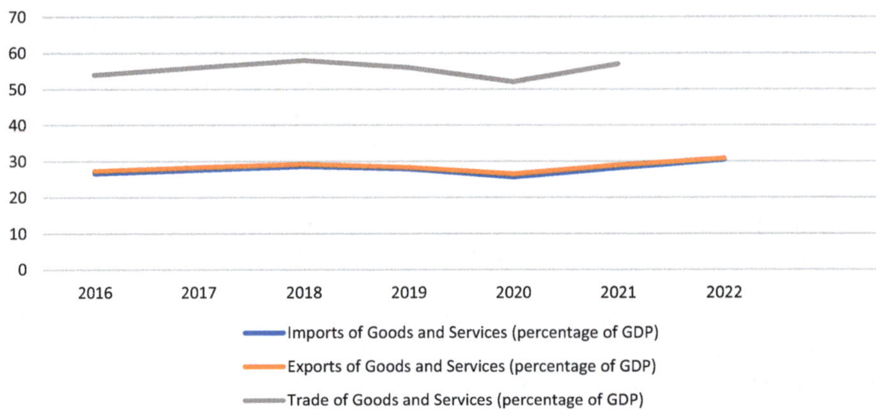

Fig. 2.9 Trade in the world (2016–2022). *Source*: World Bank national accounts and OECD National Accounts data files. https://data.worldbank.org/indicator/NE.TRD.GNFS.ZS?locations=8S

remarkable progress observed in the South Asian region over the past few decades can be attributed to the notable export expansion from this geographical area. The principal trade partners of South Asian nations include the United States, Europe, and China. These nations have experienced a slowdown in their economies because of the pandemic. The sudden decline in trade and exports resulted from an abrupt decrease in international demand. The outbreak of COVID-19 has significantly impacted the export and import activities of South Asian nations. Despite a sustained and positive trajectory in export numbers over the past few years, all countries within the South Asian region anticipate a decrease in their export volumes for the present year compared to the levels attained in 2019.

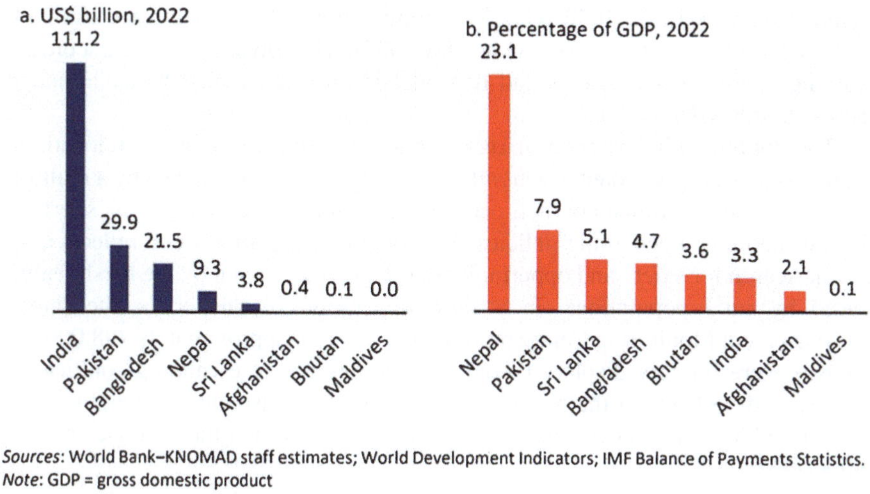

Fig. 2.10 Top remittance recipients in South Asia, 2022

According to the World Trade Organization (WTO 2024), global trade is projected to experience below-average growth in 2023 despite a modest improvement in GDP forecasts compared to the previous autumn. The global merchandise trade volume is expected to expand by 1.7% this year, drawing comparisons to the 2.7% growth rate observed in 2022. However, the trade growth fell short of earlier projections due to a significant downturn in the fourth quarter. The expansion of worldwide merchandise trade is currently impeded by several factors, including the ongoing conflict in Ukraine, persistently high inflation rates, tighter monetary policy, and prevailing market uncertainties.

Migration

In numerous South Asian countries, labour migration, both internal and international, is a widespread phenomenon. The mobility patterns observed in this region are notably complex, primarily influenced by the temporary and circular migration of low-wage labourers who move both within and across national borders (World Bank 2020a; Kapilashrami 2023). Figure 2.10 provides a detailed overview of the leading remittance recipients in South Asia for 2022[8]. While remittances constituted a modest 4% of the region's collective GDP, there was considerable variation among different countries. Notably, Nepal stood out with a remarkable 23.1% of its GDP derived from remittances, earning it a place among the top 10 countries globally known for their high remittance inflows. In comparison, Pakistan received remittances totalling 7.9% of its GDP, highlighting its economic reliance on funds sent from overseas. Sri Lanka and Bangladesh followed with remittance contributions of 5.1% and 4.7% of their GDPs, respectively. Despite being the largest recipient of

[8] For references, World Bank (2020b), World Bank (2020c), World Bank (2020d)), and IMF (2020).

remittances worldwide, India recorded a comparatively lower share, accounting for only 3.3% of its GDP in 2022 (Chandra 2023). This divergence underscores the varying economic landscapes and dependence on international financial support across South Asian nations[9].

The complex phenomenon of rural-urban migration and coerced relocation in South Asia is deeply rooted in a significant historical context, shaped by a multitude of factors such as armed conflict, persecution, natural disasters, and the shortcomings of neoliberal economic policies. This ongoing migration trend reflects a desperate search for safety and opportunity in urban areas, driven by the harsh realities faced by rural populations. In a stark illustration of this crisis, the Internal Displacement Monitoring Centre reported in 2019 that approximately 498,000 individuals were forcibly displaced from their homes due to escalating conflicts and widespread violence in the region. This alarming increase underscores the urgent need to address the underlying causes of displacement and the struggles of those affected[10].

The region under discussion is notable for having one of the highest concentrations of refugees globally, creating a complex and urgent humanitarian situation. In South Asia, mobility patterns are marked by a prevalent trend of low-wage, low-skilled temporary migration that occurs primarily within national boundaries. This includes a range of movements, such as interstate migrations and rural-to-urban transitions that occur within states. Facilitators like intermediaries and recruitment firms are crucial in enabling circular migration across regional borders, helping individuals traverse from their home countries to seek opportunities elsewhere. The economies of South Asian countries, therefore, reap substantial benefits from the contributions of these migrants. For instance, it is estimated that around 100 million internal migrants in India make a significant impact, contributing approximately 10% to the nation's Gross Domestic Product (GDP) (Deshingkar 2020). Moreover, the Gulf Cooperation Council (GCC) countries host a considerable population of South Asian expatriates who bolster their home nations' economies through remittances[11]. However, despite the crucial economic contributions made by these low-wage migrant workers, they frequently find themselves ensnared in a cycle of precariousness. This ongoing instability is characteristic of their countries of origin and destinations. The environments from which these workers come and move are often marked by a prevailing sense of poverty, informality in labour markets, and a glaring lack of job security (John and Kapilashrami 2021).

The migration patterns intricately woven over several decades in South Asia experienced a dramatic upheaval in March 2020. As the COVID-19 pandemic took hold, a substantial influx of migrants began their hurried return to their countries of

[9] Here is the link: https://blogs.worldbank.org/en/peoplemove/remittance-flows-reached-all-time-high-2022-south-asia.

[10] See World Bank (2020b) and World Bank (2020c).

[11] These financial transfers are vital, accounting for a staggering 30% of Nepal's GDP, 7.9% of Pakistan's GDP, and 5.8% of Bangladesh's GDP, highlighting the essential role of these migrant workers in sustaining their families and communities back home. See Wagle (2024).

origin, driven by sudden job losses and the stringent lockdown measures implemented to combat the virus. These individuals, hailing from the far reaches of Europe, the Gulf states, North America, and various Asian regions, embarked on poignant journeys back to their homelands, often filled with uncertainty and longing.

Many domestic migrants relied on trains, a lifeline for countless individuals, to navigate their way back to their rural towns and villages after spending time in bustling urban centres. This mass movement of people has been characterised as the Great Reverse Migration. This phenomenon is the largest mass migration in South Asia since the tumultuous partition of India in 1947. These travellers' swift and widespread return sparked alarm over the potential for COVID-19 transmission during their often cramped and challenging journeys home, highlighting the intersection of mobility, health, and community in a crisis[12].

Informal Sector and Unemployment

The informal sector in South Asia is a vibrant yet precarious component, encompassing over 90% of the region's businesses and engaging more than 80% of its workforce[13]. Workers in this sector face significant challenges, particularly compared to their counterparts in formal employment and larger businesses, who demonstrate a higher resilience in economic turmoil. Unfortunately, the onset of the COVID-19 pandemic has severely worsened these conditions, with informal businesses and their employees bearing the brunt of its impacts. In April 2020, the ramifications of the pandemic were starkly evident, as more than 44% of the Indian workforce found themselves unemployed—a dramatic and distressing reality[14]. Informal workers, characterised by their temporary or casual employment arrangements, were particularly vulnerable; they experienced a pronounced risk of job displacement compared to those who were self-employed. This trend was consistent across various industries, geographic locations, and educational backgrounds, highlighting the systemic vulnerabilities within the informal labour force. The economic hardships ushered in by the pandemic were not uniform but disproportionately impacted those engaged in informal work. Statistics reveal a troubling reduction in income for informal workers, particularly those within the middle-income range. In Bangladesh, India, and Pakistan, the poorest segments of the population—who largely depended on the informal sector—suffered significant declines in earnings, with reductions of 9%, 13%, and 16%, respectively[15]. While the wealthiest third of society faced milder financial setbacks, the middle tier of the informal workforce experienced losses of a similar magnitude, ranging from 11% to 16%[16]. Informal

---

[12] For reference, see Lee et al. (2021), available at https://www.sciencedirect.com/science/article/pii/S0047272720301766.

[13] For details, see Bussolo et al. (2020), available at https://blogs.worldbank.org/en/endpovertyinsouthasia/covid-19-has-worsened-woes-south-asias-informal-sector.

[14] See Bussolo et al. (2020).

[15] See da Silva (2022), available at https://socialprotection.org/discover/blog/gaps-coverage-missing-middle-south-asia.

[16] See Caetano, *ibid.*

workers experienced significantly greater financial losses than their counterparts in the formal sector, regardless of their wage levels. Looking to the future, it is crucial for governments to actively support the informal economy actively, acknowledging its vital contributions to livelihoods and the larger economy. In the long term, there is an urgent need to establish comprehensive and universal social security systems to provide safety nets for individuals in this sector. Policymakers should also explore proactive strategies to enhance productivity and develop human capital within the informal sector, rather than merely expecting a natural transition to formal economic activity. This approach would help alleviate the negative impacts of COVID-19 and promote sustainable growth and resilience for this essential segment of the workforce.

Education

Despite the concerted efforts by governments and educational partners to promote remote learning in countries such as India, the Maldives, Pakistan, and Sri Lanka, the prolonged school closures have created significant disparities in educational access for children throughout South Asia. The impact of the COVID-19 pandemic led to the unsettling interruption of education for a staggering 434 million children in the region. According to a comprehensive study by UNICEF (2021b), many students and their parents expressed deep concerns regarding the drastic decline in learning engagement since schools closed their doors. For example, a striking 80% of children in India, aged between 14 and 18, reported that their study habits had deteriorated compared to their previous experiences in a classroom setting. Similarly, in Sri Lanka, alarming statistics emerged, as 69% of parents with children in primary school indicated that their youngsters were learning "less" or "significantly less" during this challenging period[17]. The situation has been particularly arduous for marginalised groups, including children with disabilities, girls, and those hailing from low-income families, who have faced heightened challenges in accessing effective online learning. The combined effects of these disruptions paint a troubling picture of educational equity in South Asia during the pandemic. Furthermore, school closures in the region have forced hundreds of millions of students and their teachers to transition to remote learning, often in areas with limited connectivity and costly technology. Children may face challenges obtaining the necessary technology even when families can access devices. Consequently, students have encountered significant setbacks in their learning journey[18].

Governments worldwide have made significant efforts to transition to remote learning in response to school closures. However, these initiatives have encountered substantial challenges, particularly in developing regions. For example, 42% of

[17] See UNICEF (2021), available at https://www.unicef.org/india/press-releases/repeated-school-closures-due-covid-19.

[18] Statement by George Laryea-Adjei, UNICEF Regional Director for South Asia, available at https://www.unicef.org.uk/press-releases/deadly-new-surge-in-south-asia-threatens-to-reverse-global-gains-against-the-covid-19-pandemic-and-have-disproportionate-impact-on-children/.

Indian children aged 6–13 reported not engaging in remote learning during the pandemic-induced school closures. Similarly, in neighbouring Pakistan, 23% of younger students lacked access to the technology necessary for participating in online education. The most vulnerable families, especially those from lower socio-economic backgrounds, have been disproportionately affected, often struggling to afford even a single device to support their children's learning. Research from UNICEF[19] highlights that their usage and access are often limited, even when digital devices are available. For instance, only about 24% of Pakistani children with smartphones can use them as freely as needed. The study emphasises the crucial role of student–teacher interaction in the learning process, particularly for younger children. It found that consistent and reciprocal communication between teachers and students is a key indicator of educational success. Unfortunately, the survey (UNICEF 2021a) revealed a stark reality: most students had minimal contact with their teachers after dismissing classes. Alarmingly, only 8% of public primary school teachers in Sri Lanka reported maintaining communication with their students five days a week, compared to 52% of teachers in private primary schools. The widespread disruption caused by the pandemic and prolonged lockdowns has profoundly impacted education at all levels—from primary to secondary education—and has also affected higher education institutions. This has resulted in significant learning losses likely to have long-term implications.

2.4 Sustainable Development Goals (SDGs) and Addressing Vulnerability

The South Asian countries have faced many pre-existing challenges that significantly hindered their journey towards achieving Sustainable Development Goals (SDGs), particularly in the wake of the COVID-19 pandemic. These challenges include alarmingly high levels of hunger and poverty, a public health infrastructure that is severely underfunded, and a lack of essential services such as sanitary toilets and access to clean drinking water. Moreover, inadequate social protection measures have further compounded these issues. The pandemic has thrown a spotlight on the long-standing structural inequities within the region, and the adverse conditions that were already present laid the groundwork for the pandemic's devastating socioeconomic fallout.

The SDGs represent vital frameworks and resources that nations and their communities can leverage to respond to and recover from the immediate and lingering effects of crises like the COVID-19 pandemic. Their emphasis on establishing robust social protection systems, eradicating food insecurity, and providing universal healthcare access is particularly critical in South Asia. This significance is

[19] See UNICEF (2021), *ibid,* available at https://www.unicef.org/rosa/press-releases/repeated-school-closures-due-covid-19-leading-learning-loss-and-widening-inequities.

amplified because most of the population lives in extreme poverty. At the same time, economic activities often occur within an informal sector characterised by limited opportunities for quality employment and low participation rates of women in the workforce. As the COVID-19 pandemic unfolded, it coincided with a growing commitment to the SDGs and a gradual approach towards achieving specific regional goals. However, it became evident that numerous significant obstacles persisted, preventing the successful attainment of most SDGs within the set timelines.

In stark contrast to the global average of 9.1% of GDP allocated to healthcare spending in 2022, South Asian nations invest only 3.30% of their GDP in this sector. Among these countries, Afghanistan stands out with the highest allocation at 23.09%, while Bangladesh reports the lowest at 2.39%. The East Asia and Pacific region, excluding high-income countries, performs somewhat better, with investments averaging approximately 5.15% of GDP[20]. This significant disparity highlights the weaknesses in public health infrastructure across the region, particularly concerning supply side issues such as the availability of hospital beds and the number of healthcare professionals. These challenges primarily result from inadequate resource allocation within the healthcare sector. The pandemic has further exposed these critical vulnerabilities, revealing a fragile health system that struggles to meet its demands. Additionally, the region grapples with challenges related to limited broadband connectivity and insufficient sanitary services, which hinder the implementation of alternative working arrangements during lockdowns.

A majority of the workforce in South Asian countries is engaged in the informal economy, which lacks social security protections. This vulnerability exposes many workers to economic shocks that threaten their livelihoods due to the lack of necessary social security and insufficient state-provided protections. Consequently, what initially began as a health crisis has evolved into a complex dilemma intertwining humanitarian issues and economic difficulties. This precarious state has particularly affected vulnerable populations, including migrant workers, casual labourers, and those relying on daily wages, as they face the urgent risk of insufficient access to necessities like food, income, and other essential resources. The ongoing global pandemic has ushered in profound negative economic and humanitarian impacts that are mutually reinforcing, compounding the existing challenges. The implementation of lockdowns and various containment measures has caused significant disruptions to economic activities, leading to closures of businesses and enterprises, widespread job losses, and the potential to plunge millions deeper into extreme poverty. Consequently, the developmental achievements made over recent years are at serious risk of being rolled back. The vulnerabilities highlighted by the SDGs have posed significant challenges to the coping mechanisms of the South Asian region, making it increasingly difficult to address and manage these critical vulnerabilities effectively (ESCAP 2021)

[20] See accessed at 1:45 p.m Uzbek time on May 13, 2025.

2.5 Addressing the Job Loss and Poverty Challenges Brought on by COVID-19 in South Asia

Job Loss

The South Asian region, home to approximately 2.04 billion people in 2022, accounts for about 25% of the global population. With around 1.08 billion working-age individuals, it has the largest working-age population in the world (ILO 2022). The unemployment rate[21] in South Asia was 7.55% in 2020, reflecting a 1.32% increase from 2019. It decreased to 6.45% in 2021, marking a 1.1% decline from the previous year. In 2022, the unemployment rate dropped further to 5.15%, a 1.3% decline from 2021, and for 2023, it fell to 4.61%, showing a decrease of 0.53% from 2022 (Macrotrends 2025). The pandemic has led to a significant slowdown in economic activity, resulting in diminished profits and substantial job losses during 2020–2022. The unemployment landscape has exhibited similarities across the various nations within the region. Different industries have faced varying impacts; for instance, production-related sectors have been severely affected by lockdown measures, while others, such as information technology (IT)—where remote work was a viable option—have experienced minimal disruption (Ordonez 2020).

The pandemic disproportionately impacted informal businesses[22] and their employees across South Asia, highlighting stark contrasts with the experiences of those in the formal sector. In India, a concerning 44% of the workforce engaged in informal employment found themselves unemployed in 2020, highlighting the sector's vulnerability during such a crisis, according to a World Bank study (Bussolo et al. 2020). Similar effects were observed in neighbouring countries. The study notes that in Bangladesh, approximately 9% of individuals dependent on the informal economy experienced significant income losses, while this figure escalated to 13% in India and 16% in Pakistan. Alarmingly, the scale of job losses in India was staggering, with projections suggesting that between 30 and 100 million individuals across both formal and informal sectors lost their livelihoods. The garment industry in Bangladesh was particularly affected, with layoffs expected to impact between 2.5 and 3 million workers, underscoring the sector's critical role in the economy. Pakistan faced severe challenges as well, with nearly 18 million people reported to have lost their jobs directly due to the pandemic. Meanwhile, Afghanistan is preparing for an alarming rise in unemployment, projected to increase by approximately 40%, according to the Ministry of Economy (Kepayet 2020). The study reveals that individuals in the middle third of the income distribution experienced similar losses across these countries, with reported income loss percentages of 11%, 7%, and 16%. In contrast, the wealthiest 33% of the population faced significantly less

---

[21] Unemployment refers to the share of the labour force without work but available for and seeking employment. It is available at https://www.macrotrends.net/global-metrics/countries/SAS/south-asia/unemployment-rate accessed at 3:30 p.m. Uzbek time on May 14, 2025.

[22] More than 80% of all South Asia's workers engage in informal activities, and over 90% of the region's businesses are informal, see da Silva Luciano (2022).

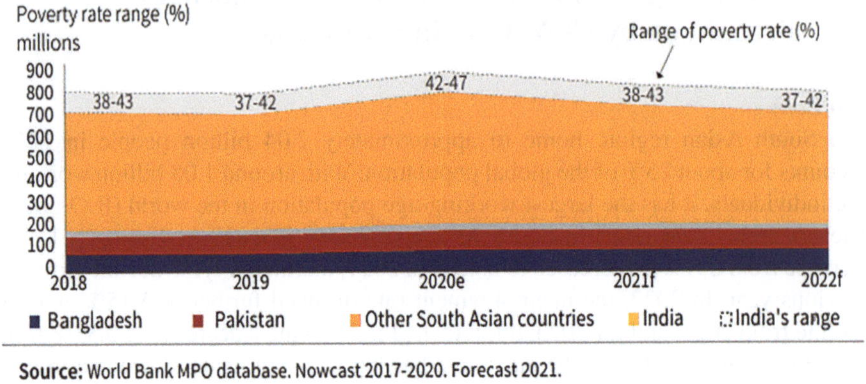

Fig. 2.11 COVID-19-induced poverty rates at the lower middle-income level falls to the range of 37–43% for the South Asian Region in 2022. *Source*: World Bank MPO database. Nowcast 2017–2020. Forecast 2021

severe impacts, highlighting a widening disparity in economic resilience among various socioeconomic groups during the crisis period.

COVID-19-Induced Poverty

A significant study conducted by the World Bank in 2021 (World Bank 2021) explored the profound effects of COVID-19 on global poverty rates, with a particular emphasis on the lower-middle-income poverty threshold of $3.20 per day from 2018 to 2021. The findings revealed that in 2020, 19% and 24% of individuals living in extreme poverty—defined by this lower middle-income standard—were in this region. This statistic starkly contrasts with pre-crisis estimates, which suggested that only 12% to 17% of the global poor fell into this category.

Furthermore, the study highlights that over two-thirds of the newly identified global extreme poor[23], categorised as those who either fell into poverty or remained trapped in it due to the pandemic, are concentrated in South Asia. Projections indicate that the poverty rate in this region, defined by living on $3.20 a day, is expected to range between 37% and 42% in 2022, a slight improvement from the previous year's estimates of 42%–47% (Fig. 2.11). Nevertheless, all countries within this region are anticipated to experience a gradual reduction in poverty levels as economic growth resumes and per capita income begins to recover[24].

[23] This estimate was based on earlier forecasts of GDP growth, which indicated a significant decline in GDP. However, the conclusion remains valid regardless of the poverty line considered: most of the newly impoverished individuals due to COVID-19 are situated in South Asia. Generally, the uncertainty surrounding India's poverty statistics affects the estimates for South Asia. For 2020, the poverty rate at $3.20 per day is estimated to be between 41% and 47% in India.

[24] However Poverty in the region will not fall as quickly as expected, given that elevated inflation, a slow recovery of employment and incomes, and the withdrawal of pandemic-era food programmes impact the poor the hardest. See,https://openknowledge.worldbank.org/server/api/core/bitstreams/efe1e55a-fe61-452f-a2da-3b01b9c9c477/content.

2.6 Region-Specific Observations, Anecdotes

At the onset of the pandemic, South Asia was thrust into a state of turmoil, facing a dramatic shock that disrupted economies and shattered livelihoods across the region. However, as the two years unfolded, most countries showed remarkable resilience and adaptability in confronting the mounting challenges brought on by the pandemic and compounded by political uncertainties, with the notable exceptions of Bangladesh, Pakistan, and Afghanistan. These pressing issues are elaborated upon in Chap. 3. Sri Lanka, in particular, witnessed a significant economic unravelling during the years 2021–2022. The adverse effects of the pandemic severely impacted critical sectors, including tourism—a cornerstone of its economy—the flow of remittances, and the renowned tea industry for which the country is famous. In a bid to promote sustainability, the government's abrupt transition to a fully organic farming model was expected to yield positive outcomes, but instead turned into a catalyst for economic distress, exacerbating the situation. Further complicating these challenges was China's so-called "debt trap diplomacy", alongside substantial tax reductions implemented for political advantages that deepened Sri Lanka's financial woes. Additionally, the fallout from the Russia–Ukraine conflict added a layer of complexity, hindering recovery efforts. Projections indicate that Sri Lanka's economic growth rate is expected to settle at around 3.5% by 2025. This forecast remains consistent with the estimates from October and is buoyed by the promising outcomes of Sri Lanka's economic reforms, particularly in strengthening public finances and building reserves. Meanwhile, other South Asian countries such as Nepal, Maldives, Bhutan, and Afghanistan are progressing and appear to be on the right track towards better economic stability. The International Monetary Fund (IMF) has a notably optimistic outlook for India, predicting that it will become the world's fourth-largest economy by 2025, surpassing Japan for the first time. The IMF's latest projections estimate India's nominal GDP will soar to an impressive $4.187 trillion in 2025, just ahead of Japan's anticipated $4.186 trillion. India's success in weathering the storm of the pandemic can largely be attributed to its effective vaccine diplomacy and emerging role as a global pharmaceutical leader. The Indian government's nimble policy frameworks, highlighted by initiatives such as Atma Nirbhar Bharat, alongside proactive economic strategies, have significantly contributed to this optimistic growth trajectory.

References

Acharya R, Porwal A (2020) A vulnerability index for the management of and response to the COVID-19 epidemic in India: an ecological study. Lancet 8:E1142–E1151. https://doi.org/10.1016/S2214-109X(20)30300-4

Acuité Ratings (2020) COVID-19 lockdown estimated to cost India $4.5 billion a day: Acuité ratings. The Hindu Business Line, Chennai, April 2

Asian Development Bank (2023) Asian development outlook. July, Manila. https://www.adb.org/sites/default/files/publication/896606/asian-development-outlook-july-2023.pdf

Babu GR, Khetrapal S, John DA, Deepa R, Narayan KV (2021) Pandemic preparedness and response to COVID-19 in south Asian countries. Int J Infect Dis 104:169–174

Baldwin R, Tomiura E (2020) Thinking ahead about the trade impact of COVID-19. Economics in the Time of COVID-19 A59, March 6

Banik A, Nag T, Chowdhury SR, Chatterjee R (2020) Why do COVID-19 fatality rates differ across countries? An explorative cross-country study based on select indicators. Glob Bus Rev 21(3):607–625

Banik A, Singla SK (2021) Wide disparity in vaccine drive across the world, The Hindu Business Line, June 17

Bussolo M, Sharma S, Timmer H (2020) COVID-19 has worsened the woes of South Asia's informal sector. World Bank blogs https://blogs.worldbank.org/endpovertyinsouthasia/covid-19-has-worsened-woes-south-asias-informal-sector

Chandra V (2023) Remittance flows an all-time high in 2022 in South Asia. World Bank blog, October 10. https://blogs.worldbank.org/en/peoplemove/remittance-flows-reached-all-time-high-2022-south-asia

C da Silva Luciano (2022) Gaps in coverage of the missing middle class in South Asia. https://socialprotection.org/discover/blog/gaps-coverage-missing-middle-south-asia

Deshingkar P (2020) Why India's migrants deserve a better deal, The Mint: New Delhi, May 18. https://www.livemint.com/news/india/why-india-s-migrants-deserve-a-better-deal-11589818749274.html

ESACAP (2021) Achieving the SDGs in South Asia: an integrated approach to accelerate SDG progress and covid-19 recovery. https://www.unescap.org/sites/default/d8files/knowledge-products/South%20Asia%20SDG%20Report%202021_261121.pdf

ESCAP (2020) COVID-19 and South Asia: national strategies and subregional cooperation for accelerating inclusive, sustainable and resilient recovery. https://www.unescap.org/sites/default/files/South%20Asia%20Covid-19%20Paper_5.pdf

FAO (2020) Responding to the impact of the COVID-19 outbreak on food value chains through efficient logistics. Rome doi:https://doi.org/10.4060/ca8466en

FAO, IFAD, UNICEF, WFP, WHO (2020) Joint statement on COVID-19—impacts on food security and nutrition, Rome

Government of India (2021) Economic survey 2020–21. Ministry of Finance, New Delhi

Government of India (2024) Ayushman Bharat Pradhan Mantri Jan Arogya Yojana. https://www.india.gov.in/spotlight/ayushman-bharat-pradhan-mantri-jan-arogya-yojana

Hale T, Angrist N, Goldszmidt R, Kira B, Petherick A, Phillips T, Webster S, Cameron-Blake E, Hallas L, Majumdar S, Tatlow H (2021) A global panel database of pandemic policies (Oxford COVID-19 government response tracker). Nat Hum Behav 5(4):529–538

Hayat M, Uzair M, Ali Syed R, Arshad M, Bashir S (2022) Status of COVID-19 vaccination around South Asia. Hum Vaccin Immunother 18(1):2016010

ILO. (2022). World Employment and Social Outlook 2022. Geneva.

International Monetary Fund (2020) International financial statistics, Washington, DC. https://data.imf.org/?sk=4c514d48-b6ba-49ed-8ab9-52b0c1a0179b&sId=1537997141415

John EA, Kapilashrami A (2021) Victims, villains, and the rare hero: analysis of migrant and refugee health portrayals in the Indian print media. Indian J Med Ethics 6(2):145–155

Kapilashrami A (2023) Pandemic, precarity, and health of migrants in South Asia: mapping multiple dimensions of Precarity and pathways to states of health and well-being. J Migrat Health 7(2–3):100180

Kepayet M (2020) An insight into the unemployment amidst COVID-19 in South Asia. Modern diplomacy, link. https://moderndiplomacy.eu/2020/05/14/an-insight-on-the-unemployment-amidst-the-covid-19-in-south-asia/

Lee JN, Mahmud M, Morduch J, Ravindran S, Shonchoy AS (2021) Migration, externalities, and the diffusion of COVID-19 in South Asia. J Public Econ 193(January):104312

Macrotrends (2025) South Asia unemployment rate 1991–2025. https://www.macrotrends.net/global-metrics/countries/SAS/south-asia/unemployment-rate

Ordonez J (2020) Almost 25 million jobs could be lost worldwide as a result of COVID-19. International Labour Organisation. https://www.ilo.org/global/about-the-ilo/newsroom/news/WCMS_738742/lang–en/index.htm

Ozili PK, Arun T (2020) Spillover of COVID-19: impact on the global economy. https://papers.ssrn.com/sol3/papers.cfm?abstract_id=3562570

Rasul G, Nepal AK, Hussain A, Maharjan A, Joshi S, Lama A, Sharma E (2021) Socio-economic implications of COVID-19 pandemic in South Asia: emerging risks and growing challenges. Front Sociol 6:629693

Rasul G, Neupane N, Pasakhala B, Gurung P, Nepal A, Sharma E (2020) Deepening regional cooperation for enhancing water, energy, and food security and addressing COVID-19 challenges in the Hindu Kush Himalayan region. In: Tiziano D (ed) Water resources and economic processes. Routledge, London. https://doi.org/10.4324/9780429025013

UNICEF (2021a) Accelerating progress towards universal health coverage in South Asia in the era of COVID-19. How universal primary care can tackle the inseparable agendas of universal health coverage and health security. https://www.unicef.org/rosa/media/17021/file/Accelerating%20progress%20towards%20Universal%20Health%20Coverage%20in%20South%20Asia%20in%20the%20era%20of%20Covid-19.pdf

UNICEF (2021b) Repeated school closures due to COVID-19 leading to learning loss and widening inequities in South Asia, Press release. https://www.unicef.org/india/press-releases/repeated-school-closures-due-covid-19

United Nations (2023) World economic situation and prospects 2023, New York. https://www.un.org/development/desa/dpad/publication/world-economic-situation-and-prospects-2023/

Wagle UR (2024) Labor migration, remittances, and the economy in the Gulf cooperation council region. CMS 12:30. https://doi.org/10.1186/s40878-024-00390-3

World Bank (2018) Sri Lanka-achieving pro-poor universal health coverage without health financing reforms, https://documents.worldbank.org/pt/publication/documents-reports/documentdetail/138941516179080537/sri-lanka-achieving-pro-poor-universal-health-coverage-without-health-financing-reforms

World Bank (2020a) Towards safer and more productive migration for South Asia. Wahington, DC. http://hdl.handle.net/10986/33559. License: CC BY 3.0 IGO

World Bank (2020b) Migration and development brief 33: covid-19 crisis through a migration lens, April 2020. KNOMAD-World Bank, Washington, DC

World Bank (2020c) Migration and development brief 33: phase II covid-19 crisis through a migration lens, October 2020. KNOMAD-World Bank, Washington, DC

World Bank (2020d) World development report, Washington, DC. https://www.worldbank.org/en/publication/wdr2020/brief/world-development-report-2020-data

World Bank (2021) South Asia vaccinates, South Asia economic focus, Spring, Washington, DC

World Bank (2023) Explaining opportunities toward inclusive growth, Washington, DC, p 88

World Trade Organization (2024) World trade outlook and statistics, Geneva. https://www.wto-ilibrary.org/content/books/9789287076335/read

Chapter 3
Exploring the Impact of Extraordinary Health Hazards on Growth, Investment, and Employment: A Deeper Dive

Abstract The COVID-19 pandemic has had a profound impact on the economies of South Asia. It has affected growth, investments, and job opportunities. As we navigate these challenging times, it is essential to examine how the pandemic has altered our economic landscape and what this means for the future. In South Asia, the pandemic presented significant challenges, resulting in major disruptions to supply chains and a decline in consumer demand. This has lowered GDP and impacted three main sectors: Agriculture, Manufacturing, and Services. Although some industries, such as IT and pharmaceuticals, have experienced growth, many others continue to struggle. The pandemic also led to a significant decline in Foreign Direct Investment (FDI) in South Asia. From 2021 to 2023, FDI dropped from $53 billion to just $36 billion. Despite this, India remained the top recipient of FDI in the region in 2023. The job market in South Asia has partially recovered. Policymakers can help lessen the long-term effects of the pandemic by providing support to regional service centres. These centres can offer job-matching services, training, and IT help for workers. This support will make it easier for people to transition into new jobs and industries. The job market is changing, influenced by rapid technological advancements and the emergence of new industries, particularly in healthcare. The future of work offers both new opportunities and challenges for workers, employers, and the economy. Key trends expected to shape jobs in South Asia include greater digital access, geopolitical tensions, and efforts to tackle climate change. Like companies worldwide, businesses in the region are investing in technologies such as artificial intelligence (AI), robotics, autonomous systems, and energy solutions.

Keywords South Asia · Pandemic · COVID-19-induced inflation · Recovery · Energy prices · Foreign exchange rates · Monetary policy · Stock market · Investment in South Asia · Employment · COVID-19-induced job losses · Skill-intensive technology · Wage inequality · Future of jobs in South Asia

A. Banik et al., *Extraordinary Health Hazards and their Socio-Economic Effects in South Asia*, South Asia Economic and Policy Studies, https://doi.org/10.1007/978-981-95-5729-5_3

3.1 Introduction

In the preceding chapter, we undertook an in-depth examination of the multitude of challenges that arose during the COVID-19 pandemic, with a particular emphasis on critical elements such as vaccination initiatives, fatality statistics, and the varying degrees of stringency adopted by governments worldwide. We scrutinised how these formidable challenges have profoundly affected the South Asian economies, a region already struggling with high poverty rates and unstable job markets. The pandemic precipitated widespread job losses, curtailed access to essential social protection systems, and exacerbated inadequate sanitation facilities, all of which intensified the hardships endured by the populace. A noteworthy consequence has been the significant decline in migration, which has historically served as a vital safety net for countless families. Furthermore, we observed the adverse impacts on micro, small, and medium enterprises (MSMEs), which serve as the backbone of the regional economy but have been profoundly affected during this tumultuous period. The once-thriving tourism sector, a key source of revenue and employment, has faced unprecedented challenges, leading to labour shortages and sudden demand shocks across various industries. The overarching effects of the pandemic have starkly highlighted the vulnerabilities inherent in these economies and underscored the urgent need for comprehensive recovery strategies that extend beyond immediate relief. In response to the pandemic, governments throughout the region reacted with remarkable speed and implemented broad-ranging measures. They employed many policy tools that were entirely new or previously untested on such an extensive scale in emerging economies. Among these measures were substantial direct income support initiatives, temporary debt moratoria, and expansive asset purchase programmes orchestrated by central banks. The variation in these programmes was striking, reflecting the disparate struggles of countries, with all except India facing significant challenges in mobilising resources due to their constrained access to credit markets during the pandemic. Moreover, the fiscal responses exhibited substantial variability, highlighting the marked differences in the readiness and capability of governments to invest in support mechanisms. It is well-documented that the majority of COVID-19 cases in developing Asia originated from South Asia. Beyond the health-related vulnerabilities and the economic fallout, which manifested as diminished demand spillovers, disruptions to supply chain production links in developing Asia contributed to a nearly 30% contraction in global output (Sawada and Lea 2021). Tourism-dependent economies in the South Asian region, particularly those in the region, bore the brunt, experiencing a stark decline in the service sector's contribution to production and trade. Nevertheless, some countries emerged as exceptions amid this global crisis. During these turbulent times, countries in the region adopted expansionary monetary policies characterised by increased government spending, predominantly directed towards the health sector, all while grappling with escalating debts (Friedrich Naumann Foundation 2020). However, the judicious and well-crafted fiscal consolidation measures distinguished the recovery efforts, enabling these economies to meet their primary objectives during the pandemic while upholding fiscal discipline (World Bank 2020a).

This chapter provides an in-depth analysis of the economic shocks experienced by South Asian economies during the COVID-19 pandemic, while also outlining their recovery strategies. The pandemic has profoundly altered the economic landscape, influencing a wide range of factors including growth metrics, investment strategies, employment opportunities, and the technological implications for future employment in the region. As we navigate these challenging times, it is crucial to evaluate how the pandemic has reshaped our economic reality and what this signifies for the future.

3.2 Envisioning a Post-COVID-19 Growth Landscape: Insights and Reflections

Impact on Gross Domestic Product, Manufacturing, Agriculture, and Services Sector

The South Asian region has encountered significant challenges due to the pandemic, resulting in severe supply chain disruptions and a marked decline in consumer demand. This upheaval has reduced GDP, particularly affecting three key sectors: Agriculture, Manufacturing, and Services. While specific industries, particularly the IT and pharmaceutical sectors, have experienced growth in production, many others continue to face ongoing challenges. Figure 3.1 illustrates the annual change in Real Gross Domestic Product (GDP) (%) during the pre- and post-COVID-19 period (2015-2024) across South Asian countries. The data reveals that, during the 2019–2020 period, all economies experienced negative growth, with the exceptions of Nepal (2.3%), Bangladesh (5.2%), and Bhutan (2.4%). In contrast, notable negative changes were observed in the Maldives (20.5%), India (9%), and Sri Lanka (6.1%).

Figures 3.2, 3.3, and 3.4 provide a detailed illustration of the annual growth rates for three vital sectors of the economy: agriculture, manufacturing, and services, spanning the years from 2017 to 2022. The onset of the COVID-19 pandemic had a profound impact on global economic activities, resulting in a sharp decline during the first half of 2020. This downturn was primarily driven by the implementation of extensive lockdowns and social distancing measures aimed at mitigating the spread of the virus. Despite these challenges, the agricultural sector demonstrated remarkable resilience, sustaining growth even as the economy recovered. In contrast, the manufacturing and service sectors have struggled significantly, experiencing reduced output that has put additional strain on overall economic performance.

Furthermore, Figs. 3.5, 3.6, and 3.7 present an insightful analysis of each sector's contribution to the Gross Domestic Product (GDP) as a percentage, highlighting the differences observed during and after the COVID-19 outbreak. This data

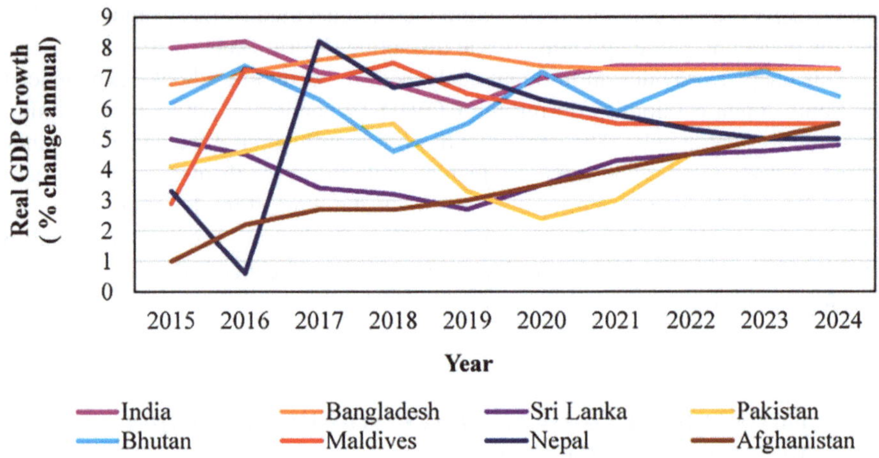

Fig. 3.1 Annual change in Real Gross Domestic Products (%) during the pre- and post-COVID-19 period (2015–2024) in South Asian Countries. *Source*: Based on the data available at the World Bank, World Development Indicators: selected indicators for the South Asian Region

underscores the shifting dynamics within the economy as it navigated the unprecedented challenges posed by the pandemic.

The current situation is exacerbated by diminished revenues from trade disruptions and a noticeable decline in tax compliance rates, which have taken a toll on government finances. Interestingly, despite the widespread struggles faced by numerous sectors during this period, the manufacturing output in India, Bangladesh, and Nepal displayed some resilience and even recorded modest growth amid the pandemic. In Bangladesh, the manufacturing sector, however, bore the brunt of significant challenges mainly due to its heavy reliance on micro, small, and medium enterprises (MSMEs), especially within the textile industry. The onset of the pandemic led to substantial supply side disruptions, severely hindering operations and resulting in a sharp decline in textile export demand.[1] Consequently, the sector faced several obstacles, including a reduced production scale and operational capacity, which significantly affected manufacturing. This downturn created a ripple effect throughout the industry, reducing turnover and income for businesses connected to the manufacturing sector. Nevertheless, optimism emerged as a gradual recovery

[1] India provided a transshipment facility to Bangladesh during a period when COVID-19 had a significant impact on the entire South Asia region. Like many other countries, Bangladesh suffered greatly from the pandemic, but its garment manufacturers began receiving orders for essential health gear, including masks, medical cloth, and gloves. Faced with flight and shipping restrictions, Bangladesh sought assistance from India. This collaboration enabled Bangladesh to enhance its manufacturing capabilities despite the challenging circumstances; see also De, Prabir, https://indianexpress.com/article/opinion/columns/rise-and-fall-india-bangladesh-transshipment-ties-9943183/

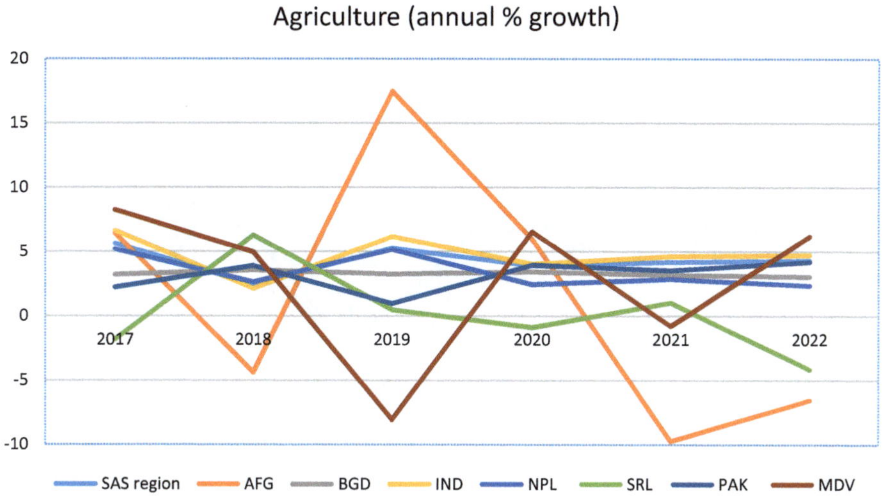

Fig. 3.2 Annual growth of the agriculture sector (%) during the pre- and post-COVID-19 period (2017–2022) in South Asian countries. *Source*: Based on the data available at the World Bank, World Development Indicators: selected indicators for the Asian Region

was observed in the aftermath of the pandemic, suggesting a potential path to revitalisation (Sen et al. 2020).

The pandemic had a profound impact on businesses, resulting in a significant slowdown in operations across various industries. This disruption particularly affected the manufacturing sector in India, resulting in a significant decline in production levels. As factories faced challenges in maintaining their usual output, the consequences rippled through the economy, diminishing turnover and reducing income for many companies. Ultimately, the effects of these low-scale operations not only strained individual businesses but also posed broader challenges for the entire manufacturing landscape in the country.[2] The Indian government implemented several relief measures during the pandemic, including the Essential Commodities Act, logistical support, and special passes for COVID-19-related travel. These initiatives significantly eased the operational burdens for various stakeholders, enabling them to conduct their daily business activities more effectively. As the initial wave of infections began to stabilise, a sense of optimism started to permeate the business landscape, particularly with the phased reopening of the economy. This newfound hope spurred positive expectations regarding business

[2] The Index of Industrial Production (IIP) also fell to a negative growth rate of 9.6%, indicating that core manufacturing activity suffered setbacks from both the first and second waves of the pandemic. The IIP typically reflects the industrial sector's overall output, including manufacturing, mining, and electricity production. If the IIP shows a decline, it suggests that the industrial sector's output is contracting, which can indicate a slowdown in economic growth. For reference, https://www.mondaq.com/india/operational-impacts-and-strategy/1086172/impact-of-covid-19-on-the-manufacturing-sector-in-india accessed at 1:08 p.m. Uzbek Time on May 20, 2025.

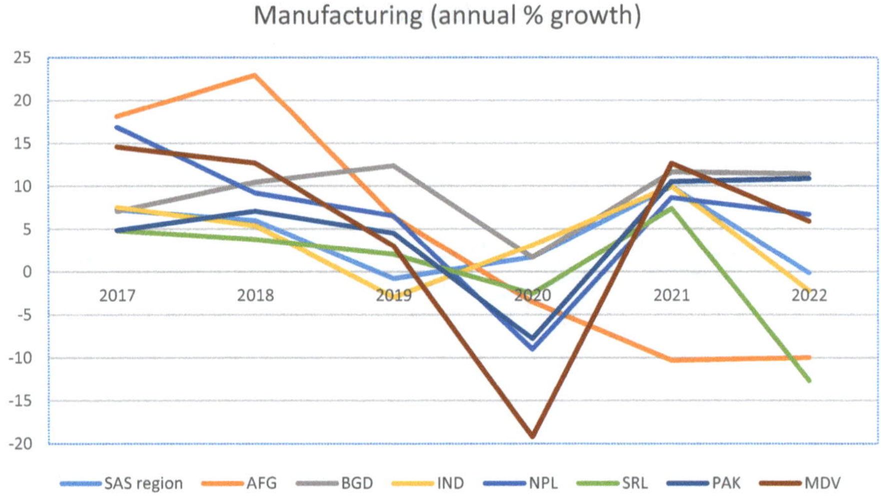

Fig. 3.3 Annual growth of the manufacturing sector (%) during the pre- and post-COVID-19 Period (2017–2022) in South Asian countries. *Source*: Based on the data available at the World Bank, World Development Indicators: selected indicators for the South Asian Region

output. The manufacturing sector, in particular, experienced significant growth as COVID-19 restrictions were gradually lifted. Factories resumed full-time production, driven by an increase in new orders and a surge in exports, marking a robust recovery and a promising outlook for the months ahead. Figure 3.8 visually represents the Purchasing Manager's Index (PMI)[3] for the manufacturing sector, a crucial indicator that reflects production activity and economic health. The data reveals a significant downturn in the manufacturing sector during 2020, attributed mainly to the widespread disruptions caused by the pandemic. However, subsequent months showed signs of recovery, indicating a gradual rebound as businesses adapted and adjusted to the new economic landscape.

The economy of Sri Lanka is intricately linked to key sectors, including tourism, tea production, rubber exports, and the influx of remittances from overseas workers. During the pandemic, the country experienced significant challenges, particularly evident in the export volume indices for various products. Notably, exports of rubber products, petroleum goods, textile and apparel items, and the overall manufactured goods sector plummeted to their lowest levels due to the crisis. Prior to the

[3]The S&P Global India Manufacturing Purchasing Managers' Index (PMI) assesses the performance of the manufacturing sector based on a survey conducted among 500 manufacturing companies. The PMI is composed of five individual indexes, with the following weightings: New Orders (30%), Output (25%), Employment (20%), Suppliers' Delivery Times (15%), and Stock of Items Purchased (10%). It is essential to note that the Delivery Times index is inverted to ensure it moves in a comparable direction. A reading above 50 indicates expansion in the manufacturing sector compared to the previous month, while a reading below 50 signifies contraction, and a reading of 50 reflects no change.

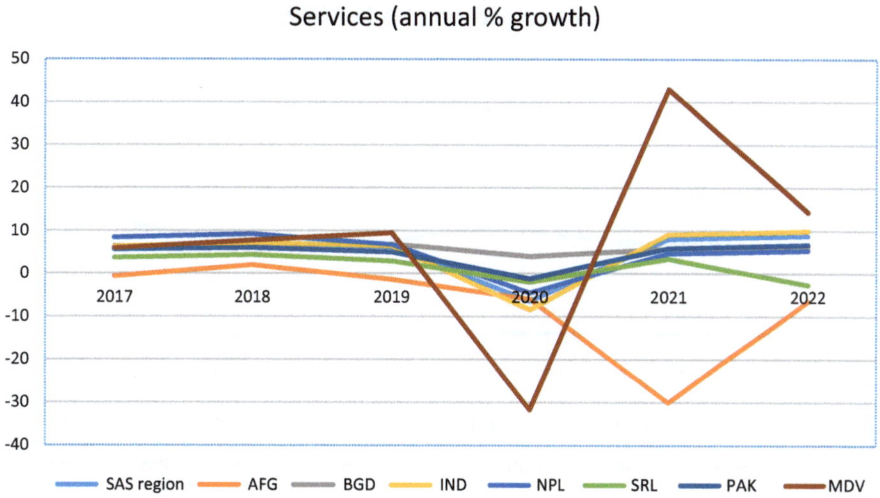

Fig. 3.4 Annual growth of the services sector (%) during the pre- and post-COVID-19 period (2017–2022) in South Asian countries. *Source*: Based on the data available at the World Bank, World Development Indicators: selected indicators for the South Asian Region

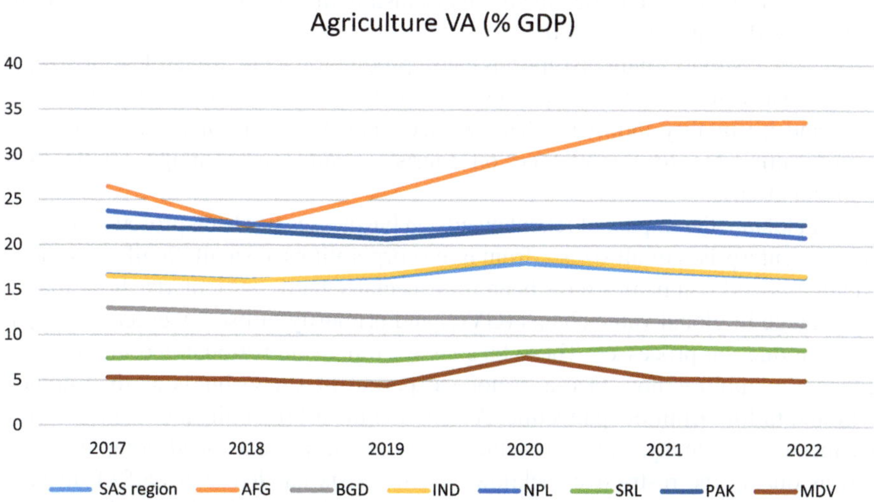

Fig. 3.5 Contribution of the agriculture sector to GDP (%) during the pre- and post-COVID-19 period (2017–2022) in South Asian countries. *Source*: Based on the data available at the World Bank, World Development Indicators: selected indicators for the South Asian Region

onset of the pandemic, the performance of these exports—particularly in the textile and apparel sector, as well as rubber goods—was modest, with figures not reaching particularly high levels, except for petroleum exports. However, the epidemic's impact was devastating, resulting in a dramatic downturn across all categories of

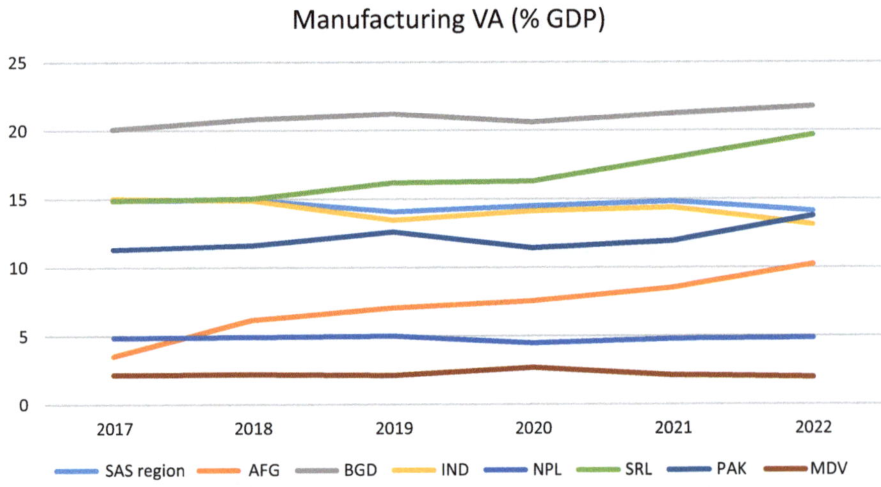

Fig. 3.6 Contribution of the manufacturing sector to GDP (%) during the pre- and post-COVID-19 period (2017–2022) in South Asian countries. *Source*: Based on the data available at the World Bank, World Development Indicators: selected indicators for the South Asian Region

manufactured goods. This decline has had a lasting impact on the economy, as highlighted by Roshana et al. (2020).

In Nepal, supply chain disruptions cause production halts. Regardless of size, all firms must deal with severe repercussions, particularly those in the aviation, tourism, and hospitality industries. The services and industrial environment suffered significantly due to its reliance on tourism, trade, and foreign employment (Khanal 2020).

In Pakistan, the impact of recent events on businesses has been profound, encompassing enterprises of all sizes—from large corporations to small, family-run shops. Medium-sized companies have been hit especially hard, particularly those that do not engage in global value chains (GVC) and primarily utilise lower technology in their production processes. These businesses, reliant on national and international economic stability, now face a prolonged period of sluggishness as they grapple with the fallout from the pandemic. Among the most brutal hits are women-owned businesses and many small manufacturing operations that faced complete shutdowns during the restrictive lockdowns. This crisis has led over half of all businesses to brace for potential layoffs, with medium-sized establishments bearing the brunt of these difficult decisions. A staggering 80% of businesses reported suffering direct repercussions from the government's lockdown measures, which had far-reaching consequences that rippled through the economy.[4] One of the most striking effects has been a significant drop in consumer demand, leading to fewer orders and diminished revenue streams. The abrupt lockdown disrupted the vital cash credit

[4] For details, https://www.unido.org/sites/default/files/files/2021-03/UNIDO%20COVID19%20Assessment_Pakistan_FINAL.pdf accessed s at 3 p.m. Uzbek time on May 20, 2025.

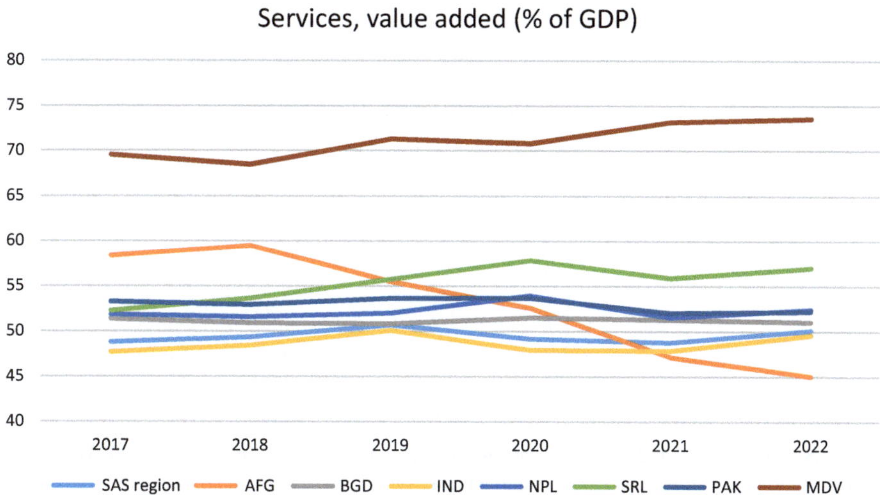

Fig. 3.7 Contribution of the services sector to GDP (%) during the pre- and post-COVID-19 period (2017–2022) in South Asian countries. *Source*: Based on the data available at the World Bank, World Development Indicators: selected indicators for the South Asian Region

cycles many businesses depend on, leaving numerous enterprises financially parched. Additionally, businesses are grappling with a critical shortage of inputs, including essential raw materials, further complicating their recovery efforts. The situation is similarly dire in the Maldives, where the nation's economy is heavily reliant on tourism, a crucial driver for the hospitality and service sectors. The pandemic-related lockdowns and travel restrictions have dealt a harsh blow to these key industries, stalling their momentum and leaving them in a precarious state (World Bank 2020b).

In the initial phases of the pandemic, South Asia was walloped, with economies faltering and countless livelihoods disrupted across the region.[5] However, over the subsequent years, South Asian countries demonstrated impressive resilience and adaptability as they navigated the ongoing challenges of the pandemic. Table 3.1 depicts the real GDP growth rates for South Asian nations in 2023, alongside projections for 2026. Overall, South Asia is on track for a promising growth rate of 5.8%. However, the growth rate drops significantly to 3.6% when India is excluded from this calculation. Notably, countries like Pakistan faced their own unique set of hurdles. Pakistan's economic landscape was particularly challenging, as it grappled with pandemic-related woes, catastrophic flooding, substantial military spending, and the geopolitical ramifications of the Russia–Ukraine conflict. As a result, Pakistan's GDP growth for the fiscal year 2025 is projected at a modest 2.7%. In stark contrast, Sri Lanka experienced a severe economic downturn during 2021–2022, primarily driven by the pandemic's detrimental impact on key sectors,

[5] See Figs. 3.1, 3.2, 3.3 and 3.4.

Fig. 3.8 S&P Global India Manufacturing Purchasing Manager's Index (2018–2023). *Source*: https://tradingeconomics.com/india/manufacturing-pmi

Table 3.1 Real GDP growth at constant price (%), 2023 (act.)–2026 (est.)-South Asian countries

	Country fiscal year	Real GDP growth at constant market prices (%)				Revision to forecast from October 2024 (Percentage points)		
Calendar year basis		2023	2024(e)	2025(f)	2026(f)	2024(e)	2025(f)	2026(f)
South Asia region		7.4	6.0	5.8	6.1	−0.4	−0.4	−0.1
South Asia region excluding India		2.8	3.5	3.6	4.3	−0.3	−0.4	−0.2
Maldives		4.7	5.5	5.7	5.3	0.8	1.0	0.7
Sri Lanka		−2.3	5.0	3.5	3.1	0.6	0.0	0.0
Fiscal year basis		22/23	23/24(e)	24/25(f)	25/26(f)	23/24(e)	24/25(f)	25/26(f)
Afghanistan	Mid-march to mid-march	−6.2	2.3	2.5	2.2	N/A	N/A	N/A
Bangladesh	July to June	5.8	4.2	3.3	4.9	−1.0	−0.7	−0.6
Bhutan	July to June	5.0	4.9	6.6	7.6	−0.4	−0.6	1.0
India	April to march	7.6	9.2	6.5	6.3	+1.0	−0.5	−0.4
Nepal	Mid-July to mid-July	2.0	3.9	4.5	5.2	0.0	−0.6	−0.3
Pakistan	July to June	−0.2	2.5	2.7	3.1	0.0	−0.1	−0.1

Source: World Bank (2025), South Asia, Washington D.C. *Note*: Last Update 23 April 2025

including tourism, remittances, and its renowned tea industry. The government's ambitious pivot towards entirely organic farming was aimed at fostering sustainability but inadvertently served as a trigger for economic turmoil. To exacerbate the situation, Sri Lanka found itself ensnared in what has been described as China's "debt trap diplomacy", coupled with significant tax reductions enacted for short-term political benefits, which deepened the country's economic plight.

The fallout from the Russia–Ukraine war further intensified these challenges, complicating recovery efforts. However, it anticipates a growth rate of 3.5% for Sri Lanka in 2025.[6] This projection is unchanged from the October forecast and is supported by the positive performance of Sri Lanka's economic reforms, particularly in strengthening public finances and accumulating reserves. Bangladesh also faced substantial economic struggles, primarily linked to disruptions in its vital textile industry, which were exacerbated by supply chain interruptions resulting from COVID-19 and the subsequent Russia–Ukraine war. The country saw a marked decline in remittances and exports, primarily due to sluggish demand from developed economies. As political uncertainties persist, the outlook for Bangladesh's economy appears dim, with expectations of a slowdown in economic growth rate. It shows a reduction in Bangladesh's real GDP growth to 3.3% in FY25, down from 4.2% in FY24, predominantly influenced by dwindling investments and ongoing domestic political instability amid broader global economic challenges.[7] Other South Asian countries, including Bhutan, the Maldives, Nepal, and Afghanistan, are projected to grow by 6.6%, 5.7%, 4.5%, and 2.5%, respectively, in 2025. The International Monetary Fund (IMF) projects India's economy to grow by 6.5% in 2025. The IMF has a more optimistic vision for India, projecting it to become the world's fourth-largest economy by 2025, surpassing Japan for the first time. The latest estimates from the IMF suggest that India's nominal GDP will reach an impressive $4.187 trillion in 2025, slightly eclipsing Japan's projected $4.186 trillion.[8]

Across the globe, energy prices have seen a significant decline from the exceptional highs recorded in recent years, leading to a notable reduction in fertiliser

---

[6] See, https://www.reuters.com/world/asia-pacific/sri-lankas-economy-grow-35-2025-despite-us-tariff-headwinds-world-bank-says-2025-04-23/#:~:text=Rates%20%26%20Bonds-,Sri%20Lanka's%20economy%20to%20grow%203.5%25%20in%202025%20despite,tariff%20headwinds%2C%20World%20Bank%20says.

[7] The country faces several significant challenges. According to the World Bank, real GDP growth is projected to further moderate to 3.3% in FY25, primarily due to a decline in both private and public investment. Political uncertainty, coupled with rising costs of borrowing and inputs, is anticipated to restrain private investment growth and maintain subdued industrial performance. Public investment is expected to decrease as the government reduces capital expenditure in FY25. The fiscal deficit is projected to remain below 5% of GDP in the medium term, with capital expenditure increasing only gradually. Additionally, inflation is likely to stay elevated in the near term. See, https://www.worldbank.org/en/news/press-release/2025/04/23/strong-economic-and-fiscal-reforms-will-help-bangladesh-sustain-growth-amid-global-uncertainty and World Bank (2025a).

[8] See the Times of India (2025) highlighted from the IMF (2025), available at https://timesofindia.indiatimes.com/business/india-business/big-achievement-india-to-become-4th-largest-economy-in-2025-overtaking-japan-will-be-3rd-largest-by-2028/articleshow/120900272.cms

costs. This decrease in energy expenses has been crucial in alleviating domestic inflationary pressures, resulting in lower import bills.[9] It has helped mitigate some of the considerable terms-of-trade losses that various countries faced over the past year (World Bank 2025b). A particularly striking aspect of this recovery is the remarkable resurgence of services exports, with tourism and business services leading the charge.[10] For instance, the Maldives, where tourist arrivals have not only rebounded but surged beyond pre-pandemic levels, is driven mainly by a significant influx of visitors from China. In India, the story of economic growth is similarly optimistic. The services sector has emerged as the standout performer in the economy, closely followed by a booming construction sector. New government initiatives have accelerated this growth trajectory to bolster infrastructure development nationwide. Additionally, many South Asian countries have embarked on fiscal consolidation processes to streamline their economies. This includes cutting inefficient subsidies, enhancing tax revenues, and enforcing stricter spending controls. These fiscal reform efforts in Bangladesh and Sri Lanka have been boosted by recently established agreements with the International Monetary Fund (IMF). Meanwhile, discussions regarding fiscal reforms in Pakistan are ongoing, highlighting a diverse range of economic recovery processes throughout the region. However, the aftermath of the pandemic has introduced significant challenges in monetary policy interventions aimed at combating inflation, including aggressive monetary tightening and interest rate hikes by central banks both globally and in South Asia. In particular, the State Bank of Pakistan has raised its policy rate more sharply than its counterparts, catapulting it from 7% to a staggering 20%. Despite these efforts, the Pakistani currency has depreciated by 27% since June 2022, resulting in a troubling depreciation-inflation spiral that has pushed real interest rates into negative territory.[11] A similar situation prevails in Sri Lanka, where the real interest rate remains negative despite an 11-percentage-point increase in the official interest rate. Several South Asian countries are facing the dual challenges of economic recovery and financial sector stress. This is exacerbated by rising asset values resulting from poor regulatory practices, soaring import costs in Bangladesh, and growing macroeconomic uncertainties associated with surging interest expenses in Sri Lanka. A report from the World Bank highlights that such restrictions can be counterproductive, suggesting that they might even encourage the resurgence of an informal exchange rate. This tactic, often employed to attract capital in informal markets, particularly

[9] In the US dollar terms. For details, https://blogs.worldbank.org/en/opendata/fertilizer-prices-stabilize-amid-lower-input-costs-and-trade-shi

[10] China also reopened its economy during this time. It has effectively restored the flow of goods and services, smoothing disruptions in global value chains and invigorating global production capabilities.

[11] According to Paradigm Shift, "The Pakistani Rupee has experienced significant depreciation, losing a substantial amount of its value, even after efforts to stabilize it. The currency has been overvalued by as much as 20% and, despite some adjustments, has depreciated by 27% since June 2022. This depreciation is attributed to a combination of factors, including political instability, rising inflation, and low foreign currency reserves." See Rafiq Imran Myra (2022), available at https://www.paradigmshift.com.pk/stability-pakistani-rupee/.

in lower-income economies following the COVID-19 pandemic, has led to a troubling trend of "informal capital outflow,' where remittances are diverted from the formal financial sector to informal channels. For instance, data from Bangladesh indicates that a mere 1% deviation between the formal and informal exchange rates can shift 3.6% of remittances into the informal financial sector, revealing that a dual exchange rate regime creates additional distortions that complicate domestic markets beyond the challenges already posed by capital controls and import restrictions.[12]

The Impact of Post-COVID-19 Inflation in South Asia: A Closer Look at the Aftermath

A trend in the annual inflation rate as a percentage from 2020 to 2024 (forecasted) for the South Asian region and its countries is shown in Fig. 3.9. Inflation in South Asia experienced a significant surge in 2022, driven by various pressures that began to ease afterward. The situation was particularly dire in Sri Lanka, with inflation skyrocketing to over 45%, resulting in an alarming annual average inflation rate of 9.2% for that year. Similarly, Pakistan grappled with escalating price pressures, exacerbated by severe flooding that disrupted supplies. This marked a historic peak for inflation, reaching the highest levels seen since 2009, when it hit 11.2%—attributed mainly to currency depreciations during the global financial crisis (World Bank 2022). This made 2022 the second-highest year for inflation in this century. Looking ahead to 2023 and 2024, inflation started to ease across most countries as commodity prices stabilised and stringent monetary policies were fully enacted. However, notable exceptions exist. In Afghanistan, inflation is projected to remain stubbornly high due to persistent supply constraints.[13] Although inflation is anticipated to linger at around 23% in Pakistan, it is expected to gradually decline as the supply chain issues stemming from the floods are resolved and international energy prices decrease. In countries such as Sri Lanka and Pakistan, where governments have implemented strict import restrictions due to depleted foreign exchange reserves, the resulting scarcity has further exacerbated inflationary pressures. These restrictions obstruct the natural price signals that typically encourage a swift market response, complicating efforts to stabilise the economy. Meanwhile, in Bangladesh,

[12]According to The World Bank, quoted by the Daily Star, "In Bangladesh, a 1% difference between formal and informal exchange rates can cause 3.6% of remittances to shift to informal channels, according to a World Bank study. This demonstrates how a dual exchange rate regime, beyond capital controls and import restrictions, adds to market distortions and complexity, particularly concerning remittances". See, https://www.thedailystar.net/business/economy/news/wide-gap-formal-informal-exchange-rates-led-forex-reserve-slide-wb-3315741. In a recent World Bank report; it states "In Bangladesh, real GDP growth moderated to 4.2% in FY23/24 from 5.8% in FY22/23, primarily driven by a sharp decline in exports. Supply chain disruptions, combined with currency depreciation and rising domestic energy prices, added to inflation pressures in 2024. Consumer price inflation peaked at 11.7% in July and remained elevated at 9.3% in February 2025. The current account balance has improved as a result of rising exports and strong remittance inflows, which have increasingly been channeled through the formal financial system as the curb market premium has narrowed", see World Bank (2025c).

[13]A lack of official inflation data in recent times prevents the creation of a point forecast for Afghanistan.

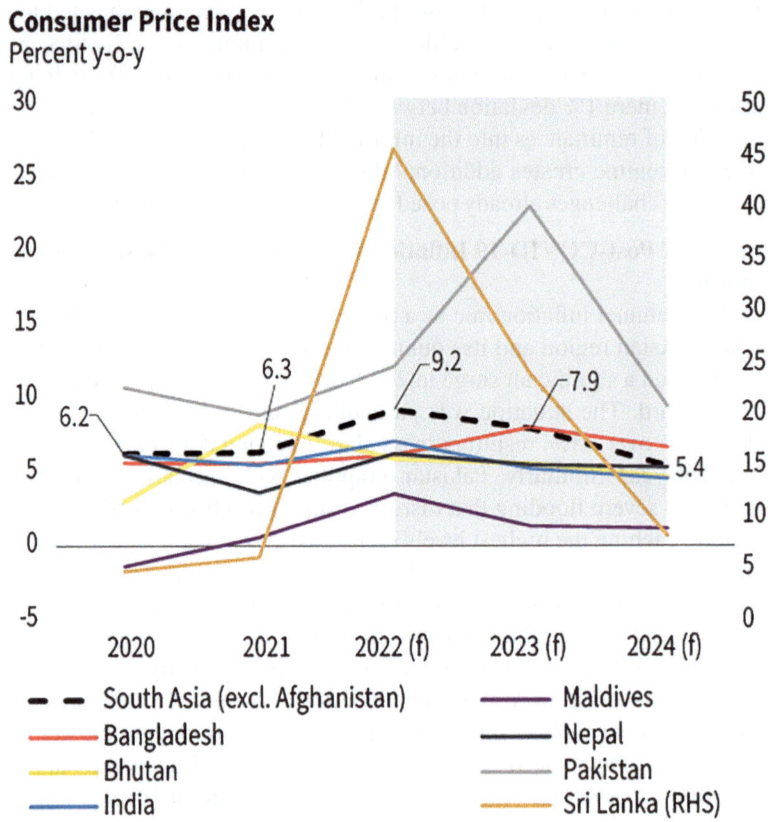

Fig. 3.9 Inflation in the South Asian Region and South Asian countries. (%): 2020–2024 (forecasted). *Source*: World Bank Macro Poverty Outlook and staff calculations. The corresponding fiscal years cited by the World Bank (2022) display individual-country inflation rates

while inflation is forecasted to stay within single-digit figures, this stability comes at the cost of limiting market responsiveness.

Much of the price suppression in Bangladesh results from a range of quantity restrictions, including fuel subsidies and artificial controls on the domestic credit market through regulated interest rates (World Bank 2022). Research indicates that several key factors significantly impact the inflation rates in Bangladesh, Sri Lanka, and Pakistan from 2020 to 2024. Notably, the depreciation of foreign exchange rates, the levels of foreign reserves, and the inflow of remittances have proven to be powerful determinants. These elements interact in complex ways, influencing the overall economic stability and purchasing power of these nations. Understanding the relationships among these factors is essential for policymakers seeking to manage inflation effectively in the region.[14]

[14] See Jui et al. (2024), https://www.sciencedirect.com/science/article/pii/S2405844024074127, and Banik (2023).

Major Stock Market Indices in select South Asian Countries

The major stock markets across the South Asian region, encompassing India, Pakistan, Bangladesh, and Sri Lanka, have experienced significant declines in their respective indices (see Fig. 3.10). Notably, the KSE 100 plummeted to its lowest level of 27,229 points on 25 March 2020. In India, the BSE SENSEX reached a remarkable peak, soaring to an all-time high of 42,273.87 in January 2020, only to experience a dramatic fall to 25,281 on 23 March 2020, marking its lowest point due to the COVID-19 pandemic. Similarly, the DSE recorded its lowest figures in Bangladesh, dropping to 3,604 on 18 March 2020. Meanwhile, Sri Lanka's CSE continued its downward trajectory, reaching 4,248 by 12 May 2020. This initial shockwave through the financial markets was profound.

However, in the following months, a sense of resilience emerged, paving the way for a remarkable recovery, as noted by Khan et al. (2022).[15] The revival of the financial markets can largely be attributed to a renewed sense of confidence among investors stemming from the decline in COVID-19 cases across the region. This improvement can be attributed to concerted efforts to control the spread of the virus, including the implementation of widespread vaccination campaigns. Countries began transitioning from stringent lockdown measures to more flexible "smart" lockdowns, allowing limited business activities to resume while prioritising public health. Proactive monetary and fiscal policies have bolstered economic performance

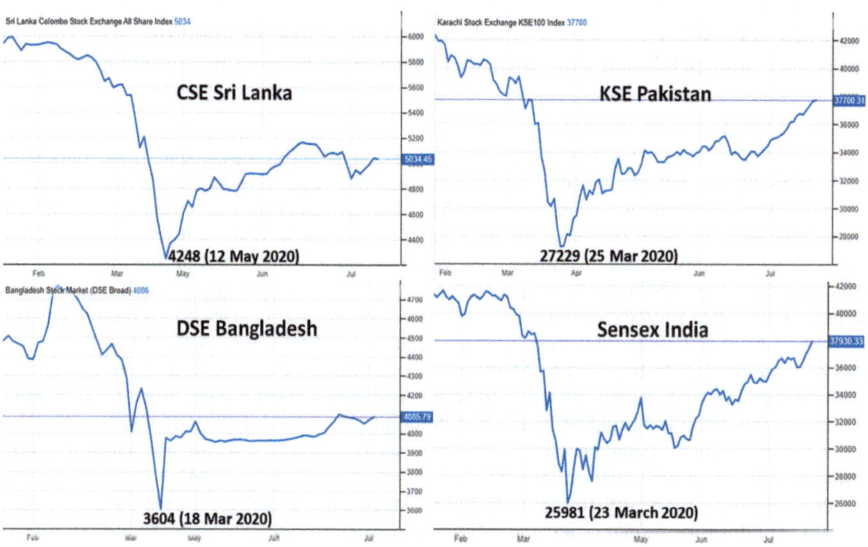

Fig. 3.10 Major stock market indices in select South Asian countries (6 months frame): 2020. *Source*: Trading Economics 2021, available at https://tradingeconomics.com/stocks. This is the original source, which is also quoted by Khan et al. (2022)

[15] Available at https://link.springer.com/article/10.1007/s11356-021-16894-9/figures/1

during this challenging time. As the pandemic's grip loosens, many countries are beginning to breathe a sigh of relief, witnessing a substantial reduction in new infections. India faced challenges as the daily infection rate approached a staggering one million. However, it has since significantly declined to around thirty thousand cases per day, according to the World Health Organization (2022).

Investment in South Asian Countries

The COVID-19 pandemic brought about unprecedented disruptions that significantly affected the global economy, leading to a notable decline in Foreign Direct Investment (FDI) inflows within South Asia. From 2021 to 2023, FDI in the region plummeted from a robust $53 billion to a mere $36 billion. Despite this alarming downturn, India managed to retain its status as the foremost recipient of FDI in South Asia during 2023. According to the United Nations Conference on Trade and Development's (UNCTAD 2024) World Investment Report 2024, India's foreign direct investment (FDI) inflows decreased by 43% compared to the previous year, totalling $28 billion. This steep decline resulted in a significant drop in India's position among global FDI recipients, falling from eighth place in 2022 to 15th in 2023.[16] This situation mirrors a broader global trend, where the overall flow of Foreign Direct Investment (FDI) declined by 2% in 2023, reflecting the ongoing challenges faced by economies worldwide. The trend in project financing mirrors these changes, as a global economic slowdown has further impacted investment in various projects across South Asia.

Over the past 5 years, from 2018 to 2022, private investment growth in South Asia has followed two distinct trajectories (Fig. 3.11). In countries like Bhutan, Pakistan,[17] and Sri Lanka, the growth has been disheartening, either negative or

[16] However, India received $81.04 billion in gross Foreign Direct Investment (FDI) during the 2024–25 fiscal year, reflecting a 14% rise from the previous year, according to provisional government data. FDI equity inflows alone surpassed $50 billion, registering a 13% year-on-year growth. The momentum, however, slowed in the final quarter of the fiscal year, with gross FDI declining 24.5% to $9.34 billion. India recorded a 13% year-on-year growth in FDI during the 2023–2024 fiscal year, attracting $50 billion compared to $44.42 billion in the previous year. Total FDI, comprising equity inflows, reinvested earnings, and other capital, rose 14% to $81.04 billion, marking the highest level in 3 years. Singapore remained India's top FDI source with $14.94 billion, followed by the US ($5.45 billion) and Mauritius ($3.73 billion). However, inflows from countries such as the Netherlands, Japan, the UK, and Germany declined. Sector-wise, growth was recorded in services ($9.34 billion), trading, telecom, automobile, construction development, non-conventional energy ($4 billion) and chemicals. However, sectors such as software and hardware, infrastructure, and pharmaceuticals experienced a contraction. Singapore, Mauritius, and the US together accounted for nearly 58% of total equity inflows. See Financial Express, May 27, 2025, available at https://www.financialexpress.com/policy/economy-fdi-rises-13-to-50-billion-in-fy24-despite-24-5-dip-in-march-quarter-3859354/.

[17] The investment climate in Pakistan following the COVID-19 pandemic has been challenging, characterized by declining Foreign Direct Investment (FDI), difficulties in domestic investment, and high unemployment rates. While Pakistan has a nominally open FDI regime, it faces infrastructure issues, a challenging business environment, and political instability, which hinder investment, as noted at https://www.state.gov/reports/2023-investment-climate-statements/pakistan/ and in the US Department of State's (2023) report.

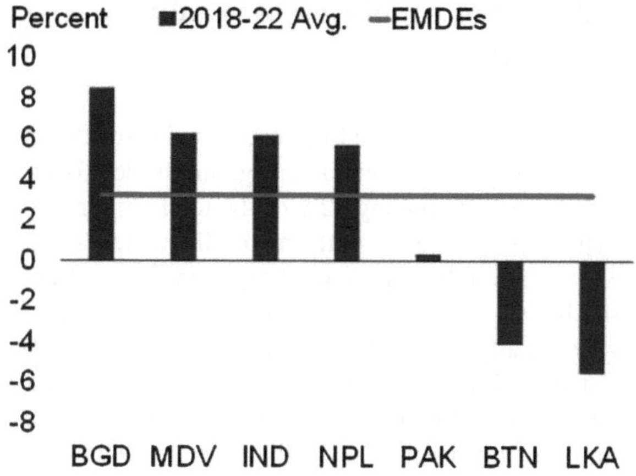

Fig. 3.11 Growth of real investment in South Asian countries: 2018–2022 (August). *Source*: Kirby (2023); Notes: EMDEs = Emerging Market Developing Economies. Figures show the annual growth of real fixed capital investment (in local currency units), with an average for the period 2018–2022. The EMDEs aggregate is computed using 2015 GDP as weights. The sample includes 123 EMDEs

stagnating at near-zero levels. In contrast, India, Maldives, Bangladesh, and Nepal have experienced a surge in investment growth, significantly outpacing the average growth seen in other emerging markets and developing economies (EMDEs).[18] Notably, both India and Bangladesh have benefited from robust public investment growth, averaging around 10% per year—three times higher than the EMDE average.[19] However, maintaining this level of public investment may pose challenges in the future as government debt increases and borrowing costs rise.

To foster and sustain private investment across South Asia, several critical factors will need to be addressed. These encompass the development of complementary infrastructure, the establishment of a supportive institutional and business environment that also includes political stability, improved access to financing, and the implementation of policies that minimise market distortions. These elements will be vital in driving economic growth and attracting further investment to the region.

[18] However, Bangladesh's commercial environment remains challenging, with foreign direct investment inflows declining due to entrenched structural and political risks. Investor confidence remains undermined by governance deficiencies, regulatory opacity, and an uneven playing field despite reformist pledges by the interim administration. Businesses are struggling with subdued economic growth, persistent inflationary pressures, and weakened consumer spending, contributing to profit declines across key sectors available at https://insight.pangea-risk.com/bangladesh-investment-climate-weakens-amid-political-and-economic-strains

[19] See Kirby (2023), available at https://blogs.worldbank.org/en/endpovertyinsouthasia/south-asias-economic-outlook-five-charts

3.3 The Landscape of Employment: Embracing the Future of Jobs

The South Asia region is characterised by three crucial sectors that play a pivotal role in employment: agriculture, manufacturing, and trade. Together, these sectors provide livelihoods for an astonishing 92% of the total labour force[20] in the region. However, employment levels are not uniform and fluctuate significantly among the various countries within South Asia. According to a report published by the World Bank (2024a), the labour force in the region is expected to reach 797 million by 2024, accounting for nearly 41% of the total population. This labour distribution is notably concentrated, with India alone contributing 608 million workers, followed by Pakistan with 84 million, Bangladesh with 78 million, Sri Lanka and Afghanistan each with nine million, Nepal with 8.42 million, Bhutan with 0.41 million, and the Maldives with 0.28 million.[21] The majority of men and women in the workforce earn their income within these primary sectors, alongside the construction industry, which predominantly employs men. Unfortunately, these sectors are also notorious for their low labour productivity and often lack decent wages, safe working conditions, and job security. A significant portion of jobs in these dominant employment sectors falls outside the protective umbrella of national social security systems, indicating a troubling absence of positive, decent work outcomes. Despite remarkable economic growth over the past 50 years, there has been little shift in the overwhelming dominance of low-productivity sectors and the persistent deficits in decent work.

Figure 3.12 illustrates a complex evolution within the labour market over the past 30 years. Notable progress has been made in increasing the proportion of formal employment and reducing working poverty. However, these advancements have been significantly challenged by the COVID-19 pandemic, resulting in stagnation or even a reversal of many previously achieved gains. The labour market continues to display a stark duality, characterised by a pronounced divide between sectors. For instance, the modern sector—particularly in information technology (IT), technology adoption in the health sector, pharmaceuticals, and business services—has

[20] The term “Labor force,” as defined by the International Labour Organization (ILO), refers to the group of individuals aged 15 and older who actively contribute to the economy by providing labor for the creation of goods and services within a specific timeframe. This group encompasses not only those who are currently employed but also individuals who are unemployed and seeking employment, as well as those who are entering the job market for the first time. On the other hand, the Labor force participation rate is a crucial indicator that measures the proportion of the population aged 15 and older that is actively engaged in economic activities. It represents all individuals who are supplying labor for the production of goods and services during a designated period. This rate helps illustrate the level of population involvement in the workforce, shedding light on the dynamics of employment and economic participation. For further reference, the link is https://www.ilo.org/resource/labour-force#:~:text=The%20labour%20force%20is%20the,employment%20plus%20persons%20in%20unemployment.

[21] See ILO (2022b).

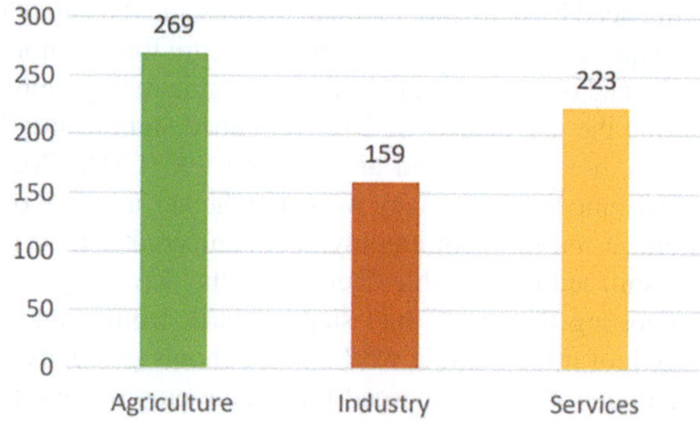

Fig. 3.12 Composition of total employment by broad sector group, 2019 (million): South Asia. *Source*: International Labour Organization, ILOSTAT database. Data as of January 2021. Accessed via World Development Indicators Database (21 May 2025) and ILO (2022a)

experienced remarkable workforce growth. These industries have attracted a more highly skilled labour pool, reflecting a shift towards increased productivity and innovation. Nevertheless, despite this growth, the overall share of workers engaged in these modern sectors remains disappointingly low compared to total employment figures. In contrast, the traditional sector is marked by low skill requirements and lower productivity. In 2021, the total labour force in the region, consisting of individuals aged 15 and older, was estimated at 677 million, resulting in a labour force participation rate of 47.3%.[22]

Of this labour force, women accounted for approximately 22.2%, with a participation rate of 21.6%. In contrast, men exhibited a significantly higher labour force participation rate of 71.6%, highlighting an ongoing gender disparity. Further analysis reveals that the total employment of individuals aged 15 and older in South Asia reached approximately 636 million in 2021, resulting in an employment-to-population ratio of 44.5%. Breaking down employment by broad sector, agriculture emerged as the predominant employer, engaging 41.3% of the total workforce. This was followed by the industrial sector, which accounted for 24.4%, and the services sector, which represented 34.3% as of 2019 (ILO 2022a).

The journey towards regaining employment following the pandemic's upheaval has proven to be remarkably uneven, exposing stark disparities across different sectors and countries. In 2020, South Asia experienced a severe economic downturn, categorising it as one of the regions most devastated by the global crisis. The pandemic left an indelible mark on employment, peaking in 2020 when strict lockdown measures were implemented worldwide. During this tumultuous period, South Asia was particularly hard-hit, witnessing a dramatic decline in jobs that resulted in the employment rate sinking 3.7 percentage points below its 2019 level (ILO 2022a).

By 2022, the situation began to improve, reflecting an overall recovery that had allowed the region not only to regain the employment lost in 2020 but also to attain positive job growth, even surpassing pre-pandemic employment figures. However, this growth unfolded at a slower pace compared to the robust surge seen in the latter half of 2022. A closer inspection of employment trends reveals striking disparities

[22] See World Bank (2022a), https://data.worldbank.org/indicator/SL.TLF.TOTL.IN?locations=8S.

influenced by both geographical regions and the nature of employment. In India, for example, a survey conducted by the Centre for Monitoring Indian Economy (CMIE) at the end of 2021 revealed a disheartening reality: female labour force participation during the last quarter of 2021 remained significantly below pre-pandemic benchmarks, hovering around an alarming 9% (CMIE 2021).[23] This data pointed to a worrisome trend, as many women, whether in urban or rural areas, shifted towards more casual forms of employment compared to their previous roles. This concerning shift led to a notable decrease in the percentage of female permanent workers, suggesting that many had stepped back from stable, salaried positions, often in search of more flexible work. With schools gradually reopening around mid-2022, a glimmer of hope emerged for female employment to rebound to the levels seen before the pandemic—a recovery pattern observed in various other countries as well. Simultaneously, the crisis triggered a significant change in the labour dynamics for many young Indian workers aged under 25, compelling them to transition into more casual and temporary roles that offered little to no job security. By 2021, a notable segment of employed youth in India found themselves in positions such as helpers, agricultural and plantation workers, sales assistants, and shop attendants—occupations marked by lower productivity and significantly reduced wages (ILO and IHD 2024).

Recently, however, the tides have begun to shift. There has been a marked increase in the share of permanent salaried jobs within India's overall job market, inching closer to the levels experienced before the pandemic. Notably, during September and October 2022 alone, over 8.5 million salaried positions were created, primarily concentrated in urban locales. Conversely, a troubling trend has emerged: the number of self-employed individuals has increased.[24] At the same time, the number of individuals holding regular salaried jobs has declined in 2022, raising urgent concerns about the quality of the newly created job opportunities. Despite overall progress, this recovery remains uneven, particularly within the services sector, which is heavily intertwined with rural retail trade, where job losses have continued to pose significant challenges.

Findings from COVID-19 phone surveys[25] conducted across the diverse nations of Bhutan, Nepal, Pakistan, Bangladesh, and Sri Lanka reveal a significant positive shift beginning in mid-2021. However, the economic landscape in Sri Lanka has plunged into a notable downturn, a scenario exacerbated by a complicated mix of

---

[23] The Consumer Pyramids Household Surveys (CPHS) are high-frequency, large-scale surveys that have become widely used, particularly to assess short-term changes in the economic conditions of households, such as the impact of COVID-19 pandemic policies on the economy.

[24] "More Than 8.5 million Jobs Added During Sept-Oct 2022: Report", according to a report from the Centre for Monitoring Indian Economy (CMIE), as highlighted by The Business Standard. This surge in employment underscores a significant rebound in the job market, available at https://www.businessworld.in/article/more-than-85-million-jobs-added-during-sept-oct-2022-report-453705.

[25] Available at Household Monitoring Systems to Track the Impacts of the COVID-19 Pandemic, World Bank (2022b).

declining economic activity and a marked increase in resignations, migrations, and retirements. This worrying trend was highlighted in a 2023 report from the Central Bank of Sri Lanka (Central Bank of Sri Lanka 2023), which painted a stark and concerning picture of the employment market. In striking contrast, Afghanistan is grappling with a cyclical economic slowdown, primarily influenced by the seasonal change characteristic of winter. This has resulted in a gradual but worrying decline in employment opportunities. The repercussions of this downturn have severely impacted the income-generating capacities of self-employed individuals and casual labourers, as highlighted in a 2023 report from the World Bank (2022c). Meanwhile, Bhutan faces critical challenges, particularly in the realm of youth employment. The youth unemployment rate skyrocketed to a distressing 29% in 2022, a significant increase from 21% the previous year. This alarming trend has prompted waves of outward migration as young individuals seek better prospects and more appealing opportunities beyond their borders—a phenomenon highlighted in a report published by the Royal Government of Bhutan and the World Health Organization (Royal Government of Bhutan and the World Health Organization 2022). The sluggish pace of job creation, coupled with a deterioration in the quality of existing employment, has significantly hampered private consumption. This has led to lackluster economic activity throughout the region. The presence of informality in South Asia's economic structure has only worsened these challenges. The closure of factories and restaurants, coupled with a sharp decline in tourism and a decrease in consumer demand for goods and services, has severely limited the economy's ability to absorb labour. Consequently, unemployment rates have escalated, and household incomes have plummeted, pushing millions of families into a precarious state of increased vulnerability to poverty. Data from the Centre for Monitoring Indian Economy (CMIE) in 2020[26] sheds light on this urgent situation, highlighting the pressing need for comprehensive strategies aimed at revitalising the labour market and improving the quality of employment opportunities in India. Despite these concerning developments, there are some silver linings to consider. Positive structural trends offer hope for the long-term future. For instance, women, who often take on the role of primary caregivers, are generally more willing and able to engage in remote work. Home-based jobs present significant opportunities in the rapidly growing, market-oriented services sector, particularly in areas such as e-commerce. Additionally, data suggests[27] that, even prior to the pandemic, a larger proportion of South Asian youth were employed in manufacturing and less contact-sensitive service sectors. Many young people and women have expressed a strong appreciation for the newfound flexibility in working hours that jobs in digital technology now offer.

It is essential to note that, during the pandemic, the agricultural sector experienced relatively less disruption, while the manufacturing sector rebounded fairly

[26] See World Bank (2024b), https://thedocs.worldbank.org/en/doc/400139d320ead96a0ec624d3608d9b56-0310012025/original/India-Country-Economic-Memorandum-2024-0227c.pdf.

[27] See ILO (2021).

quickly within a few months. However, there was pronounced variability in how the services sector recovered. For instance, the growth of "business services"—which includes professional, financial, and real estate services—along with public services surged impressively. In stark contrast, sectors heavily reliant on in-person interactions and deemed "COVID-sensitive", such as tourism-related services, including accommodations, restaurants, recreation, and entertainment, witnessed a dramatic decline, leaving many workers jobless for extended periods. As of late 2022, while activity in these sectors was beginning to recover, it remained significantly below pre-pandemic levels. One consistent trend observed in the South Asian employment landscape is that the recovery of labour markets has remained far from complete as nations grapple with a series of global challenges, including the economic fallout from the war in Ukraine. However, it is unsettling to note that the three fastest-growing service subsectors during this period—non-contact intensive "business services" and certain public services—are characterised by lower labour intensity, lower average wages, and higher skill requirements. This suggests a widening gap in earnings compared to pre-COVID levels, leading to increased income inequality and a post-COVID recovery that has not been inclusive. The aforementioned analysis employs a "nowcast" approach,[28] assuming that all workers can swiftly return to their previous jobs and maintain the same level of productivity as before the pandemic. However, this assumption fails to reflect the reality experienced by many due to "scarring effects".[29] These effects refer to the inability of workers to return to their former productivity levels, often resulting from new family obligations, health issues, or the necessity to sell assets during lockdowns to make ends meet.

In this context, it is important to highlight a significant initiative by the Indian central government in response to COVID-19: the provision of free food grains to approximately 81.35 crore (0.8335 billion) beneficiaries under the Pradhan Mantri Garib Kalyan Anna Yojana (PMGKAY). This programme commenced on 1 January 2024, and is set to run for 5 years, representing a historic milestone in social welfare. PMGKAY stands out as one of the world's most prominent programmes aimed at ensuring food and nutrition security for 81.35 crore individuals, with an estimated expenditure of Rs. 11.80 lakh crore[30] throughout its duration.[31] Many experts interpret this decision as a strong testament to the Prime Minister's commitment to

[28] The nowcast approach involves using real-time data to estimate the current or near-term state of an economic indicator, such as GDP, before the official data is released. It is essentially a prediction of the "present" or "now" using available data. This method is beneficial for indicators that are published with a significant delay.

[29] The scarring effect refers to the negative long-term impacts on labor market outcomes that result from an adverse experience, such as unemployment, especially early in one's career. This means that experiencing unemployment, for example, can increase the probability of future unemployment and lower future earnings compared to someone who has not been unemployed see Nilsen and Reiso (2021).

[30] Equivalent to US$ 141 billion based Foreign exchange rate US$ 1 = 83.33 on February 9, 2024.

[31] See GoI (2024), available at, https://www.pib.gov.in/PressReleasePage.aspx?PRID=1980689.

effective and targeted welfare, emphasising the importance of meeting the population's fundamental food and nutritional needs.[32]

Understanding the challenges faced by India's population of 81.35 crore is crucial, particularly in terms of economic hardships and their repercussions. The post-COVID landscape has exacerbated these challenges, leading to an increase in both farm and non-farm labourers. According to the latest Periodic Labour Survey released in September 2024, the unemployment rate for individuals aged 15–29 has reached 10.2%, with a concerning rise to 13% among graduates in this age group.[33] As a result, the share of manufacturing in overall employment has declined while the agricultural sector's contribution has increased. This shift signifies a "reversal of structural transformation", transitioning from a higher productivity sector to one characterised by lower productivity. Consequently, real wages for semi-skilled and unskilled workers in India have declined, with the decline particularly severe in rural areas due to the surplus labour supply that emerged after the COVID-19 pandemic. For instance, the wages of self-employed individuals decreased from Rs 9,454 in 2017-18 to Rs 8,591 in 2023–2024, while those of salaried employees fell from Rs 12,665 to Rs 11,858 during the same period. Studies indicate that approximately 550 million individuals are affected by these changes (GoI 2025). The current economic landscape raises critical questions regarding the quality of jobs created in India.[34] Alarmingly, government data show that the manufacturing sector's share in the country's Gross Domestic Product (GDP) has remained stagnant since the financial year 2013–2014, holding steady at 17% as of 2024–2025. Furthermore, India's export of goods and services as a percentage of GDP has declined, decreasing from 25.2% in 2013–2014 to 22.45% in 2024–2025.[35]

In this context, examining what has happened to the labour share of GDP is essential. Intriguingly, a study focusing on India, which utilised KLEMS (Capital, Labour, Energy, Materials, and Services) data, reveals that the overall economy-wide labour share declined from 54% in 1980 to 49% in 2016. This research thoroughly analysed labour share at the sectoral level, encompassing both formal and informal sectors across the entire economy (Basu and Veeramani 2021).[36] The shift-share decomposition analysis[37] findings suggest that internal and external sectoral

[32] For example, here is the link, https://www.udayindia.in/news/free-foodgrains-for-8135-crore-beneficiaries-for-five-years-cabinet-decision.

[33] Available at, https://www.pib.gov.in/PressReleasePage.aspx?PRID=2074262, GoI (2024b).

[34] See Business Standard (2024). Available at https://www.business-standard.com/budget/news/real-earnings-fell-for-salaried-self-employed-in-past-6-years-eco-survey-125013101362_1.html.

[35] See India Briefing (2025). Available at https://www.india-briefing.com/news/india-manufacturing-tracker-2024-25-33968.html/.

[36] See also Abraham and Sasikumar (2017).

[37] It is worth noting that "shift-share decomposition" is a statistical method applied in regional economics to dissect changes in an economic variable, such as employment or income, within a region into three components: a national effect (overall economic growth), an industry mix effect (the comparison of a region's industry composition to the national average), and a regional competitive effect (how well a region performs within its industries relative to the other areas). This

factors have contributed to these trends in aggregate labour share. However, a more detailed examination at a disaggregated level indicates that the decline in labour share within sectors cannot be attributed solely to technological advancements or increased trade exposure. Instead, it is primarily driven by two specific sectors: real estate and construction, which have demonstrated resilience against technological changes and the influences of international trade. On the other hand, the between-sector component of this decline highlights a structural transformation within the economy that has disproportionately benefited high-skilled service sectors while largely neglecting manufacturing. Within the organised manufacturing sector, there has been a noticeable increase in the value-added share of capital-intensive sectors, which typically have a lower labour share, accompanied by a decline in unskilled manufacturing. This shift has contributed to a reduction in the overall labour share within formal manufacturing. Furthermore, a sectoral-level analysis reveals that the composition of capital-intensive and high-skilled sectors is correlated with a decrease in the sectoral wage share, even when controlling for variables such as trade openness and capital intensity. Such findings underline the complex interplay of structural changes within the economy, reinforcing concerns about the future of job quality and equity in income distribution.

The recent Economic Survey (GoI, op. cit.) offers a wealth of intriguing insights that shed light on the current state of India's economy. A particularly striking finding is the projected decline in India's labour share of GDP for the year 2024. This indicates that a smaller portion of the nation's income is being allocated to workers, in contrast to a rising share going to capital owners. This shift is primarily attributed to the increasing prevalence of automation in various sectors and the expansion of the informal workforce. Notably, this decline in labour share is occurring even as the overall unemployment rate shows signs of improvement. The survey's analysis highlights the alarming trend of declining real wages, which should serve as a wake-up call for policymakers at all levels of government. The widening wage gap is becoming increasingly concerning, characterised by falling incomes for unskilled and semi-skilled workers alongside rising wages for skilled professionals. This diverging wage trend highlights a significant national challenge. Furthermore, the phenomenon known as the "servicification of manufacturing"[38]—where there is a growing reliance on specialised services within the manufacturing sector—emerges as a related issue of concern. As India's population approaches 1.4 billion, with more than half of its citizens under 30 (Kapoor 2023), it becomes clear that relying solely on the services or agricultural sectors for job creation is insufficient. India must reassess its manufacturing policies to sustain momentum in poverty alleviation and economic growth. This issue also significantly impacts the South Asian coun-

method enables analysts to ascertain which factors have contributed most significantly to regional changes.

[38] Servicification of manufacturing refers to the growing integration of services with traditional manufacturing processes, where manufacturers offer value-added services alongside their products. This trend involves manufacturers expanding their offerings to include services like maintenance, consulting, customization, and digital solutions.

tries of Bangladesh, Pakistan, Sri Lanka, Nepal, and Afghanistan. Each of these nations grapples with a distinct array of complex challenges that are deeply rooted in their unique cultural backgrounds, economic conditions, and religious education. Additionally, traditional educational curriculums often do not align with the current job market demands, creating further obstacles to growth and development. These interwoven factors contribute to a multifaceted landscape that each country must navigate in pursuit of a brighter future. The details of this issue are thoroughly discussed in Chap. 7.

3.4 Planning for the Future

The recovery of South Asia's employment market is currently incomplete. Policymakers in the region can help mitigate the long-term effects of the pandemic by directing resources to regional service centres that offer essential job-matching infrastructure, training, and IT support for workers. This assistance would reduce the costs and challenges associated with job transitions, facilitating a smoother shift into new sectors. The job market is undergoing a transformative shift that is reshaping our understanding of employment, driven by rapid technological advancements and the emergence of new industries, particularly in healthcare services. The future of work presents both exciting opportunities and unique challenges for workers, employers, and the broader economy. Key trends anticipated to influence the future of jobs in India and South Asia include increased digital access, geopolitical tensions, and efforts to mitigate climate change. Much like their global counterparts, companies in the region are heavily investing in technologies such as AI, robotics, autonomous systems, and energy solutions (World Economic Forum 2025). For instance, employers in India anticipate that their adoption of specific technologies will exceed global trends, with 35% expecting advancements in semiconductors and computing technologies, and 21% forecasting that quantum computing and encryption will revolutionise their operations. The fastest-growing job roles—such as Big Data Specialists, AI and Machine Learning Specialists, and Security Management Specialists—are closely aligned with these trends. To fulfill their talent needs, companies in India plan to tap into diverse talent pools (67%, compared to 47% globally) and implement skills-based hiring practices, such as eliminating degree requirements (30%, versus 19% globally). Currently, available data show significant declines across various aspects of human capital, highlighting the urgent need to prioritise this area. Human capital, encompassing health, knowledge, skills, and experiences accumulated throughout a lifetime, is crucial for driving productivity and economic growth (Schady et al. 2023). Additionally, strong human capital allows individuals to adapt to unexpected challenges. However, such shocks can disrupt the development of human capital, disproportionately affecting those in poverty and exacerbating inequality. The acquisition of human capital is a cumulative and sequential process. Early setbacks, if not addressed, can have lasting effects into adulthood, potentially hindering the accumulation of human capital for future generations.

References

Abraham V, Sasikumar SK (2017) Declining wage share in India's organized manufacturing sector: trends, patterns and determinants, ILO Asia-Pacific working paper series. International Labour Organisation, Geneva

Banik A (2023). In tackling inflation, the country cannot ignore the world, The Daily Star, October 8

Basu A, Veeramani C (2021) Labour share in the Indian economy: an exploratory analysis of the role of trade, technology, and structural transformation, WP-2021-027, Indira Gandhi Institute of Development Research, Mumbai, December

Business Standard (2024) Salaried, self-employed real wages below 2017–18 levels: eco survey, January 31

Central Bank of Sri Lanka (2023) Annual economic review of the central bank 2023, Colombo

CMIE (2021) CMIE's consumer pyramids household survey, Mumbai

Friedrich Naumann Foundation (2020) South Asia amidst the covid-19 crisis, policy brief, Islamabad, May

Government of India (2024a) Free foodgrains for 81.35 crore beneficiaries for five years: cabinet Decision, Ministry of Consumers Affairs, Food and Public Distribution, New Delhi, Posted on November 29

Government of India (2024b) Periodic labour force survey (PLFS)—quarterly bulletin [July–September 2024, Ministry of Consumers Affairs, Food and Public Distribution, New Delhi, Posted in November 18

Government of India (2025) Economic survey 2024–25. Ministry of Finance, New Delhi

ILO (2021) Statistical brief, June 2021, Geneva

ILO (2022a) Southern Asia: the employment-environment-climate nexus, November, Geneva

ILO (2022b) Asia–Pacific employment and social outlook 2022 rethinking sectoral strategies for a human-centered future of work, Geneva

ILO, IHD (2024) India employment report 2024 youth employment, education, and skills, New Delhi

IMF (2025) IMF country report no. 25/109 on Pakistan, Washington, DC

India Briefing (2025) India manufacturing tracker 2025, June 2, 2025

Jui NF, Hossain MJ, Das A, Sultana N, Islam MK (2024) Analyzing the impact of remittance, FDI and inflation rate on GDP: a comparative study of Bangladesh, Pakistan, and Sri-Lanka using VAR and BEKK-GARCH approach. Heliyon 10(11):e31381

Kapoor M (2023) As India's population approaches 1.4 billion, with more than half its citizens under 30, DW.Com, April 3

Khan MA, Naqvi HA, Hakeem MM (2022) Economic and financial impact of the covid-19 pandemic in South Asia. Environ Sci Pollut Res 29:15703–15712. https://doi.org/10.1007/s11356-021-16894-9

Khanal N (2020) Impact of corona virus pandemic on different sectors of Nepalese economy. Manag Dyn 23(2):243–254

Kirby P (2023) South Asia's economic outlook in five charts. World Bank, Washington, DC

Nilsen OA, Reiso KH (2021). Scarring effects of unemployment, IZA DP No. 6198, December

Rafiq IM (2022) Bringing stability to the Pakistani rupee, Paradigm Shift, August 16

Roshana M, Kaldeen M, Banu AR (2020) Impact of COVID-19 outbreak on Sri Lankan economy. J Crit Rev 7(14):2124–2133

Royal Government of Bhutan and World Health Organization (2022) The people's pandemic: how the himalayan Kingdom of Bhutan staged a world-class response to COVID-19. Ministry of Health, Thimpu

Sawada Y, Sumulong LR (2021) Macroeconomic impact of covid-19 in developing Asia, ADBI working paper series, no. 1251, Asian Development Bank Institute (ADBI), Tokyo

Schady N, Holla A, Sabarwal S, Silva J, Yi Chang A (2023) Collapse and recovery: how the covid-19 pandemic eroded human capital and what to do about it. © World Bank. http://hdl.handle.net/10986/39403 License: CC BY 3.0 IGO

Sen S, Antara N, Sen S, Chowdhury S (2020) The unprecedented covid-19 on the apparel workers by shivering the apparel supply chain. J Text Apparel Technol Manag 11(3):1–20

Times of India (2025) Big achievement! India to become fourth largest economy in 2025, overtaking Japan; will be third largest by 2028, May 5, 2025. https://timesofindia.indiatimes.com/business/india-business/big-achievement-india-to-become-4th-largest-economy-in-2025-overtaking-japan-will-be-3rd-largest-by-2028/articleshow/120900272.cms. Accessed at 4 p.m. Uzbek time on May 20, 2025

UNCTAD (2024) World investment report 2024, New York

US Department of State (2023) 2023 investment climate statements: Pakistan, Washington, DC

WHO (2022) India situation report, 101, New Delhi

World Bank (2020a) The economic impact of covid-19 on South Asia, South Asia economic focus-Spring 2020, Washington, DC

World Bank (2020b) COVID-19 and tourism in South Asia: opportunities for sustainable regional outcomes, Washington, DC

World Bank (2022). Pakistan Development Update, October 2022: Inflation and the Poor. Washington, DC

World Bank (2022a) South Asia Economic Focus, Managing the aftershocks (chapter II), Washington DC. https://openknowledge.worldbank.org/server/api/core/bitstreams/9130be66-181e-5bb4-8c65-6f9ff3ec93b0/content

World Bank (2022b) Household monitoring systems to track the impacts of the covid-19 pandemic, Washington, DC

World Bank (2022c) Chapter 1. The economic impacts of the COVID-19 crisis, Washington, DC. https://www.worldbank.org/en/publication/wdr2022/brief/chapter-1-introduction-the-economic-impacts-of-the-covid-19-crisis

World Bank (2024a) South Asia development update, April 2024: jobs for resilience. © World Bank.` http://hdl.handle.net/10986/41212 License: CC BY 3.0 IGO

World Bank (2024b) India-becoming a high-income economy in a generation, Washington, DC

World Bank (2025a) Strong economic and fiscal reforms will help bangladesh sustain growth amid global uncertainty, press release, April 23. https://www.worldbank.org/en/news/press-release/2025/04/23/strong-economic-and-fiscal-reforms-will-help-bangladesh-sustain-growth-amid-global-uncertainty

World Bank (2025b) Fertilizer prices stabilize amid lower input costs and trade shifts. World Bank blogs, Washington, DC. https://blogs.worldbank.org/en/opendata/fertilizer-prices-stabilize-amid-lower-input-costs-and-trade-shi

World Bank (2025c) South Asia development update taxing times, Washington, DC, April. https://documents1.worldbank.org/curated/en/099740404232536373/pdf/IDU-57df111d-3695-43ba-a852-173326850600.pdf

World Economic Forum (2025) Future of jobs report, Geneva, January

Chapter 4
COVID-19 and Economic Hardship in South Asia

Abstract This chapter discusses how COVID-19 increased health vulnerability and poverty. The literature suggests strong correlation between poverty and income mediated by health factors. High out-of-pocket expenditure, migration, and increasing urbanisation strengthened this further in SA regions. This chapter underscores role of policy intervention, which entails financial investment, continuous monitoring, and innovative and inclusive policy design. Prompt policy actions and numerous tailored schemes, in this direction in SA region, helped to contain the spread of COVID-19 in the early stage of infection. India, in particular, has taken a prominent role in these initiatives. This chapter lists governments' prompt actions in the SA region to mitigate, which took varied forms ranging from lockdown measures to rolling out tailored insurance schemes. It highlights that the pre-COVID standards of living were already alarming enough to necessitate urgent policy interventions aimed at addressing the underlying issues. Thus, many countries in the region had already designed suitable schemes pre-COVID, but rolled it out in massive scale as soon as COVID hit the countries, e.g. India launched Ayushman Bharat in 2018—world's largest health insurance scheme.

Keywords COVID · Vulnerability · Poverty · Multidimensional Poverty Index · Health insurance · Urbanisation and migration · Out-of-pocket expenditure · Catastrophic health shock

4.1 Introduction

In the previous chapter, we discussed the long-term impacts of COVID-19-induced shocks across South Asian economies. It is also helpful to investigate the possibility of creating synergies using the healthcare frameworks already in place in South Asian economies. Several studies have been conducted on the worldwide and regional COVID-19 performances, the measures countries have taken, and the economic aftershocks caused by this pandemic. Despite this, the COVID epidemic has

A. Banik et al., *Extraordinary Health Hazards and their Socio-Economic Effects in South Asia*, South Asia Economic and Policy Studies,
https://doi.org/10.1007/978-981-95-5729-5_4

resulted in many unique characteristics and relatively few shared characteristics among locations. Because of this, it has undoubtedly been difficult for policymakers to learn from each other's experiences to devise beneficial policies tailored to each situation. Another significant factor contributing to the difficulty of making meaningful comparisons throughout the globe is the absence of high-quality data. On the front of the development, slow progress on achieving the Sustainable Development Goals (SDGs) (SDG-4: education; SDG-6: access to drinking water and sanitation; SDG-7: energy) combined with a lack of quality and accessibility in health facilities and rendered the South Asian region a hotbed for the epidemic. Pandemic performances and national vulnerabilities should not be judged solely based on a country's policy intervention during the pandemic. The pre-pandemic socio-economic configuration and the conditionalities in place at the time significantly impacted the outcome. These played an essential part in coping with the unprecedented shock, ultimately influencing the country's performance. This chapter will discuss and highlight these developmental factors, such as poverty, to compare outcomes throughout, and post the COVID-19 epidemic.

4.2 General Poverty Scenario in South Asian Countries

The international poverty line, used to quantify extreme poverty, was established in 2011 at USD 1.9 per person per day. The new poverty line, which was close to $1.9 per day, was arrived at by averaging the following four steps: (i) selecting the national poverty lines of 15 poor countries; (ii) inflating those poverty lines to 2011 levels using the consumer price index (CPI) of those countries; (iii) converting those inflation-adjusted poverty lines to US dollars using purchasing power parity (PPP) for 2011; and (iv) averaging those US dollar-denominated. Referencing Ferreira et al. (2016), the reference group includes Chad, Ethiopia, the Gambia, Ghana, Guinea-Bissau, Malawi, Mali, Mozambique, Nepal, Niger, Rwanda, Sierra Leone, Tajikistan, Tanzania, and Uganda.

The World Bank established a global poverty line to regularly monitor extreme poverty, which has been adjusted for variations in buying power parity. The line underwent its most recent update in 2015 and subsequently experienced an increase to a value of $2. The official poverty level of a country is determined based on its per capita income rather than per capita consumption, which serves as the primary welfare measure. Comparing poverty rates and official poverty lines between countries is not straightforward due to the lack of direct comparability at the national level. Consequently, the National poverty headcount ratio is frequently utilised to facilitate cross-country comparisons. This metric denotes the proportion of individuals residing below the national poverty line(s) within a given population. The national estimates are derived from household surveys by utilising population-weighted subgroup estimates.

Analysing the data in Table 4.1, we find the following patterns among the South Asian countries. In 1995, India exhibited a poverty headcount ratio of 45.3%, which suggests a substantial segment of the populace residing beneath the country's poverty threshold. Over time, the poverty headcount ratio exhibited a downward trend, with a recorded value of 37.2% in 2000 and decreasing to 29.8% in 2010. The poverty rate in Bangladesh was 50.1% in 1995, making it one of the countries with the highest poverty rates per capita. Over time, there has been a discernible decline in the poverty headcount ratio, evidenced by significant decreases to 48.9% in 2000, 40% in 2005, and 31.5% in 2010. Pakistan also exhibited a considerable poverty headcount ratio in 2000, whereby 64.3% of the populace resided below the national Poverty threshold. Like other nations, Pakistan has experienced a reduction in poverty levels, with figures declining to 50.4% in 2005, 36.8% in 2010, 24.3% in 2015, and 21.9% in 2018.

According to comparative data, Sri Lanka exhibited a comparatively lower poverty headcount ratio than other nations. The poverty headcount ratio exhibited a notable increase from 28.8% in 1995 to 46.8% in 2000, followed by a subsequent decrease to 28.4% in 2005, 16% in 2010, and a further decline to 14.3% in 2015. In 1995, Nepal exhibited a poverty headcount ratio of 41.8%. As with other nations, Nepal has undergone a reduction in its poverty headcount ratio over time, with figures dropping to 30.9% in 2005 and 25.2% in 2010. The table does not furnish poverty headcount ratio data for Maldives except for 2019 (5.4%), which is substantially lower than Pakistan and Sri Lanka. Except for 2011 (38.3%) and 2016 (54.5%), the table also lacks poverty headcount ratio statistics for Afghanistan. Afghanistan consistently had the most significant percentage of needy people compared to other countries.

While the overall trend shows a reduction in poverty headcount ratios, it is crucial to note the disparities across nations. In 1995, Bangladesh and Pakistan had high poverty headcount ratios but have made significant progress. Sri Lanka has consistently maintained lower poverty levels, while India and Nepal have substantially declined. This disparity underscores the need for targeted interventions and strategies.

Table 4.1 Poverty headcount ratio at national poverty lines (% of population)

Country name	1995	2000	2005	2010	2015	2019
Afghanistan				38.3[(f)]	54.5[(g)]	
Bangladesh	50.1	48.9	40[(b)]	31.5	24.3[(g)]	
Bhutan			31.7		8.2[(h)]	
India	45.3[(a)]		37.2c	29.8[(e)]		
Sri Lanka	28.8	46.8[(b)]		28.4[(e)]	16[(g)]	14.3
Maldives						5.4
Nepal	41.8		30.9[(d)]	25.2		
Pakistan		64.3	50.4	36.8	24.3	21.9[(i)]

Source: Compiled by authors from World Bank data. *Notes*: (a) refers to 1993; (b) refers to 2002; (c) refers to 2004; (d) refers to 2003; (e) refers to 2009; (f) refers to 2011; (g) refers to 2016; (h) refers to 2017; (i) refers to 2018

The issue of poverty is multifaceted, but understanding the poverty gap is crucial. The term "poverty gap" in academic literature refers to the difference between the established poverty threshold and actual earnings. It is essential to differentiate between absolute and relative poverty. Absolute poverty is the gap between an individual or household's earnings and a pre-established poverty line. In contrast, relative poverty is the difference in earnings between an individual or household and the average or median income of the overall population.

The poverty gap metric is a valuable tool for comprehending the magnitude and gravity of poverty in a particular society. An increased discrepancy between individuals residing in impoverished conditions and the poverty threshold implies an elevated degree of poverty. Conversely, a narrowed poverty gap may indicate a comparatively less severe occurrence of poverty.

Table 4.2 provides an overview of these nations' poverty and shared prosperity conditions, highlighting the estimated number of people living in poverty, the poverty rates, and the poverty gaps. Among the countries mentioned, India boasts the highest population, trailed by Pakistan and Bangladesh. Bhutan and Maldives are characterised by having the least populous nations. India has the highest incidence of poverty, with an estimated 175.7 million individuals living below the poverty line. Bangladesh is home to a significant number of impoverished individuals, with a staggering 24.4 million people residing below the poverty line, thereby ranking second in the world in terms of poverty incidence. Pakistan, Nepal, Sri Lanka, Bhutan, and Maldives exhibit a notable reduction in the prevalence of poverty, with figures ranging from 0.2 million to 9.9 million individuals. According to available data, Sri Lanka exhibits a poverty rate of 0.77%, which suggests a comparatively small segment of the populace experiencing poverty. Bangladesh exhibits the highest poverty rate at 15.16%, indicating a relatively greater prevalence of poverty than the remaining nations. India exhibits a poverty rate of 13.42%, which can be

Table 4.2 Poverty and shared prosperity report—2018

Country	Survey year(s)	Population (millions)	Number of poor (millions)	Poverty rate (%)	Poverty gap (%)	Poverty gap/rate (%)
India	2011.5	1311.19	175.7	13.42	2.4	17.7
Bangladesh	2010 and 2016	160.53	24.4	15.16	2.8	18.1
Pakistan	2013.5 and 2015.5	190.38	9.9	5.23	0.7	13.2
Nepal	2010.17	28.57	2.0	7.03	1.4	19.8
Sri Lanka	2012.5 and 2016	25.00	0.2	0.77	0.1	11.7
Bhutan	2012 and 2017	0.81	0.0	1.66	0.3	16.3
Maldives	2009.5	0.37	0.0	4.08	0.8	20.3
Afghanistan	NA	35.53	NA	NA	NA	NA

Source: Adopted from https://worldbank.github.io/SARMD_guidelines/poverty-measures.html

classified as moderately high. In contrast, Pakistan and Nepal demonstrate relatively lower poverty rates of 5.23% and 7.03%, respectively. According to available data, Sri Lanka exhibits the smallest poverty gap of 0.1%, which suggests that the average deficit in income or consumption among impoverished individuals is relatively minor. Pakistan exhibits a poverty gap of 0.7% of the poverty rate, indicating a comparatively lesser degree of poverty depth than other nations. The nations of Bangladesh, India, Nepal, Bhutan, and Maldives exhibit poverty gaps that range from 1.4% to 4.08% of the poverty rate. The poverty gap in Maldives is the highest among all countries, and it is expressed as a percentage of the poverty rate, at 20.3%. This suggests that the extent of poverty in Maldives is relatively more severe than the poverty rate. Nepal and Bangladesh exhibit relatively high percentages of poverty gap/rate, indicating a considerable intensity of poverty in comparison to their poverty rates. According to available data, Sri Lanka exhibits a poverty gap/rate percentage of 11.7%, which suggests a comparatively shallow poverty level about the poverty rate.

A disparity in poverty levels can be ascribed to a convergence of multiple factors. Several instances include an imbalanced distribution of income, insufficient healthcare, discrimination based on gender, heightened unemployment rates, and a scarcity of social welfare systems. The persistence and expansion of poverty and wealth disparity can be attributed to structural elements such as deficient governance, insufficient infrastructure, and corruption.

4.3 Post-COVID-19 Scenario of Poverty

It is much researched and well evidenced now that COVID-19 created a reversal of the poverty trend, unprecedented and exacerbated by rising inflation triggered by COVID-19-induced supply chain disruption and the Russia–Ukraine war. Poorer households spend more on food than on non-food, and almost 80% of countries on which data is available, the World Bank report suggests, have witnessed higher food inflation than non-food inflation. People living in extreme poverty spend two-thirds of their resources on food, whereas a person with an income of $50 daily——typically evidenced in high-income countries—spends 25% on food. This data has many implications for rising food prices, which economic crises like situations, war, or natural calamities can trigger. COVID-19 was undoubtedly such a situation. The impact of COVID-19, as evidenced, has been the largest on the poorest. As per WB estimate (Mahler et al., 2022), 97 million more people now live on less than $1.90 per day in 2021 due to the pandemic (an increase in the poverty rate to 9.1 per cent), and 163 million more are living on less than $5.50 a day (an increase in $5.50 poverty rate to 42.1 per cent). Also, across all regions, there has been an increase in the number of poor people. It is also essential to mention that this COVID-induced poverty has lost the progress and efforts in reducing extreme poverty, and this has been quite severe for some countries. As evidenced by high-frequency survey data, the income shock due to job loss or other related reasons during COVID-19 led to further vulnerable scenarios like running down assets and savings and subsequent recurrent income losses. This increased 57% the chances of going a whole day without eating, which has long-run implications on cognitive and physical development. Erosion of entrepreneurial capital is another factor that could lead to possible vulnerability to poverty.

Following Oxford's Multidimensional Poverty Index (MPI) addresses three key questions: (1) What was the MPI trend before COVID-19 in the SA region? (2) Impact of COVID on SA, and (3) COVID response to mitigate poverty in SA. It follows the SDG poverty targets viz., make MDI poverty by national definition half by 2030 in all ages (target 1.2), and end $1.9 per day monetary poverty by 2030 (Table 4.3).

The graphical representation in Fig. 4.1 indicates that poverty rates were considerably lower before the COVID-19 pandemic. In contrast, Fig. 4.2 illustrates that poverty rates at the subnational level were also relatively elevated.

Child mortality and nutrition are prominent factors that contribute significantly to the Multidimensional Poverty Index (MPI) in the South African region (Fig. 4.3). As per pre-COVID levels, the MPI reveals that India and Sri Lanka exhibit superior subnational performance in South Asia, while Pakistan and Afghanistan demonstrate comparatively inferior performance. The research conducted by Alkire et al. (2020) has revealed that a noteworthy observation can be made regarding the findings, which indicate that 47 out of 75 countries have made progress towards halving the global MPI between 2015 and 2030. These countries, namely, India, Nepal, and Bangladesh, are being referred to. Pakistan was among the 18 nations that deviated from the intended course. The study did not encompass Afghanistan; however, all tasks proceeded according to the established timeline.

4.4 Estimates on Poverty

According to reports from the World Health Organization (WHO, 2021b) and the World Bank, the COVID-19 pandemic has impeded two decades of global advancement towards Universal Health Coverage (UHC). The findings indicate that before the pandemic, a significant number of individuals, exceeding 500 million, were compelled or even further into poverty due to the necessity of personally financing healthcare expenses. The interruption of services and shift in prioritisation towards impoverished populations disrupted the immunisation process, marking the first occurrence in a decade. This disruption was accompanied by a significant rise in Fatalities attributed to tuberculosis, malaria, and related illnesses. This phenomenon has been observed in low-income and middle-income countries and numerous emerging middle-income countries. According to reports, the pandemic has exacerbated the situation to an unprecedented degree since the crisis of 1930, as it has altered individuals' preferences for expenditure on healthcare services. Similarly, individuals who were required to bear the cost of unanticipated medical expenses

Table 4.3 Multidimensional Poverty Index: developing countries

	Multidimensional Poverty Index		Population in multidimensional poverty							Contribution of deprivation in dimension to overall multidimensional poverty			Population living below income poverty line# (%)	
Countries	Year and survey	Value	Headcount*(%)	Intensity of deprivation (%)	Number of poor in the year of the survey (thousands)	Number of poor (2020) (thousands)	Inequality among people with low incomes (value)	Population in severe multidimensional poverty (%)	Population vulnerable to multifaceted poverty (%)	Health	Education	Standard of living	National poverty line (2009-2020)	PPP $1.90 a day (2009–2021)*
Afghanistan	2015/2016 D	0.272	55.9	48.6	19,365	21,789	0.020	24.9	18.1	10.0	45.0	45.0	54.5	
India	2019/2021 D	0.069	16.4	42.0	230,739	228,907	0.010	4.2	18.7	32.2	28.2	39.7	21.9	22.5
Maldives	2016/2017 D	0.003	0.8	34.4	4	4		0.0	4.8	80.7	15.1	4.2	5.4	0
Nepal	2019 M	0.074	17.5	42.5	5047	5137	0.010	4.9	17.8	23.2	33.9	43.0	25.2	15
Pakistan	2017/2018 D	0.198	38.3	51.7	84,228	87,089	0.023	21.5	12.9	27.6	41.3	31.1	21.9	3.6
Sri Lanka	2016 N	0.011	2.9	38.3	626	634	0.004	0.3	14.3	32.5	24.4	43.0	4.1	0.9
Bhutan	2010 M	0.175	37.3	46.8	263	288	0.016	14.7	17.7	24.2	36.6	39.2	8.2	1.5
South Asia	—	0.091	20.5	44.6	381,056	385,103	0.014	6.9	17.9	28.0	33.7	38.3	22.6	19.0

Sources: UNDP, 2022: https://hdr.undp.org/content/2022-global-multidimensional-poverty-index-mpi#/indicies/MPI and the World Development Indicators database. Washington DC. Http://data.worldbank.org. Accessed 7 August 2022. *Notes*: *Asterisk* refers to SDG 1.1 and # refers to SDG 1.2. All the estimates are based on surveys for 2016–2021

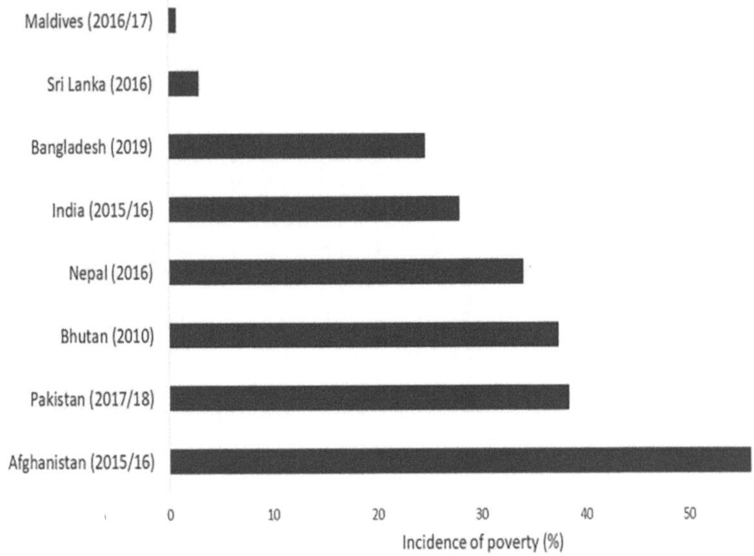

Fig. 4.1 Pre-COVID poverty rates across the countries. *Source*: Oxford Poverty and Human Development Initiative

experienced a significant financial burden, resulting in many of them falling into a state of severe impoverishment.

4.5 Catastrophic Health Shock in South Asia: Estimates, Anecdotes, Reasons

The correlation between health and poverty is both direct and indirect. To effectively address this issue, researchers and policymakers must comprehensively understand the channels this connection operates. This includes estimating the extent of influence via different channels and determining the strength of transmission channels. Based on this knowledge, policy interventions can be designed and implemented. The direct pathway involves decreased work productivity and increased opportunity cost, resulting in a loss of income due to poor health. The escalating expenses for health services and products and the limited access to these services have resulted in a higher expenditure for alternative means of obtaining the necessary health care. This is an example of the indirect relationship between channels of health impoverishment. Out-of-pocket expenditure (OOP) is a commonly used term to refer to such expenditures, and it serves as a significant indicator for public policy and health sector intervention. This phenomenon may also arise due to decreased public spending or a disproportionate increase in public expenditure relative to the growing public demand for said services. Individuals with more

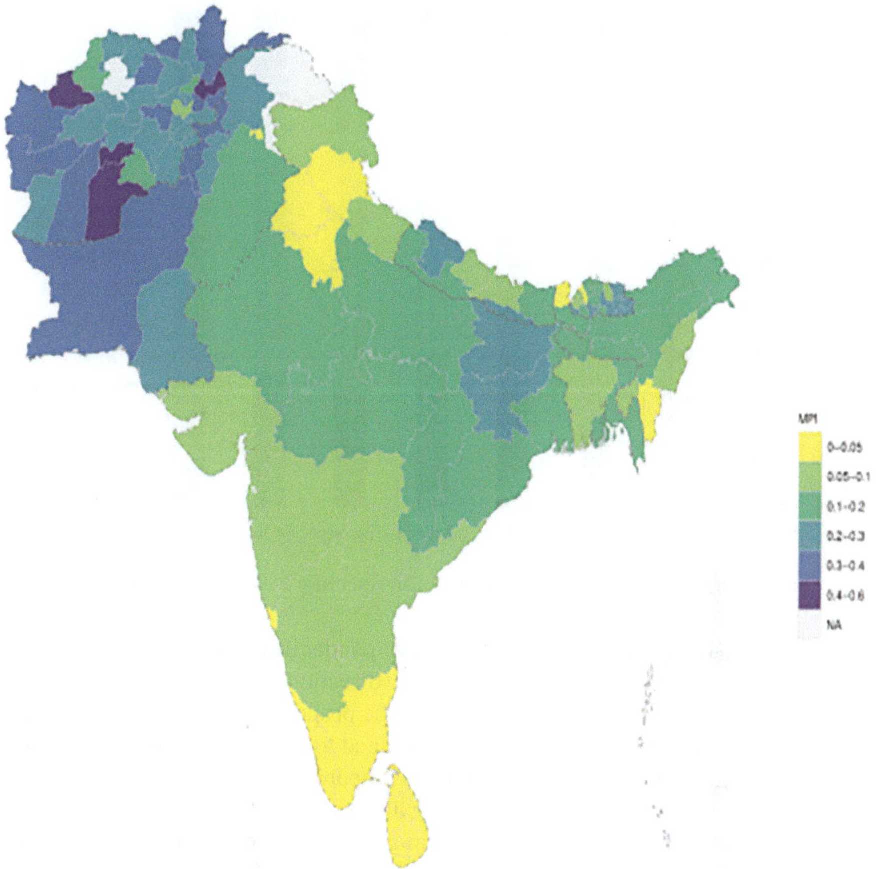

Fig. 4.2 Subnational level of Multidimensional Poverty Index (MPI). *Source*: https://data.humdata.org/dataset

significant financial resources will experience minimal or no adverse effects from catastrophic events, while those with limited income or who have experienced income fluctuations will bear the burden of sudden increases in out-of-pocket expenses. Since 2015, the World Health Organisation (WHO) and the World Bank (WB) have reported indicators to measure and mitigate financial hardship. Catastrophic health spending (CHS) is characterised by individuals or households who incur significant out-of-pocket (OOP) overall household consumption or income expenses. The statement conforms to the SDG indicator, wherein two distinct thresholds of 10% and 25% have been employed to delineate the "large" category. The objective of eradicating poverty through comprehensive measures is a crucial matter to be deliberated upon. In this regard, it is imperative to identify the underlying causes of out-of-pocket expenditure (OOP) that result in financial adversity to ensure no impoverished individual is neglected, as stated in a World Health Organisation (WHO, 2020) publication.

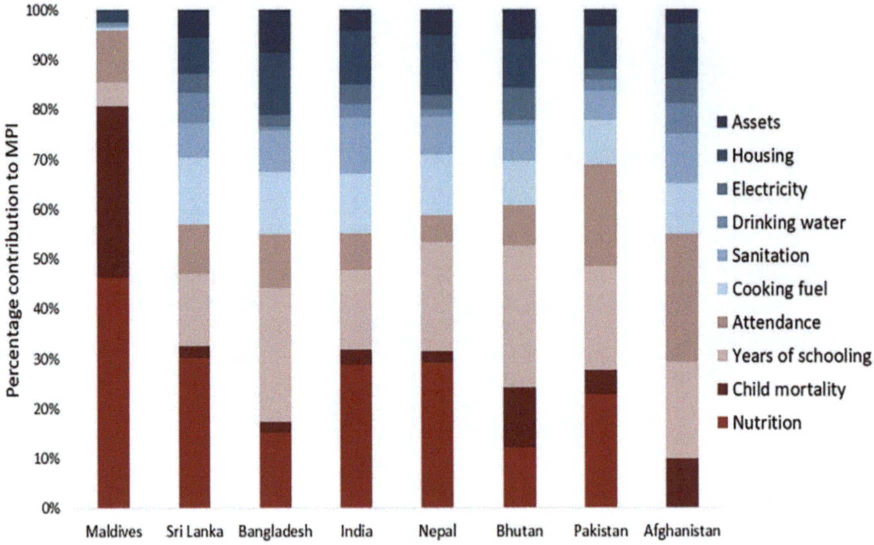

Fig. 4.3 Contribution to MPI across the South Asian countries. *Source*: UNESCAP (20)

According to estimates from the WHO, pre-pandemic catastrophic health expenditure (CHE) was trending in an unfavourable direction. Specifically, between 2015 and 2017, there was a significant increase in the proportion of the population experiencing CHE exceeding 10%. This was attributed to two factors: first, a higher rate of growth in out-of-pocket (OOP) spending compared to the development of private consumption, and second, an increase in OOP expenditure per person on health. Before the onset of the COVID-19 pandemic, specific trends were already evident and necessitated policy intervention, particularly regarding the growing demand for enhanced public funding in health financing. Countries with higher incomes tend to allocate more of their budget towards public spending. However, there appears to be no discernible decrease in health expenditure that leads to impoverishment. In 2017, an estimated 500 million individuals worldwide experienced extreme poverty. Notably, most individuals who experienced catastrophic health spending in 2017 were concentrated in the Asian region. Conversely, the population that was pushed into extreme poverty was primarily focused in the African and Asian areas, mainly due to demographic factors. Countries that rely more on public spending tend to have lower population concentration and financial hardship. An analysis conducted at the national level indicates that efficient health financing mechanisms and the comprehensiveness of such packages are crucial factors in mitigating health financing difficulties. As supported by empirical evidence, ageing has been identified as a significant contributing factor to health finance difficulties. The World Health Organization's recent report emphasises that the ageing process has exacerbated the financial burden associated with healthcare expenditures. A pressing requirement exists for high-frequency household data to facilitate more accurate analyses and appropriate policy interventions.

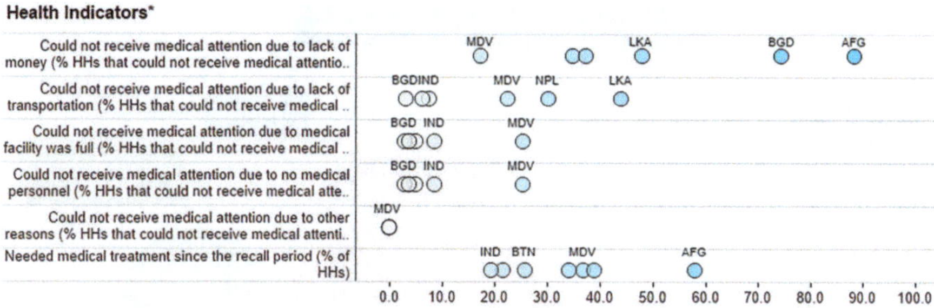

Fig. 4.4 Could not receive medical attention due to lack of money in the SA region. *Source*: World Bank, Covid-19 High-Frequency Monitoring Dashboard, The World Bank Group, Washington DC, 2023. https://www.worldbank.org/en/data/interactive/2020/11/11/covid-19-high-frequency-monitoring-dashboard

During the latter half of 2020, as the COVID-19 pandemic began to unfold and intensify, a significant economic downturn disproportionately affected the most impoverished and vulnerable households. In response to the financial impact of the COVID-19 pandemic, the government implemented various fiscal packages, which the International Monetary Fund recognised as stimulus packages. Certain nations have delayed their objectives and schedules for fiscal consolidation, while others have utilised escape clauses to generate fiscal leeway to accommodate the unparalleled increase in public spending. The survey findings from April 2021 indicate that certain nations witnessed individuals persisting with out-of-pocket payments for COVID-related tests and services despite significant government intervention. The COVID-19 pandemic has resulted in significant shifts in the demand for and supply of health services. According to the high-frequency survey conducted by the World Bank, financial barriers have played a significant role in this phenomenon.

Figure 4.4 shows the percentage of households that "could not receive medical attention when needed" in 2020. The report underscores that there needs to be a doubling of efforts towards financial protection, and there is a vast difference between economic hardship and financial protection. The report defined CHS following the SDG indicator 3.8.2 at the 10% threshold, and impoverished health spending was determined using the extreme poverty line ($1.90 a day in PPP). Out-of-pocket health spending is defined as: "any spending incurred by a household when any member uses a health good or service to receive any care (i.e. preventive, curative, rehabilitative or long-term care), provided by any provider, for any disease, illness or health condition, in any setting (e.g. outpatient, inpatient, at home). It includes formal and informal expenses directly related to the cost of seeking care as mapped in division 06 of the UN classification of individual consumption according to purposes (COICOP-2018)" (WHO 2021a). The CHS is considered a significant OOP that exceeds 10% or 25% of household share in total consumption or income, following the SDG 3.8.2 goal. It is essential to understand and target population proportion and its dynamic transition for suitable and impactful policy intervention. The conceptual framework developed by the WHO and WB for their high-frequency survey and general policy perspective is provided in Fig. 4.5.

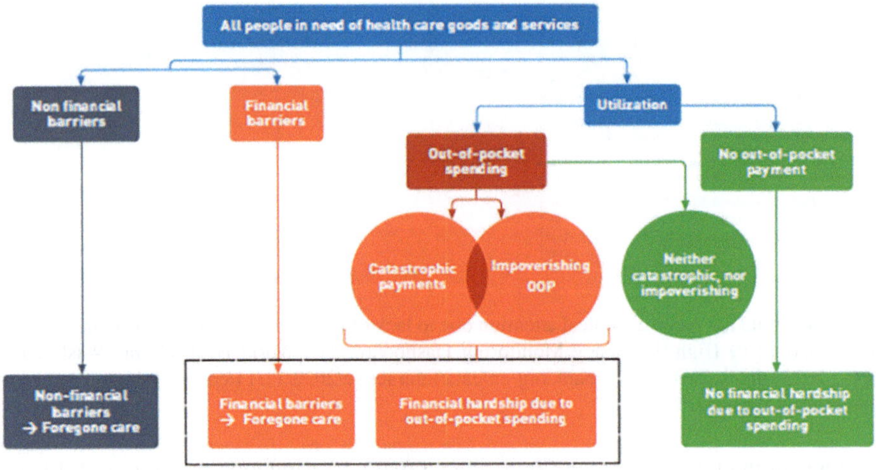

Fig. 4.5 Financial hardship and OOP. *Source*: WHO-WB 2021 publication

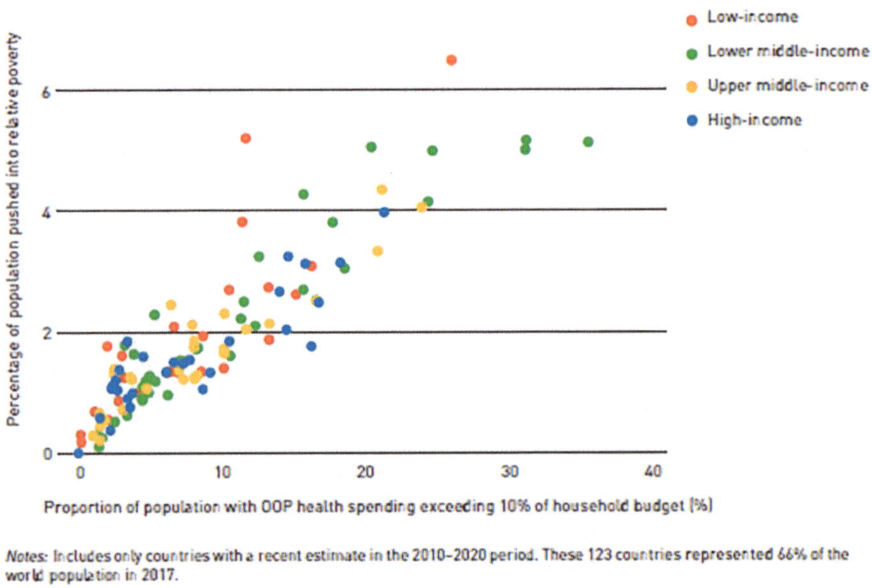

Fig. 4.6 Correlation between CHS and OOP. *Source*: WHO-WB 2021 publication

Figure 4.6 shows the correlation between CHS and OOP. According to the data presented in the graph, the countries encountered a dual challenge of not only having a significant percentage of individuals with high out-of-pocket (OOP) expenses but also a considerable proportion of individuals being driven into poverty, regardless of their income bracket. Nonetheless, it is worth noting that in numerous low-income and lower-middle-income nations, a proportion exceeding 4% of the populace is forced into a state of relative poverty.

4.6 The Post-COVID-19 Poverty Shocks

The pre-COVID poverty on MPI and other counts and CSH and impoverishing health expenditure counts were already very high in many regions; SA was among them, with wide variability within the area. The post-COVID scenario has been drastically different in that it magnified the poverty extent not only in quantity terms—total counts but on several dimensions—on quality terms. These dimensions of poverty vulnerability so far were unprecedented on several grounds; for example, poor people in most of the SA regions, by a large extent, live in slums, which are congested places lacking clean environment, they have limited access to handwash, internet and related health and non-health services and devices deemed to be essentials in the new-normal period for carrying out basic functions. The UNESCAP Report 2020 shows inequality by geography can be stark in the SA region on at least two counts out of 3: nutrition, water, and cooking fuel.

4.7 Concept of Demand-Side Financing

This section will try to understand how poverty increases health vulnerability and poverty. Is it a trap? It is imperative to grasp the correlation between poverty and income first to comprehend this notion. According to scholarly discourse, a causal relationship exists between poverty and income, mediated by health factors. Low wages or high unemployment may trigger poverty, increasing the working poor population. The susceptibility to health shocks can be attributed to poverty, inadequate awareness and access to nutritious food, and insufficient emphasis on preventive healthcare services and medications. This phenomenon significantly impacts an individual's income, resulting in the loss of workdays and reduced earning capacity. The provision of health insurance and the allocation of funds for healthcare expenses to individuals who are economically disadvantaged and susceptible to health risks are highly significant measures to be implemented as demand-side interventions in the healthcare industry. The healthcare industry is vulnerable to market failures due to various factors such as adverse selection, moral hazard, asymmetric information, externalities, and free riding. Implementing governmental initiatives to subsidise a significant portion of insurance premiums would likely incentivise individuals to engage in routine preventative health check-ups and prioritise healthcare interventions. The policy interventions on the demand side are of utmost importance as they can generate a surge in demand for healthcare services, thereby leading to favourable externalities for society. The discourse surrounding research and policy initiatives frequently emphasises supply side interventions, including identifying gaps and loopholes within the health infrastructure and shortages of staff and professionals. However, the demand side of healthcare is often overlooked in academic literature and policy networks. The principal objective of health sector policy in its intervention or mechanism design is to alleviate the gap between demand and supply. In some geographic regions, the limited availability of healthcare professionals may emerge as a crucial concern and necessitate prioritisation as a policy intervention. Conversely, in specific regions or sub-regions, the primary factor contributing to the discrepancy between supply and demand is the surplus demand resulting from the proliferation of insurance and subsidised health premiums. Consequently, the policy strategy for effective health sector intervention to alleviate the demand-supply discrepancy will inherently differ between these two scenarios. Properly comprehending and developing mechanisms require meticulous attention, mainly when financial limitations exist, and any intervention carries high costs and irreversible consequences, resembling a "one-shot game". However, the potential benefits of these interventions, such as improved health outcomes, reduced healthcare costs, and increased productivity, should instil optimism and hope in our audience.

4.8 Urban Poor and Health Issues in South Asia

Increasing urbanisation and expanding urban agglomeration are other factors behind growing poverty and health concerns. This comes with the considerable cost of the growing slum population in the suburbs, which calls for immediate adaptation policies to hygienic housing arrangements. Growing urbanisation as a side effect causes the urban poor to increase significantly, fueling health sector challenges that demand urgent attention. At the same time, countries strategise on developing cities and the development of urban agglomerations. A glance at the urban landscape in the developing world, including the SA region, shows how iniquitous and distressful commonality exists amidst prosperity and abundance. Urban high-tech hospitals mostly remain inaccessible to the street dwellers, which is too evident across most of the cities in the region. Affordability, accessibility, and social exclusion, along with speedy development and technology diffusion in all sectors, including the health sector, increasing urban poor and perpetual lower quality of life, are among some strange features of most parts of the SA region. Immigration and lack of regulatory measures towards monitoring and maintaining quality of life are other factors behind urban population growth and the growth of the urban poor. According to the UN, an urban agglomeration is an "area containing the city proper, suburbs and continuously settled commuter areas. It may be smaller or larger than a metropolitan area, comprising the city proper and its suburban fringe or thickly settled adjoining territory". Several research articles argue that all countries faced challenges during COVID-19. Still, the SA region, in particular, faced challenges on account of the high population and poverty rate—the world's one-third of the poor population lives here (ESCAP 2020), deplorable health infrastructure, inadequate social protection, limited access to water and sanitation, insufficient living space, etc. (Rasul 2020; Hossain et al. 2020). The world's most dense cities are located in this region: Dhaka, Mumbai, Karachi, and Delhi. World's largest slums are located in SA, for example, Dharavi in Mumbai (1 million), Orangi in Karachi (2.5 million), and Rohingya camps in Cox's Bazaar, Bangladesh (1 million) (Rasul 2020). The population living here are more vulnerable due to exposure to COVID-19 and infectious diseases, with poor work and living conditions, absorbed either in the informal sector or self-employed without health or social protection (ICIMOD 2020). The world's inferior healthcare infrastructure further fuels this. For example, Afghanistan has 2.8 physicians per 10,000 people, Bhutan 3.8, Bangladesh 5.3, and Nepal 6.5, one-tenth of the number in advanced economies. India has the most robust health system in the region, with 7.8 physicians per 10,000 people (Rasul, 2020). We discuss urbanisation and slum growth, which bring several health and other challenges. As per the World Bank's official estimate (Ellis and Roberts 2016), "South Asia's urbanisation has been messy as seen in the widespread prevalence of slums. At least 130 million South Asians—equivalent to more than the entire population of Mexico—live in informal urban settlements characterised by poor construction, insecure tenure, and underserviced plots".

4.9 Varied Dimensions of COVID-Induced Poverty and Vulnerability in South Asia

Common underlying causes exist for escalating poverty, which consequently requires tailored strategies for alleviation. There is substantial evidence, derived from casual empiricism and anecdotal accounts, that inequality has become pervasive within the current neoliberal economic and policy framework, characterised by rapid economic growth and significant changes. As a result of these circumstances and the absence of opportunities, individuals experiencing poverty resorted to adapting their means of survival and strategies for sustenance. The phenomenon of migration and the influx of individuals is a consequential outcome. Empirical evidence suggests that the South American region has experienced significant poverty and health shocks from large-scale influxes and migrations. The current COVID-19 pandemic and the ensuing "new normal" can be viewed as continuing this trend. According to a research study, approximately 33% of the population in India can be classified as migrants based on the Census definition for migration in the country. Approximately 16% of urban residents in Pakistan are classified as migrants. The SAAPE Poverty and Vulnerability Report SAAPE (2020) states that comparable migration statistics can be observed in other South Asian nations. The factors above give rise to many challenges, encompassing not only housing and habitation but also socio-economic and political issues, including but not limited to social strife, the proliferation of slums, population expansion, health crises, and the spread of diseases. Hence, it is imperative to address this matter through policy intervention, which entails financial investment, continuous monitoring, and innovative and inclusive policy design. This approach aims to alleviate the challenges associated with migration and integrate migrants into mainstream economic activities and outcomes. Community health workers have played a significant role in influencing outcomes during neoliberal economic expansion and the emergence of a new-normal situation.

The correlation between migration and poverty has been thoroughly examined and debated in academic and policy circles, particularly in South Asia, owing to the substantial interconnectedness between these phenomena. Figure 4.7 shows how much of the urban population in South Asia lives in slums. According to the data, Afghanistan exhibits the highest proportion (73.3%) of its populace residing in slum areas, with Pakistan (56%) and Bangladesh (51.9%) following closely behind. In India, it is observed that nearly half of the urban populace (49%) resides in slum areas. The 2020 SAAPE Poverty Report, titled "Migration in South Asia: Poverty and Vulnerability", presents a theoretical structure for comprehending the primary factors contributing to poverty in the South Asian area from the perspective of migration. The report offers suggestions for alleviating the area's unfavourable socio-economic impacts of migration.

It is a widely acknowledged fact that individuals residing in urban slums who are classified as impoverished are considerably more susceptible than their rural counterparts across all dimensions. This encompasses various shocks, such as health, livelihood, and economic shocks, which are particularly prevalent in urban areas

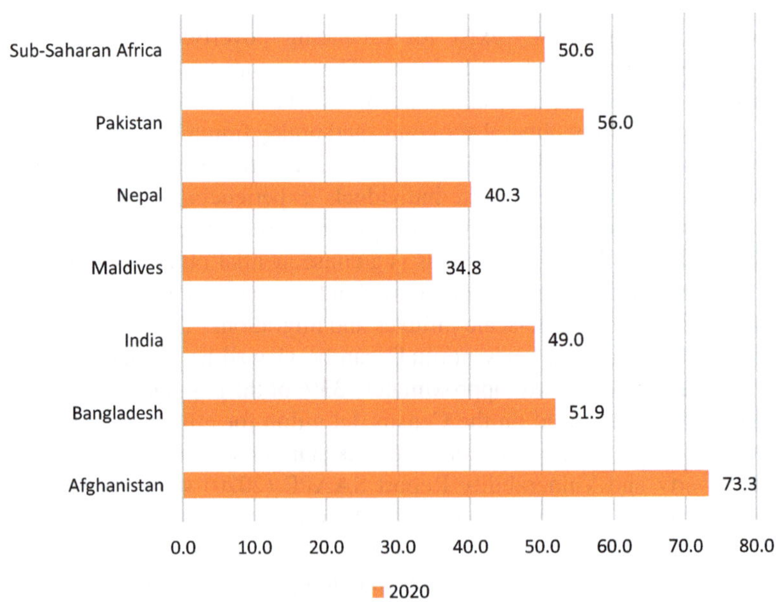

Fig. 4.7 Urban poor indicator (population living in slums). *Source*: World Development Indicators, 2020, UN-HABITAT

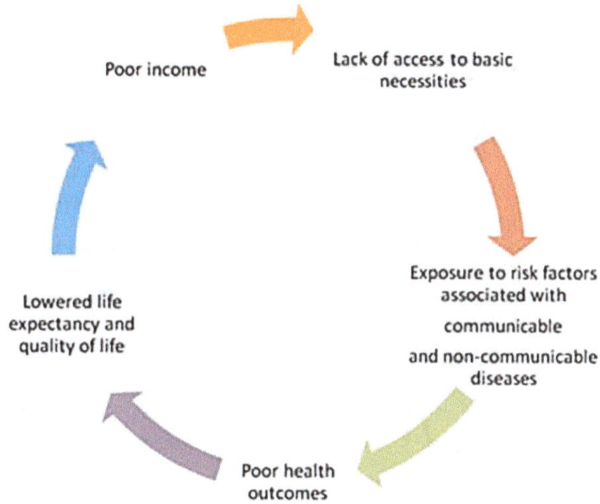

Fig. 4.8 Vicious circle of poverty and health outcomes.

due to the high cost of living. The disease burden encompasses a range of health conditions, including communicable and non-communicable diseases, injuries, and various other sources of physical and mental distress. Numerous collaborative research efforts between national specialists and the World Health Organization have revealed that the prevalence of overweight, hypertension, insufficient intake of nourishing sustenance, and susceptibility to alcohol and tobacco use is significantly greater among impoverished urban populations. The subsequent theoretical structure delineates the cyclical pattern of deprivation experienced by impoverished urban populations, as illustrated in Fig. 4.8. Correspondingly, policy emphasis should align with the framework depicted in Fig. 4.9.

Individuals residing in urban poverty are subject to various occupational exposures and hazards that can be classified into distinct categories:

Physical and mechanical: The physical and mechanical hazards that pose a risk to individuals include heat stress, radiation, cold temperatures, and extreme weather events. These hazards are especially concerning for outdoor workers, street vendors, and beggars. Additionally, injuries, musculoskeletal strain, fatigue, and exposure to dust and smoke are also potential hazards.

Chemical: The chemical substances of concern include industrial effluents, contaminated water, and industrial chemicals such as solvents and dyes, as well as domestic cleaners.

Biological: The biological hazards that individuals may encounter include exposure to untreated sewage, consumption of contaminated water and food, and handling of waste materials (including hazardous industrial and hospital waste)—particularly relevant for rag-pickers and waste handlers. Additionally, individuals may be at risk of contracting infections through hospital work or engaging in sex work, as well as vector-borne diseases.

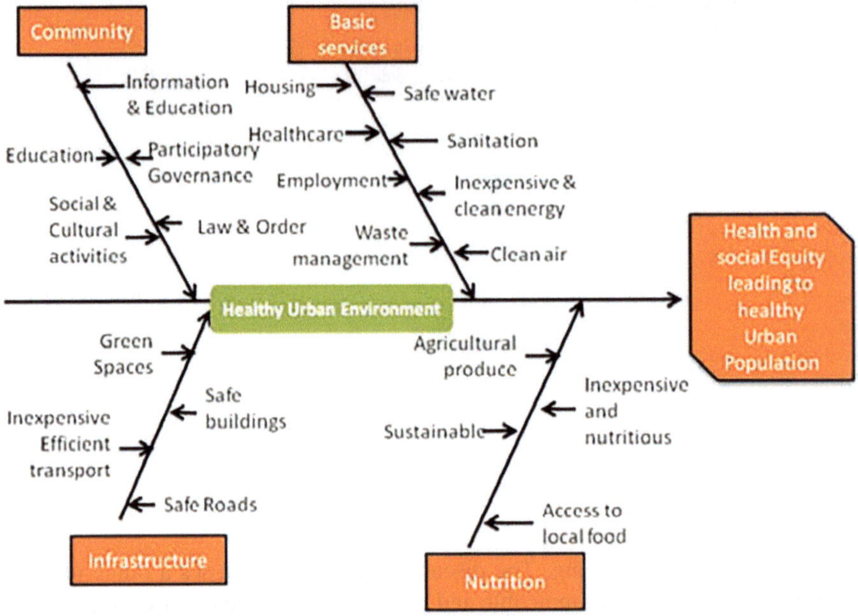

Fig. 4.9 Convergence of focused policy actions and initiatives. *Source*: WHO (2011)

Article 25 (1) of the Universal Declaration on Human Rights stipulates that every individual is entitled to a standard of living adequate for the health and well-being of oneself and one's family. This provision has a positive impact on the broader community. Hence, national policies and governance must be harmonised with the SDG objectives.

Ergonomic: The improper application of ergonomics can result in both acute and chronic injuries, such as sprains and strains from overexertion and repetitive motion injuries.

Psychosocial: The psychosocial factors that can negatively impact the workplace include harassment, exploitation, an unsupportive work environment, inadequate job security, a lack of mechanisms for addressing grievances, gender inequality, and violence.

4.10 COVID-19 Prompt Policy Actions in South Asia and Impacts

The COVID-19 pandemic spread starting from the first case varied widely across all the countries around the globe; most of the SA countries had their first COVID case much later than the advanced countries had, primarily induced by return migration and tourism-related contact services. However, as soon as the cases started to rise, mainly in quarter 1 of the 2020 financial year, governments adopted prompt actions to mitigate, which took varied forms. Table 4.4 gives a brief on that. It shows that lockdown and movement restrictions imposed as a policy measure to reduce contacts and infection have had economic repercussions in terms of income shocks and many more; anecdotal evidence shows how migrants from all over megacities in India travelled back to their native places. This also suddenly increased pressure on agricultural lands and rural livelihoods.

In the chapter discussing poverty in South Asia (SA), it becomes evident that poverty is a defining characteristic of the region and serves as a critical indicator of the persistent socio-economic dualism that plagues it. This dualism manifests starkly; on one side, the region is experiencing rapid growth across various politico-economic indicators, while on the other, the health vulnerabilities that affect its population remain deeply entrenched and are even worsening. The onset of the COVID-19 pandemic has exacerbated these vulnerabilities, highlighting the fragility of the region's socio-economic fabric.

Despite the challenges posed by the pandemic, it is important to recognise that the pre-COVID standards of living were already alarming enough to necessitate urgent policy interventions aimed at addressing the underlying issues. In response, the governments throughout SA have developed numerous tailored schemes, both in the lead-up to and during the COVID-19 crisis. India, in particular, has taken a prominent role in these initiatives.

A pivotal facet of these efforts lies in insurance—especially health and life insurance—which significantly influences the demand for sustainable and adequate health services. Such services not only provide immediate health benefits but also generate a host of externalities and societal advantages that ripple through the community. In Chap. 6 of this book, we will delve deeper into the demand dynamics within the health sector and the associated policy initiatives.

For instance, India launched Ayushman Bharat in 2018, heralded as the world's largest health insurance scheme. This ambitious initiative aims to accommodate over 10.47 crore impoverished and vulnerable families, now known as the PM Jan Arogya Yojana (PM-JAY). The scheme offers crucial insurance coverage of up to ₹5 lakh per family, with potential benefits extending to approximately 50 crore citizens. One of the central objectives of PM-JAY is to alleviate the financial burden of catastrophic medical expenses, which spiral approximately six crore Indians into poverty annually. The innovative aspect of this scheme lies in its active involvement of the private health sector, particularly in scenarios where public health institutions may falter. To achieve this, the scheme includes carefully structured incentive mechanisms to ensure participation from private healthcare providers.

In Sri Lanka, various schemes have been established to support public sector employees, such as the Public Servants Pension Scheme, insurance provisions for widows, widowers, and orphans, the Public Servants Provident Fund, and the Agrahara Medical Insurance. For workers in the private sector, there are corresponding initiatives like the Employee Provident Fund and the Employee's Trust Fund, which aim to safeguard the financial well-being of their beneficiaries.

Table 4.4 Measures taken by the Governments in South Asia to contain the spread of COVID-19 in the early stage of infection

Country	Lockdown measures (duration)	International borders/travel restrictions	Air travel	Land transport	Maritime transport
Afghanistan	Complete lockdown from 22 March till 24 May	Closed, open only for immigrants	Passive restriction enforced by neighbouring countries at the border	Passive restriction enforced by neighbouring countries at the border	Not applicable
Bangladesh	It started on 26 March, continued to 16 May, and extended to May 30. Hotspot lockdowns imposed	Closed	Domestic flights opened on 1st June. International flights are closed till 15th June. Cargo flights only	Freight trains	Essential good only
Bhutan	Restriction on entry of tourists from 6 March to 23 March—international borders sealed lockdown from April 1 to 21	Closed	Not allowed	Essential goods only	Not applicable
India	25 March to 31 May lockdown extended till 30th June in containment zones. Many activities were allowed after 8 June 2020	Closed	Domestic flights resumed, but passive restrictions for international flights	Passive restriction enforced by neighbouring countries at the border	No data
Maldives	A public health emergency was declared on 19 March. Lockdown from 1 April to 12th June in greater Malé	Closed	Permission required	Not applicable	Allowed
Nepal	23 March to 2 June. Further extended to 14 June	Closed	Permission required	Conflicting information	Not applicable

(continued)

Table 4.4 (continued)

Country	Lockdown measures (duration)	International borders/travel restrictions	Air travel	Land transport	Maritime transport
Pakistan	1 April to 9 May. lockdown lifted	Closed	International flights allowed cargo flights only	Prohibited	Allowed
Sri Lanka	Public holiday declared from 15 March lockdown from 20 March to 11 May	Closed	Cargo flights	Prohibited	No data

Source: Adapted from Rasul et al. (2021)

In Pakistan, among the various programmes initiated in 2019, the government introduced the Ehsaas programme, a comprehensive security and poverty alleviation initiative, which involved amendments to the constitution to bolster its framework. Notably, these schemes resonate with cash transfer programmes observed in Latin America, emphasising a development approach driven by demand rather than relying solely on supply side interventions. Through targeted monitoring and tailored support, these initiatives strive to foster economic upliftment and address poverty in a more effective and responsive manner.

References

Alkire, S., Dirksen, J., Nogales, R., & Oldiges, C. (2020). Multidimensional poverty and COVID-19 risk factors: a rapid overview of interlinked deprivations across 5.8 billion people.: https://www.unescap.org/sites/default/files/Session_3_Sabina_Alkire_COVID-19_and_MPI_South_Asia.pdf

Ellis P, Roberts M (2016) Leveraging urbanization in South Asia: managing spatial transformation for prosperity and livability. © World Bank. http://hdl.handle.net/10986/22549 License: CC BY 3.0 IGO

ESCAP (2020) COVID-19 and South Asia: national strategies and subregional cooperation for accelerating inclusive, sustainable and resilient recovery. COVID-19 response. Economic and Social Commission for Asia and the Pacific (ESCAP), United Nations

Ferreira FH, Chen S, Dabalen A, Dikhanov Y, Hamadeh N, Jolliffe D et al (2016) A global count of the extreme poor in 2012: data issues, methodology and initial results. J Econ Inequal 14:141–172

Hossain MS, Ferdous S, Siddiqee M (2020) Mass panic during COVID-19 outbreak—a perspective from Bangladesh as a high-risk country. J Biomed Anal 3(2):1–3

ICIMOD (2020) COVID-19 impact and policy responses in the Hindu Kush Himalaya. International Centre for Integrated Mountain Development, Lalitpur, Nepal

Mahler DG, Yonzan N, Hill R, Lakner C, Wu H, Yoshida N (2022) Pandemic, prices, and poverty. World Bank Blog. https://blogs.worldbank.org/en/opendata/pandemic-prices-and-poverty#_ftn1

Rasul G (2020) A framework for improving policy priorities in managing COVID-19 challenges in developing countries. Front Publ Health 8:589681. https://doi.org/10.3389/fpubh.2020.589681

Rasul G, Nepal AK, Hussain A, Maharjan A, Joshi S, Lama A, Sharma E (2021) Socio-economic implications of COVID-19 pandemic in South Asia: emerging risks and growing challenges. Front Sociol 6:629693

SAAPE (2020). Migration in South Asia Poverty and Vulnerability. SAAPE Poverty and Vulnerability Report: https://ruralindiaonline.org/en/library/resource/migration-in-south-asia-poverty-and-vulnerability/

WHO (2011) Addressing health of the urban poor in South-East Asia region: challenges and opportunities. World Health Organization, Regional Office for South-East Asia

WHO (2020) Health systems | Universal Health coverage. World Health Organization

WHO (2021a) Global monitoring report on financial protection in health 2021. World Health Organization

WHO (2021b) More than half a billion people pushed or pushed further into extreme poverty due to health care costs. World Health Organization. https://www.who.int/news/item/12-12-2021-more-than-half-a-billion-people-pushed-or-pushed-further-into-extreme-poverty-due-to-health-care-costs

Chapter 5
Vaccine Initiative in South Asia

Abstract There are research findings that differences in COVID-19 can be partially explained by BCG vaccination policies: is it so that the countries with universal vaccination policies are associated with lower incidence and death rates from COVID-19? Vaccination drives were quite robust in the South Asian economies with substantial economic benefits in the medium run, apart from health benefits, though concerns remain over very low overall health expenditure and inadequate infrastructure in the SA region. However, often these benefits are contingent on solid international collaboration and initiatives from developed countries. Based on the evidence available and anecdotes, this chapter provides an interesting discussion on the critical aspects of vaccination and related health policies, supply constraints, policy designs, etc., in the South Asian region during the COVID-19 pandemic. The chapter underscores that in spite of the SA region having high poverty rates, literacy too low, and hence vaccine hesitancy high, timely proactive policies and success rates are commendable.

Keywords Vaccination · BCG vaccine · Vaccine R&D · Immunisations · Lockdown · Immunity · Health management · Vaccination campaign

5.1 Introduction

A few recently published ecological papers discuss differences in COVID-19 impacts that could be partially explained by BCG vaccination policies; countries with universal vaccination policies are associated with lower incidence and death rates from COVID-19 (for example, Banik et al., 2020). The World Bank estimates in their recent report that a cumulated 10% of GDP loss will be prevented in 2022 and beyond by the current vaccination drive in the South Asian economies;

A. Banik et al., *Extraordinary Health Hazards and their Socio-Economic Effects in South Asia*, South Asia Economic and Policy Studies,
https://doi.org/10.1007/978-981-95-5729-5_5

therefore, substantial economic benefits are foreseen in the medium run apart from health benefits. However, it's crucial to note that these benefits are contingent on solid international collaboration and initiatives from developed countries. With the uncertainty of the COVID scenario concerning its changing variants, experts suggest building excess capacity in vaccine production. Given that public health expenditure in the South Asian region is only 2% of GDP, lower than even the same in the Sub-Saharan African area, and the tax base is shallow, the mobilisation of additional financial resources to meet this expenditure is beneficial and necessary. Also, capacity building towards a more efficient administrative and delivery system, proper cold-chain management, and a strategic preventive and primary care approach are needed to reduce comorbidities and economic losses during the pandemic. Based on the evidence available and anecdotes, this chapter provides an interesting discussion on the critical aspects of vaccination and related health policies in the South Asian region during the COVID-19 pandemic.

5.1.1 Vaccination Scenario Pre-COVID: South Asia in Global Comparison

See Figs. 5.1 and 5.2.

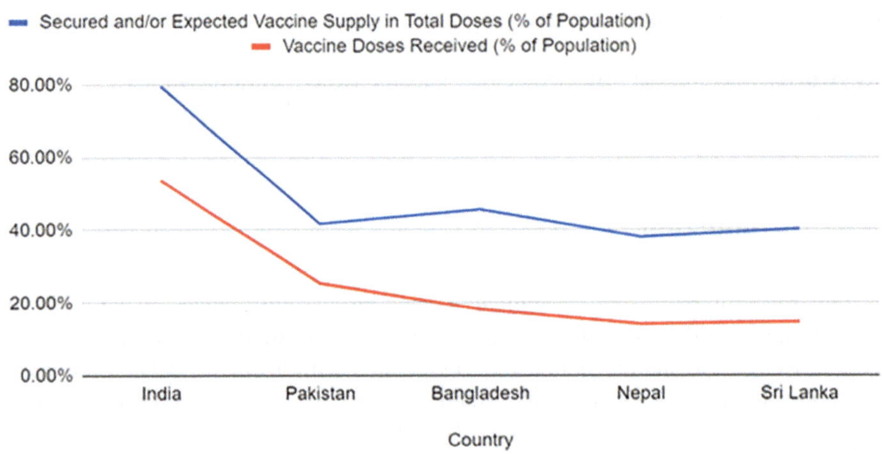

Fig. 5.1 Supply of vaccines in South Asia countries. *Source*: World Health Organization (WHO)

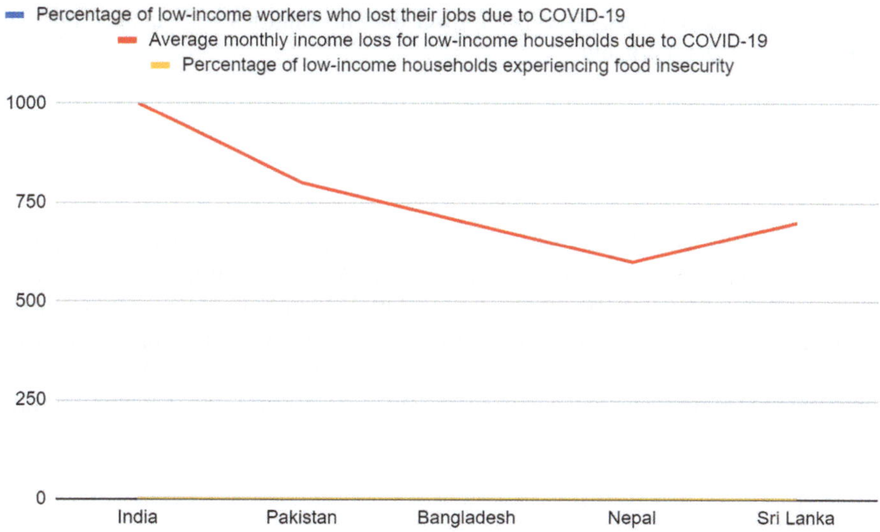

Fig. 5.2 Data on low-income groups affected by COVID-19 in South Asia. *Source*: IMF ["South Asia Regional Economic Outlook: Sustaining the Recovery" (April 2021)] & UNDP ["The Impact of COVID-19 on Poverty in Pakistan"] (June 2021)

5.2 Public Health Infrastructure and COVID-19

Healthcare systems are inadequate in South Asian nations. Only 2.8 physicians are available for every 10,000 people in Afghanistan, compared to 3.8 in Bhutan, 5.3 in Bangladesh, and 6.5 in Nepal. Only 7.8 doctors are available worldwide, even in India, which has one of the best health systems (Rasul 2020). Due to inadequate health infrastructure and resources, the South Asian nations have implemented stringent policy measures to stop the spread of the coronavirus and preserve lives. Except for a few necessities, all economic activity has ceased, travel is prohibited, goods and services are constrained, and cross-border travel is not permitted. Borders have been closed, and national, regional, and international supply lines have been disrupted, primarily in South Asia. Labour, the primary factor of production, has been isolated.

5.3 Social Factors and Post-COVID-19 Effects

5.3.1 Age Factor and COVID-19

In patients with COVID-19, older age is linked to higher mortality risks (Zhou et al. 2020). More than half of the South Asian population is below 24 years old (UNICEF 2019). Though the absolute number of deaths has been on the higher side in South

Asia, in percentage terms, it has been lower than in countries with an aged population like Italy, Denmark, etc.

5.3.2 Poverty

One-third of the world's poorest people live in South Asia, where most live in rural areas and depend primarily on agriculture. South Asia is one of the world's poorest regions. Before the COVID-19 pandemic, 649 million individuals in South Asia experienced moderate to severe food insecurity, of which 271 million experienced severe food insecurity. Similar to this, 16% of the kids had severe malnutrition, and 36% of the kids were stunted, and due to COVID-19, poverty, and inequality further increased (Rasul 2020).

5.3.3 Population

23.75% of the world's population lives in South Asia, where COVID-19 transmission has remained active. Due to the very high population density and congested settlements like Dharawi in India, the virus spread more rapidly. This was responsible for many cases and deaths, in absolute terms.

5.3.4 Vaccine Hesitancy

Due to low levels of literacy, superstitions, and the fact that vaccines were coming from India, there was vaccine hesitancy amongst the South Asian population, especially in rural areas (Hayat et al. 2022).

5.3.5 BCG Vaccination

BCG vaccine is mandatory in countries like India. Due to COVID-19 in South Asian economies, the scale of the destruction would have been very significant. However, the BCG vaccine and other factors like age composition have partially offset the loss in these economies (Banik et al. 2020).

Despite all the above constraints, South Asian economies successfully handled the pandemic through proactive policies like lockdowns, country-wide vaccination drives, and diplomacy.

5.4 India's Initiative on Vaccine R&D and Supply

On 30 January 2020, the first COVID-19 case in India was reported. Subsequently, the first wave of COVID-19 infections peaked in April 2020, and the second wave peaked in the same month of 2021. In April 2020, the Indian government enacted a rigorous nationwide lockdown, which it continued to execute until May 2020. The second COVID-19 outbreak in India severely strained the nation's healthcare infrastructure.[1]

As of 06 July 2023, 4,49,94,449 confirmed cases have been registered in India. 98.81% have been discharged, and the death rate is 1.18%.[2] After the nationwide lockdown, India adopted a vaccination method to prevent mortality from COVID-19. Based on India's experience with the most extensive immunisation programme currently in place, the "Universal Immunisation Programme" (UIP), which annually targets close to 26 million newborns to administer vaccines against 12 diseases that can be prevented by vaccination.[3] India came up with the idea to launch the COVID-19 immunisation programme right once, utilising the infrastructure already in place to supply, store, and deliver vaccines to the last mile, under the UIP, where over 600 million doses are given to children annually. Large-scale immunisation campaigns have been carried out in the past by the universal immunisation programme. For more than 20 years, the nation has conducted extensive polio programmes.[4] According to data from several studies in India, 80%–90% of people had received the measles and rubella vaccine, demonstrating the success and broad reach of immunisation campaigns (Newtonraj et al. 2019).

The COVID-19 Vaccine Global Access Facility (COVAX) was established as a unique facility. The responsibility of COVAX is to support the purchase of vaccines through GAVI. India leads the research and development of vaccines through its participation in the COVAX Advance Market Commitment (AMC), the Vaccine Alliance, and the Coalition for Epidemic Preparedness Innovations (CEPI). To speed up the development, production, and equitable access to COVID-19 diagnostics, medications, and vaccines, the WHO has also created a framework called the Access to COVID-19 Tools (ACT) accelerator. This framework was developed through international cooperation between the WHO, the European Commission, France, and The Bill and Melinda Gates Foundation (WHO 2020a, b). India is the largest producer of vaccines in the COVAX coalition.

The Cabinet Secretariat in India established a National Expert Group on Vaccine Administration for COVID-19 on 7 August 2020. Its responsibility was to decide which vaccinations the nation should utilise, oversee the extensive acquisition budget, and choose which population groups should get the initial doses of each

[1] https://www.ncbi.nlm.nih.gov/pmc/articles/PMC9633268/#:~:text=India%20has%20followed%20a%20need,the%20age%20of%2018%20years.

[2] https://www.mygov.in/covid-19/.

[3] https://main.mohfw.gov.in/sites/default/files/5628564789562315.pdf.

[4] https://www.nhp.gov.in/pulse-polio-programme_pg.

vaccine. Indian businesses inked contracts with Novavax for supply, licencing, and production arrangements with AstraZeneca for 100 million vaccine doses. India created two locally produced candidate vaccines for the vaccine race: COVAXIN and ZyCov-D.

The Indian drugs regulator initially approved (under Emergency Use Authorisation) Covishield, a chimpanzee adenovirus vector encoding the SARS-CoV-2 spike glycoprotein, and Covaxin, inactivated entire virions produced in Vero cells, as two vaccines for use in an emergency. Nearly 88% of all doses administered nationwide have been of the Covishield vaccine, which is like the Oxford-AstraZeneca (ChAdOx1 nCoV-19) vaccine in composition and immunogenicity.[5]

Bharat Biotech and the National Institute of Virology (NIV) of the Indian Council of Medical Research (ICMR) collaborated on developing COVAXIN, an indigenous COVID-19 vaccine. The BSL-3 (Bio-Safety Level 3) high containment facility at Bharat Biotech is the development and manufacturing site for this locally produced, inactivated vaccine.

The Serum Institute of India (SII) and the Indian Council of Medical Research jointly developed Covishield (COVID-19 Vaccine). It has the same formulation as the AstraZeneca vaccine. This has acted as the vaccine that vaccinated more than 88% of the Indian population and served as the main instrument of vaccine diplomacy through the "Vaccine Maitri" programme. Other vaccines against COVID-19 used in India include Sputnik V, Corbevax, Covovax, ZyCOv-D, etc. The Department of Biotechnology, under Mission COVID Suraksha, in January 2023, delivered four vaccines. The four vaccines are ZyCoV-D, the first indigenously developed DNA vaccine globally, and CORBEVAXTM, the first protein subunit vaccine in India. GEMCOVACTM-19, the first indigenously developed mRNA vaccine in the world, and iNCOVACC, the first indigenously developed intranasal COVID-19 vaccine in the world.[6]

Figure 5.3 shows the number of COVID-19 vaccine doses administered in India as of first September 2022. As of 06 July 2023, India has administered 2,206,741,404 doses of COVID-19 vaccination.[7] As of July 2022, India has provided approximately 235 million doses of COVID-19 vaccinations to 98 nations worldwide as part of the "Vaccine Maitri" project.[8] The nations that benefited from the Vaccine Maitri programme were Bangladesh, Myanmar, Nepal, Bhutan, Maldives, Mauritius, Sri Lanka, Brazil, Morocco, South Africa, Afghanistan, Mexico, DR Congo, Nigeria, the United Kingdom, and many others. Only 4 days after launching its vaccination programme, India began sending the vaccines abroad on 20 January 2021. Bhutan and the Maldives were the first nations to get vaccines as a grant from India. This played a pivotal role in India's vaccine diplomacy.

[5] https://dashboard.cowin.gov.in/.

[6] https://www.pib.gov.in/PressReleasePage.aspx?PRID=1894167.

[7] https://www.mygov.in/covid-19/.

[8] https://www.business-standard.com/article/current-affairs/india-supplied-over-235-mn-total-supplies-of-covid-vaccines-to-98-countries-122071500116_1.html.

India has administered the highest total COVID-19 vaccine doses among South Asian countries. In addition, India has supplied these countries with vaccines, especially Covishield under Vaccine Maitri and the COVAX facility. India has acted as the regional leader in vaccine supply.

5.5 Other South Asian Countries Initiative on Vaccine R&D and Supply

Similar to Fig. 5.3, Fig. 5.4 shows the number of COVID-19 vaccine doses (including all doses and boosters) administered in South Asian countries other than India as of 6th July 2023.

5.5.1 Bangladesh

On 27 January 2021, COVID-19 immunisations were given in Bangladesh. The AstraZeneca vaccine, created in India, was first administered to the general populace on 7 February 2021. Other vaccines include Pfizer, Sinopharm, and Moderna. Since the start of the pandemic, COVID-19 has been the subject of widespread rumours, ignorance, and misinformation among the general people in Bangladesh due to the lacklustre reception to online registration. Some people voiced a dislike for vaccination because they feel they do not need it, while others expressed scepticism because it is an Indian product.

Due to low literacy rates, low faith in the healthcare system, and inadequate adherence to health safety standards, a considerable prevalence of vaccine refusal

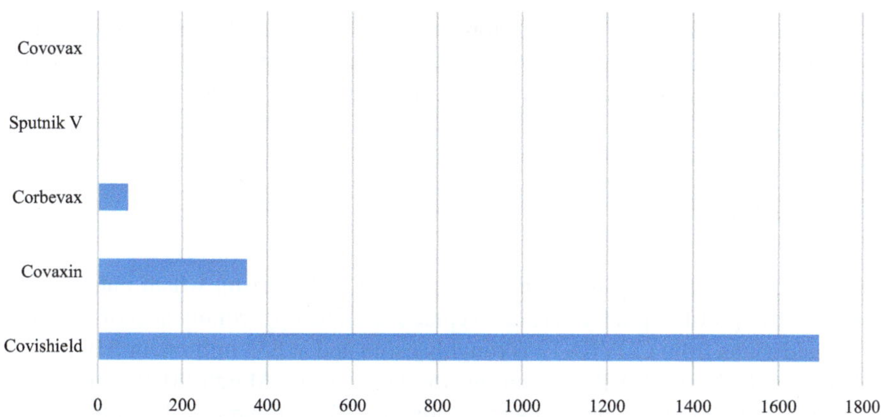

Fig. 5.3 COVID-19 Vaccine doses administered in India (in millions). *Source*: https://www.statista.com/statistics/1248301/india-covid-19-vaccines-administered-by-vaccine-type/

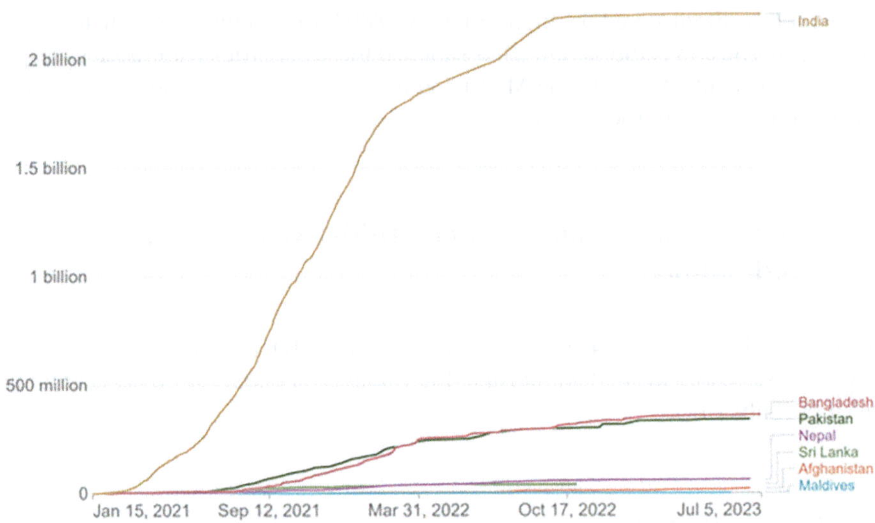

Fig. 5.4 Total COVID-19 vaccine doses administered in South Asian countries. *Source*: https://ourworldindata.org/grapher/cumulative-covidvaccinations?

and reluctance was seen among rural and slum communities. The ongoing app-based vaccination registration has stoked scepticism and resistance among the less informed people. Because poor socioeconomic and educational levels are shared by most people living in rural areas, and all slum residents (Abedin et al. 2021).

5.5.2 *Bhutan*

On 27 March 2021, India donated 500,000 AstraZeneca vaccinations to Bhutan, beginning with the AstraZeneca-Oxford vaccination dosage. This marked the beginning of the country's first phase of its mass vaccination programme. China, India, and the USA provided the other vaccines, Sinopharm and Moderna.

5.5.3 *Maldives*

The Maldives' economy relies heavily on travel and tourism, which puts them in danger of importing illnesses prone to epidemics. The opportunity cost of shielding the Maldivians from COVID-19 is roughly estimated at $33 million, or 510 million Maldivian Rufiyaa (MVR), according to statistics for March 2019. But among countries where tourism accounts for more than 10% of exports, the Maldives has outperformed those with no such dependence in terms of delaying the pandemic's arrival (Suzana et al. 2020).

On 1 February 2021, the Covishield vaccine from AstraZeneca was distributed to the general public owing to a grant from India of 100,000 doses. The COVAX facility also administered the Pfizer-BioNTech vaccine and the AstraZeneca (AZD1222) vaccine (donated by Japan). Ninety per cent of the nation's front-line tourism workers were immunised. All residents over 18 received the first dose of an AstraZeneca vaccine, the second dose of a Sinopharm vaccine, and both doses of an AstraZeneca vaccine (Hayat et al. 2022).

5.5.4 Nepal

People were vaccinated with AstraZeneca, Sinopharm, Pfizer, J&J/Janssen (1.5 million doses) Single-Shot COVID-19 vaccine. This was done through Vaccine Maitri, COVAX, help from the World Bank, etc. Only 56.6% of Nepal's population is literate, and the majority still adheres to superstitions. This makes it simple for them to believe in myths, which has led to people breaking laws governing public health. Both Nepal's socioeconomic standing and healthcare system are subpar. Over 65% of all healthcare spending is accounted for by the out-of-pocket (OOP) model. Authorities in Nepal were often at odds with one another over political issues, which delayed decisions for the COVID-19 response and lowered public confidence (Adhikari, 2021).

5.5.5 Pakistan

Pakistan received the first doses of the Sinopharm vaccine from its neighbour China on 1st February 2021. Through the COVAX programme, it also received the Pfizer-BioNTech vaccination. Pakistan received Moderna and AstraZeneca-Covishield vaccines from the COVAX facility. Multilateral organisations, including the Asian Development Bank, supported the effort.

Because the perception of vaccination causes serious worries for specific people, there were issues with the COVID-19 vaccine in Pakistan, including scepticism and doubt fuelled by incorrect information (Malik et al. 2021).

5.5.6 Sri Lanka

On 29 January 2021, the coronavirus immunisation programme was launched after India donated 0.5 million doses of the AstraZeneca vaccinations. After the COVID-19 pandemic's setbacks, Sri Lanka and China agreed to a credit arrangement of $500 million. This financing will help with the country's economic recovery. Similar agreements were also struck with Australia, Japan, the ADB, the World Bank, etc.

5.6 Policy Initiative Towards Vaccination and Success Story

Countries adopted initial measures like lockdowns at the national and state levels. A vaccination drive with the help of Vaccine Maitri, COVAX, and multilateral bodies like the ADB, World Bank, China, etc., followed this. There has been vaccine hesitancy in the South Asian population. Some countries also followed unique policies. For example, starting 15th September 2020, all Sri Lankans over 30 must carry their vaccination cards in public areas to stop the COVID-19 outbreak from spreading.

5.6.1 *Success Story of India*

The first COVID-19 case in India was reported on 30 January 2020. The second wave of COVID-19 infections peaked in April 2021, the same month the first wave of infections peaked in April 2020. The Indian government implemented a strict statewide lockdown in April 2020 and carried it out until May 2020. Phased closures followed this in case of an increase in cases.

Punitive actions and nudges, such as dialler tone and advertisements, promoted non-clinical interventions like wearing masks and social distancing. Innovative strategies like "Har Ghar Dastak" and "Jan Bhagidari" supplemented this.

India developed its vaccines in the form of Covishield and Covaxin and emerged as the global supplier of vaccines through COVAX and Vaccine Maitri. In India, digital health infrastructure like the COWIN portal, e-Sanjeevani, etc., played a vital role in decentralising the process. The government followed a prioritisation approach for administering the vaccine depending upon the vulnerability of the groups. India followed a Barbell strategy, wherein the government took an agile approach to tackle the pandemic. Measures like the Atma Nirbhar Bharat Scheme, Pradhan Mantri Garib Kalyan Ann Yojana, etc., were launched.[9]

The COVID-19 pandemic has posed significant challenges to nations worldwide, including India. Given the rapid transmission of the virus, the Indian government has implemented various measures to manage and alleviate its impact on the public's welfare. These measures have been implemented to reduce the spread of the virus, enhance the capacity of healthcare systems, and help vulnerable populations. This document provides a comprehensive overview of the primary steps taken by the Indian government to mitigate the transmission of COVID-19 (GOI 2021).

[9] Economic Survey of India 2020–2021.

1. **Nationwide Lockdown:** The implementation of a nationwide lockdown refers to imposing strict restrictions on the movement and activities of individuals across an entire country. In March 2020, the government of India implemented a comprehensive lockdown across the nation as a whole, intending to mitigate the transmission of the virus. During the lockdown period, stringent measures were implemented to limit the movement of individuals. These measures included closing educational institutions, offices, and non-essential businesses. Additionally, public transportation services were temporarily suspended. During the initial phase of the lockdown, it became necessary to extend the duration on multiple occasions. This decision was made in response to the ongoing severity of the outbreak. However, as time progressed, certain areas began to witness a gradual relaxation of restrictions. The extent of relaxation varied depending on the severity of the outbreak in each specific area.
2. **Testing and Contact Tracing:** To detect and isolate individuals who have contracted COVID-19, the Indian government has implemented extensive measures to expand testing and contact tracing endeavours. The expansion of testing capacity was achieved by establishing testing laboratories in various locations throughout the country. Contact tracing was implemented to ascertain and locate individuals who had been near individuals with confirmed cases of a particular disease. These identified individuals were then subjected to quarantine or isolation measures as deemed appropriate based on the level of risk involved.
3. **Healthcare Infrastructure:** In response to the imperative to enhance healthcare infrastructure, the Indian government implemented a series of measures. In response to the escalating number of individuals affected by the COVID-19 pandemic, temporary hospitals, and isolation centres were established. These facilities were specifically designed to provide adequate accommodation and care for patients afflicted with the virus. Various measures were undertaken to enhance the capacity of existing healthcare facilities. These measures primarily focused on augmenting the number of beds, ventilators, and other essential medical equipment. Equipping the healthcare facilities with these additional resources bolsters their ability to provide adequate medical care and support to needy patients. To strengthen the capabilities of healthcare professionals, various initiatives were undertaken to provide training and facilitate recruitment.
4. **Vaccination Campaign:** In January 2021, India initiated an extensive vaccination campaign to combat the COVID-19 pandemic. This campaign is one of the most significant global efforts in scale and magnitude. The government's objective was to administer vaccinations to a substantial proportion of the population, prioritising healthcare workers, frontline workers, and individuals belonging to vulnerable groups. Throughout the nation, a network of vaccination centres was established to facilitate the widespread administration of vaccines. These centres were strategically positioned to ensure accessibility and convenience for the general population. In parallel, rigorous evaluations were conducted to assess the safety and efficacy of various vaccines. Consequently, multiple vaccines were approved, providing healthcare professionals with different options to combat the targeted diseases. The approval process involved comprehensive

assessments of the vaccines' safety profiles and their ability to prevent the targeted infections effectively. This meticulous evaluation ensured that only vaccines meeting the highest standards were available to the public.

5. **Public Awareness and Communication** have been identified by the Indian government as essential strategies in effectively managing the transmission of COVID-19. Recognising their significance, the government has strongly emphasised these tools to mitigate the spread of the virus within the population. Regular updates and guidelines were disseminated via official channels like press conferences and social media platforms. Public health campaigns were initiated to disseminate knowledge and promote awareness among the general populace. These campaigns aimed to educate individuals on the importance of adopting preventive measures, including using masks, maintaining hand hygiene, and implementing social distancing practices.

5.6.2 How Bangladesh Controlled the Spread of COVID-19?

The Government of Bangladesh has implemented various measures to mitigate the transmission of COVID-19 within the nation. These measures have been implemented to safeguard the well-being and welfare of the general populace and minimise the pandemic's adverse effects on the healthcare infrastructure and the economy. This document provides an overview of the significant measures implemented, supported by references to reputable sources.

1. **Early Detection and Surveillance:** The topic of early detection and surveillance is of paramount importance. The Institute of Epidemiology, Disease Control and Research (IEDCR) in Bangladesh has been diligently engaged in the monitoring and surveillance of COVID-19 cases. The establishment of a hotline (16263) to report suspected cases and the creation of a network of laboratories dedicated to the testing of virus samples have been implemented by the World Health Organization (2021a, b).

   In addition, the government's national testing strategy encompasses testing individuals displaying symptoms, individuals who have been near confirmed cases, and the strategic testing of high-risk areas (Directorate General of Health Services 2020).
2. **Quarantine and Isolation:** The government's establishment of quarantine centres and isolation facilities aims to provide suitable accommodations for individuals who have received positive test results for COVID-19 or have had close contact with confirmed cases. According to the Ministry of Health and Family Welfare, 2020 (Government of India 2021), these establishments offer medical assistance to patients with the additional objective of curbing the spread of the virus. Individuals who have travelled internationally must undergo either mandatory institutional quarantine or home quarantine, contingent upon their level of risk (Directorate General of Health Services 2020).

3. **Public Health Messaging and Education:** The Ministry of Health and Family Welfare, in conjunction with the World Health Organisation and other stakeholders, has initiated a comprehensive public health initiative to enhance knowledge and understanding of preventive measures against COVID-19. This encompasses advocacy for proper hand hygiene, the use of masks, adherence to physical distancing measures, and staying well-informed regarding the most recent developments (World Health Organization 2020a, b).
4. **Travel Restrictions and Border Control**: To effectively communicate accurate and timely information regarding COVID-19 and combat misinformation, the government has employed diverse media platforms, including television, radio, and social media. To mitigate the transmission of COVID-19, Bangladesh has implemented travel restrictions and enhanced border control measures to regulate the influx of individuals originating from countries with a significant prevalence of According to the Directorate General of Health Services (2020), there are measures in place that require mandatory testing and quarantine for individuals who are arriving from these countries.

   To mitigate the transmission of the virus, the Ministry of Civil Aviation and Tourism (2021) has implemented measures such as suspending international flights and imposing restrictions on domestic travel.
5. **Vaccination Campaign:** Bangladesh has initiated a nationwide campaign to administer COVID-19 vaccines to its populace. The government has procured vaccines from multiple sources, including the COVAX facility. According to the guidelines set forth by the Directorate General of Health Services (2021), priority has been given to the vaccination of healthcare workers, frontline workers, and individuals belonging to vulnerable populations.

   According to the World Health Organization (2021a, b), the Ministry of Health and Family Welfare has proactively promoted the uptake of vaccinations among the general population. Additionally, the ministry has established nationwide vaccination centres to facilitate convenient accessibility.

The measures implemented by the Government of Bangladesh are intended to mitigate the transmission of COVID-19, safeguard public health, and uphold the welfare of its populace. Individuals must adhere to these measures and diligently follow the guidelines provided by health authorities to combat the ongoing pandemic effectively.

5.6.3 Measures Taken to Control the Spread of COVID-19 by Pakistan

Pakistan, like numerous other nations, has enacted a range of measures to mitigate the transmission of COVID-19. These measures have been implemented with the primary objective of ensuring the protection and preservation of the physical and mental health of the populace and alleviating the adverse consequences arising from the ongoing pandemic. This document aims to present an overview of the critical measures implemented by Pakistan, with supporting references.

1. **Implementation of Travel Restrictions:** Pakistan promptly enforced travel restrictions to mitigate the potential transmission of COVID-19. In response to the prevailing circumstances, the government has implemented measures to reduce the spread of infectious diseases. These measures include the temporary suspension of international and domestic flights, the closure of land borders, and the imposition of stringent quarantine protocols for individuals entering the country. The measures implemented were consistent with the guidelines outlined by the World Health Organisation (WHO) and the International Civil Aviation Organisation (ICAO) (WHO 2021a, b).
2. **Testing and Contact Tracing:** To promptly identify and isolate cases of COVID-19, Pakistan has significantly increased its testing capacity. This enhanced capability allows for the efficient detection of individuals who may be infected with the virus. By promptly identifying these cases, appropriate measures can be taken to isolate and treat affected individuals, thereby minimising the spread of the disease within the population. To enhance the efficacy of testing efforts, the government implemented a strategic initiative to establish testing centres in various locations throughout the nation. Additionally, a concerted effort was made to augment the daily number of tests conducted. The enhancement of contact tracing endeavours has been implemented to effectively identify and locate individuals who may have had proximity to individuals with confirmed cases of a particular disease or infection. Implementing targeted quarantine and isolation measures has been instrumental in mitigating the spread of the virus, as evidenced by the findings of the National Institutes of Health (NIH 2021).
3. **Public Health Awareness Campaigns:** Pakistan initiated comprehensive public health awareness campaigns to disseminate knowledge and raise awareness among the general population regarding the COVID-19 pandemic. These campaigns were designed to educate individuals about the virus's nature and encourage the adoption of preventive measures. The campaigns employed various mediums, including television, radio, social media, and print. Extensive dissemination of information about symptoms, preventive measures, and vaccination campaigns has been undertaken to foster widespread public compliance and comprehension of the prevailing circumstances (GOP 2021).
4. **The COVID-19 Vaccination Drive:** Pakistan has witnessed notable advancements in this context. The government has strategically designed the vaccination campaign to prioritise certain groups of individuals. These groups include healthcare workers, elderly individuals, and individuals with comorbidities. By prioritising these specific populations, the government aims to ensure that those at higher risk of contracting and experiencing severe complications from the virus receive the vaccine promptly. This prioritisation strategy is based on scientific evidence and expert recommendations to maximise the overall impact of the vaccination programme. A network of vaccination centres has been established

throughout the country to facilitate the widespread distribution of vaccines. Concerted endeavours have enhanced the ease of access for individuals seeking immunisation. The government has collaborated with international partners to obtain and expedite the vaccination process (NHSRC 2021).

Compliance with health guidelines is of utmost importance in Pakistan, and the government has taken significant steps to ensure adherence to these guidelines. Stringent enforcement measures have been put in place to achieve this objective. Implementing specific measures has been deemed necessary to mitigate the spread of infectious diseases. These measures encompass the compulsory utilisation of masks in public settings, the observance of physical distancing, and the promotion of hand hygiene by providing sanitisers and handwashing facilities. Individuals who fail to adhere to the prescribed guidelines outlined in this document may be subjected to monetary fines and other punitive measures, as stated by Dawn (2021).

References

Abedin M, Islam MA, Rahman FN, Reza HM, Hossain MZ, Hossain MA, Hossain A (2021) Willingness to vaccinate against COVID-19 among Bangladeshi adults: understanding the strategies to optimize vaccination coverage. PLoS One 16(4):e0250495

Adhikari K (2021) Third wave of COVID-19 in Nepal: challenges and way forward. J Chitwan Med College 11(2):1–2

Banik A, Nag T, Chowdhury SR, Chatterjee R (2020) Why do COVID-19 fatality rates differ across countries? An explorative cross-country study based on select indicators. Glob Bus Rev 21(3):607–625

Dawn. (2021). Govt warns against violation of COVID-19 SOPs. Retrieved from https://www.dawn.com/news/1623786

Directorate General of Health Services. (2020). COVID-19: National Guidelines on Infection Prevention and Control

Directorate General of Health Services. (2021). COVID-19 vaccination update. Retrieved from http://dghs.gov.bd/index.php/en/home/6221-covid-19-vaccination-update

Government of India (2021) National Family Health Survey-2019-20 (NFHS 5). Ministry of Health and Family Welfare, New Delhi

Government of India (GOI). (2021). COVID-19 vaccination. https://www.cowin.gov.in/home

Government of Pakistan (GOP). (2021). COVID-19 awareness campaign. Retrieved from http://covid.gov.pk/awareness-campaign/

Hayat M, Uzair M, Ali Syed R, Arshad M, Bashir S (2022) Status of COVID-19 vaccination around South Asia. Hum Vaccin Immunother 18(1):2016010

Malik A, Malik J, Ishaq U (2021) Acceptance of COVID-19 vaccine in Pakistan among health care workers. PLoS One 16(9):e0257237

Ministry of Civil Aviation and Tourism. (2021). Travel advisory for air passengers

Ministry of National Health Services Regulation and Coordination (NHSRC). (2021). COVID-19 vaccination in Pakistan. Retrieved from http://covid.gov.pk/vaccine/

National Institute of Health (NIH). (2021). COVID-19 dashboard. Retrieved from http://covid.gov.pk/

Newtonraj A, Vincent A, Selvaraj K, Manikandan M (2019) Status of coverage of MR vaccination, after supplementary immunization activities in a rural area of South India: a rapid immunization coverage survey. Rural Remote Health 19(3):1–5

Rasul G (2020) A framework for improving policy priorities in managing COVID-19 challenges in developing countries. Front Publ Health 8:589681. https://doi.org/10.3389/fpubh.2020.589681
Suzana M, Moosa S, Rafeeg FN, Usman SK (2020) Early measures for prevention and containment of COVID-19 in the Maldives: a descriptive analysis. J Health Soc Sci 5(2):251–264
UNICEF (2019): More than half of South Asian youth are not on track to have the education and skills necessary for employment in 2030, Press release: https://www.unicef.org/rosa/press-releases/more-half-south-asian-youth-are-not-track-have-education-and-skills-necessary
World Health Organization. (2020a). COVID-19: Bangladesh situation updates - weekly bulletin
World Health Organization (2020b) Boost for global response to COVID-19 as economies worldwide formally sign up to COVAX facility. World Health Organization, p 21
World Health Organization. (2021a). Bangladesh: COVID-19 Vaccination Campaign Begins
World Health Organization (2021b). Coronavirus disease (COVID-19) advice for the public. Retrieved from https://www.who.int/emergencies/diseases/novel-coronavirus-2019/advice-for-public
Zhou F, Yu T, Du R, Fan G, Liu Y, Liu Z, Xiang J, Wang Y, Song B, Gu X, Guan L, Wei Y, Li H, Wu X, Xu J, Tu S, Zhang Y, Chen H, Cao B (2020) Clinical course and risk factors for mortality of adult inpatients with COVID–19 in Wuhan, China: a retrospective cohort study. Lancet 395:1054–1062. https://www.thelancet.com/action/showPdf?pii=S0140-6736%2820%2930566-

Chapter 6
Health Care System in South Asia: Addressing Demand-Side Challenges

Abstract This chapter explores demand-side strategies to combat the healthcare issues prevalent within South Asian economies. Most of the literature on health outcomes focuses on the supply constraints, shortages, and policy interventions on the supply side of the health sector. In comparison, discussion on the demand side is scanty. The discussion thoroughly examines various factors, including the regulatory frameworks governing healthcare, the condition and accessibility of transportation networks, the intricacies involved in insurance policy design, and the efficacy of pricing control systems. The coronavirus catastrophe brought two forms of employment loss: temporary lockdown-induced job loss and permanent impact job loss. The impoverished in rural areas and those living in urban slums who depend on daily income are some of the worst affected by COVID-19. The chapter discusses in several SA country context, the urgent need for improvements in social health protection, as even though many nations have expanded their coverage, insufficient or erratic funding remains a significant concern. Proper monitoring, incentive designing, and awareness campaigns are essential to create suitable demand-side intervention in such healthcare services because of their public good nature. The chapter shows that active involvement of the respective governments in the SA countries has been visible for the last decade or so, via innovative schemes and initiatives.

Keywords Demand side · Job loss · Regulation · Insurance policy · Universal health coverage · Out-of-pocket expenditures · Public good · Adverse selection · Moral hazard

6.1 Introduction

The concept of the demand side in healthcare has emerged as a crucial response to the urgent need for enhanced accessibility and effective utilisation of healthcare services, particularly in the context of developing nations. In these regions, many

A. Banik et al., *Extraordinary Health Hazards and their Socio-Economic Effects in South Asia*, South Asia Economic and Policy Studies,
https://doi.org/10.1007/978-981-95-5729-5_6

individuals grapple with significant financial constraints that hinder their ability to seek necessary medical care. This pressing concern has sparked a deeper investigation into the demand side of health services, emphasising the resilience, determination, and commitment needed to tackle these challenges head-on.

The devastation brought about by the COVID-19 pandemic has had a profound and multifaceted impact on healthcare systems throughout South Asia. One of the most troubling consequences has been the widespread loss of employment, resulting in many individuals and families losing their employer-sponsored health benefits. This loss has starkly revealed the vulnerabilities inherent in existing healthcare frameworks, exposing gaps that need urgent attention. Even as efforts to establish universal health insurance plans have been initiated, the region continues to confront significant supply side deficiencies, such as a shortage of adequately trained medical professionals and the dilapidated infrastructure of healthcare facilities. These shortcomings render such initiatives insufficient in meeting the diverse healthcare needs of the population.

Moreover, the exorbitant costs associated with health insurance premiums have left a substantial segment of the populace without any form of coverage, thereby worsening the crisis of long-term healthcare security. This financial barrier creates a cycle of exclusion, depriving many individuals of the essential healthcare services required to maintain their well-being over time.

In light of these daunting challenges, this chapter will explore demand-side strategies to combat the healthcare issues prevalent within South Asian economies. The discussion will thoroughly examine various factors, including the regulatory frameworks governing healthcare, the condition and accessibility of transportation networks, the intricacies involved in insurance policy design, and the efficacy of pricing control systems. Each of these elements plays a vital role in shaping access to healthcare and ultimately influencing the overall health and well-being of the population.

6.2 Job Loss in South Asia During the COVID-19 Pandemic and its Aftershocks

The COVID-19 pandemic resulted in significant employment reductions in Southeast Asia, reaching its apex during the second quarter of 2020. The coronavirus catastrophe brought two forms of employment loss: temporary lockdown-induced job loss and permanent impact job loss. Temporarily lost jobs included more than three million in manufacturing, five million in transportation, three million in construction, and seven million in the micro, small, and medium-sized enterprises (MSME) sector (The Financial Express 2020).[1]

[1] Jobless recovery might put progress of last decade at risk: Study. The Financial Express. https://www.thefinancialexpress.com.bd/economy/bangladesh/jobless-recovery-might-put-progress-of-last-decade-at-riskstudy-1593175397.

The unemployment rate in India has exhibited a notable decline since April 2020. However, the emergence of novel coronavirus variants and the imposition of periodic lockdowns have engendered a fluctuating pattern of unemployment. The exacerbation of this situation has been attributed to the emergence of novel variants of the coronavirus and the implementation of lockdown measures. A trickle-down effect[2] was also observed during the COVID-19 outbreak in India. During the period spanning from February to April 2020, the proportion of households that encountered a decline in their income surged to approximately 46%. It was anticipated that there would be an increase in inflation rates for various goods and services, such as food products and fuel, in the latter part of 2020. Implementing social distancing measures has reduced employment opportunities, particularly among individuals in the lower economic stratum of Indian society. Several households have discontinued their utilisation of domestic help services, which can be characterised as an informal employment arrangement involving monthly remuneration. Many individuals in India devoted a significant portion of their time to performing domestic tasks during the lockdown period, rendering it the most observed activity. Indian government launched various programmes and campaigns to help economically backward classes, such as women, farmers, senior citizens, and construction workers. Under the Pradhan Mantri Garib Kalyan Yojana, 312 billion Indian rupees were provided to 331 million beneficiaries. More aid was announced in mid-May to support small businesses fighting the crisis.

Sri Lanka, a developing nation, has experienced three surges of the coronavirus outbreak. The ongoing COVID-19 pandemic has presented noteworthy obstacles to Sri Lanka, persisting even following the implementation of lockdown measures during the initial and subsequent waves of the outbreak. Since 21 May 2021, the entire island nation was under travel restrictions. Sri Lanka's economy experienced significant repercussions due to the initial and subsequent waves. The discernible fluctuations in the contraction of the GDP rate by 3.6% and the unemployment rate by 5.2% in 2020 are evidence of the country's economic devastation.[3]

Like numerous other developing nations, Pakistan experienced a substantial reduction in employment opportunities amidst the pandemic. The economy continues to experience the repercussions of the COVID-19 pandemic, as evidenced by the persistent impact of reduced wage rates, which have reached their highest levels. The gap can be attributed to the absence of a well-established supply and demand chain, significantly impacting production-related issues. Additionally, the unavailability of the labour force due to social distancing measures has further exacerbated the situation.[4] The shock has resulted in a significant debt burden for developing

[2] https://www.statista.com/statistics/1111487/coronavirus-impact-on-unemployment-rate.

[3] https://www.scirp.org/journal/paperinformation.aspx?paperid=119812.

[4] https://www.researchgate.net/publication/370871739_Determinants_of_Job_Loss_in_Covid-19_A_case_study_of_Pakistan.

nations such as Pakistan, as the Food and Agriculture Organisation reported in 2020. Pakistan Bureau of Statistics revealed that the lockdowns imposed during the pandemic significantly impacted the workforce, affecting approximately 27.31 million individuals. The study further indicates that 20.6 million individuals have experienced job loss, while 6.7 million have faced a reduced income. According to the Pakistan Bureau of Statistics (2020), job loss rates in Pakistan have remained significantly lower in both formal and informal sectors compared to other developing nations.

Between 12 and 17 million people were thought to have lost their jobs temporarily due to the 2-month lockout.[5] This job loss results from the shutdown of the economy's four main sectors. An extra 10 million people in the agricultural sector have lost their jobs.[6] If that number were increased, the total number of temporary employment losses would be nearly 25 million. Estimates of the number of permanently impacted jobs lost in Bangladesh due to COVID-19 are summarised in Table 6.1 by several development agencies and think tanks. The impoverished in rural areas and those living in urban slums who depend on daily income are some of the worst affected by COVID-19 (Sakamoto et al. 2020). Since the coronavirus outbreak, the average income of low-income people has decreased by more than 80%. The average daily income loss for rural poor people was 56 taka ($0.67), a decline of 79% from their prior income of 89 takas ($1.07). At the same time, slum dwellers lost 82% of their daily income, or about 81 Bangladeshi takas ($0.97), from their prior income of 108 takas ($1.30) in February.[7]

Table 6.1 Estimates of permanent Job loss during the COVID-19 outbreak

Source	Unemployed (in million)	Individuals impacted financially (in million)
World Bank	7	28
Asian Development Bank (ADB)	4	16
Policy Research Institute of Bangladesh (PRI)	12	58
Centre for Research and Information Dhaka (CRI)	6	24
Centre for Policy Dialogue (CPD)	–	56
Power and Participation Research Centre (PPRC)/ BRAC Institute of Governance and Development (BIGD)	–	70
News interviews	–	50

Source: Compiled by authors

[5] https://opinion.bdnews24.com/2020/06/04/bangladesh-at-work-job-creation-and-inclusive-growth-in-the-eraof-covid-19.

[6] https://www.lightcastlebd.com/insights/2020/03/29/theeffect-of-covid-19-on-bangladeshs-apparel-industry.

[7] https://www.aa.com.tr/en/asia-pacific/coronavirus-poor-income-drops-80-in-bangladesh/1808837.

6.2.1 Job Loss and Employees' Benefits in South Asia

Employee benefits refer to the additional perks and advantages offered to employees in addition to their regular compensation or remuneration. Benefits provided to employees can take the form of monetary or non-monetary compensation. They may be legally mandated under the employment law known as Statutory Benefits or offered voluntarily by the employer. The provision of benefits is a crucial aspect of a job offer, given the significant differences that may exist in the types and extent of benefits provided. Certain benefits are contingent upon the country of origin, such as healthcare coverage in the United States and meal vouchers in Luxembourg. Employers provide these benefits to foster a sense of organisational affiliation among employees and enhance their ability to attract and retain top talent.

The scenario of employees' benefits largely varies in Southeast Asian countries (Table 6.2). India's contribution to the Employee's Provident Fund is comparatively lower than that of three other countries (excluding the Philippines, which lacks a Statutory Provident Fund). India and Malaysia face significant challenges in providing adequate Social Security Benefits to their workforce, mainly since most are employed in the unorganised sector. The Philippines is notable for its abundance of offerings compared to other regions. It has a much more comprehensive range of benefits in each area than the other four countries, making it the most employee-friendly market in South-East Asia. Although it is not customary for Malaysian employers to offer health insurance to their employees, they typically provide a range of medical benefits at no cost or a reduced rate. These benefits may include generalist outpatient care, specialist consultations, dental and optical services, maternity expenses, and hospitalisation and surgical benefits for employees and their eligible dependents.

According to the report published by the International Labour Organisation (ILO), a significant proportion of the population in Asia and the Pacific region, totalling 1.6 billion individuals, lack adequate social health protection. The inaugural report "Extending Social Health Protection: Accelerating Progress towards Universal Health Coverage in Asia and the Pacific" comprehensively analyses the region's advancements, hindrances, and insufficiencies. The report underscores the urgent need for improvements in social health protection, as even though many nations have expanded their coverage, insufficient or erratic funding remains a significant concern. The rise in middle-class expectations for superior services, particularly from private providers not covered by social health insurance schemes, increases out-of-pocket expenditures. The report recommends enhancing institutional capacity and refining scheme design and administration to improve coverage and benefits.

Even though over 75% of the population in Asia and the Pacific region are legally entitled to receive health protection, significant gaps in legal coverage, lack of awareness of rights, and practical barriers hinder access to healthcare services. As a result, millions of individuals are forced to pay for healthcare services, which often leads to impoverishment. The report reveals significant discrepancies in healthcare

Table 6.2 Employees' benefits in Southeast Asia

	India	Philippines	Singapore	Thailand	Malaysia
Financial benefits					
Provident fund	3.67%	N/A	17% (Combined)	10%	12%
Social security scheme (life/disability insurance)	0.5%	7.37%		5%	1.77%
Healthcare/Health insurance	Statutory; N/A, Voluntary: Group Medical Cover (GMC)	Insurance (1.375%)	Inpatient insurance (not fixed) + Outpatient consultations	Not fixed	Free-of-cost/Subsidized inpatient & outpatient consultation
Stock options/Mutual funds (voluntary)	Employee Stock Ownership Plan (ESOP)	Stock options, a common practice	Employee Stock Ownership Plan (ESOP)	Employee Stock Ownership Plan (ESOP)	Employee Stock Purchase Plan
Educational/Home loans	House Building Advance (HBA) for Central & State Govt. Employees	Home loans under Pag-IBIG	Not prevalent	Not prevalent	Educational assistance for employee's own education
Non-financial benefits					
Wellness program	Fitness centre/Gym subscriptions	Fully integrated health/wellness programs	Flexi benefits (Health Screening, Dental Care and Fitness Club Subscription)	At nascent level, but an increasing trend	Wellness/Fitness sessions

(continued)

Vacation	18–24 vacation days per year based on years of service	13-Day vacation leave, with additional 1 day every year starting on the 3rd year of service. Maximum vacation leave is 18 days	14- to 20-day vacation leave subject to years of service	10 vacation days on a prorated basis for 1–3 years of service	12 vacation days on a prorated basis for less than 2 years of service
Leaves	- Sick leave - Maternity leave - Paternity leave - Marriage leave - Compassionate leave - Adoption leave	Sick leave - Paternity leave - Compassionate leave - Solo parent leave - Magna Carta leave - Calamity leave - Leave for victims of violence against women & children	Childcare leave - Paternity leave - Maternity leave - Marriage leave - Compassionate leave - Sick leave	- Sick leave - Paternity leave - Maternity leave - Monkhood leave - Hajj leave - Compassionate leave - Marriage leave - Hospitalization leave	- Sick leave - Paternity leave - Maternity leave - Marriage leave - Compassionate leave - Hospitalization leave - Child Marriage leave
Miscellaneous	- Internet reimbursement - Telephone allowance - Reimbursement of travel expenses	- 13th month pay - Mid-year bonus - Rice allowance - Prolonged sickness benefits - Loyalty token - Kapwa Tulong Club	- 13th month pay - Relocation package - Per Diem	- Gift on marriage - Funeral expenses reimbursement (insufficient data)	- Vehicle purchase subsidy - Gifts on birthday, retirement, childbirth - Long service award

Source: Ali (2020)

coverage across the Asia-Pacific region. It indicates that a minority of the labour force in the region possesses lawful income protection in the event of illness, with less than 50% meeting this criterion. Additionally, only 45.9% of females are safeguarded during pregnancy. The phenomenon of coverage gaps disproportionately impacts self-employed individuals who work in the informal economy and are migratory workers, as well as their families. The demographic group that experiences the most significant degree of suffering consists of individuals employed in agricultural and domestic occupations, as well as their respective family members.[8] The report underscores the significance of social health protection in safeguarding individuals' health, employment, and financial stability, particularly in the COVID-19 pandemic.

6.3 Factors Driving the Demand Side of the Health Sector: The Fundamentals

Most of the literature on health outcomes focuses on the supply constraints, shortages, and policy interventions on the supply side of the health sector. In comparison, discussion on the demand side is scanty in the literature, which is equally important to analyse, study, and understand for suitable policy intervention on mitigating health sector mismatches, crises, and market failures. Typically, it is said that the supply shortage and lack of hospital staff and service providers, beds, and equipment cause the health sector scenarios to worsen and underperform. However, careful investigation and analysis reveal that "shortage" is a relative concept. It might happen that the demand for health services is not in good shape and is fundamentally misdirected. To exemplify, there is plenty of evidence in developing countries and developed countries like the USA; over-testing and over-medication are commonly practised by medical practitioners, resulting in excess demand for health care services and, quite often, excess supply. An in-depth understanding of its fundamentals will help us analyse the outcome better. Health, by its very nature, is a public good since it has most of the public good characteristics, such as positive and negative externalities, non-excludability, non-rivalry, and asymmetric information, which trigger the reasons for market failure. These are primarily adverse selection problems, moral hazards, and free riding. Let us explain the case of infectious diseases and preventive health care services. The demand for such services will be lower than the social optimum since private demand will not consider the social benefits. People have limited incentive to spend on preventive services such as

[8] During the report's presentation, Guy Ryder, the Director-General of the International Labour Organisation, asserted that investing in social health protection plays a crucial role in achieving universal health coverage. According to Chihoko Asada-Miyakawa, the Assistant Director-General and Regional Director for Asia and the Pacific at ILO, many individuals in the regions still lack healthcare coverage or adequate access to healthcare services. The COVID-19 pandemic has exacerbated this circumstance.

cleanliness-related expenses, especially when they involve costs. In countries where a large proportion of the population is poor, practices an unhygienic standard of living, or lives in congested localities like slums, people will have natural tendencies to avoid incurring such costs because the private benefits are not visible. In contrast, they have no reason to care for the societal benefits. Here, practising cleanliness and taking care of preventive health will create a positive externality; therefore, the societal benefit is much more significant than the private benefit. Here, government intervention is indispensable, which is probably why countries are deeply engaged in designing incentives for shaping demand for or incentivising the supply of preventive healthcare services. Infectious disease has similar characteristics; the private individual having such disease will have limited incentive to take care of the negative externality he/she spreads on the society, and precisely for this reason, active public health care spending towards such health services is typically observed. Active monitoring, incentive designing, and awareness campaigns are essential to create suitable demand-side interventions in such healthcare services because of their public good nature. Active involvement of the respective governments in the SA countries has been visible for the last decade or so via innovative schemes and initiatives.

6.3.1 Role of Asymmetric Information, Moral Hazard and Adverse Selection, and Market Failure

To understand the demand side of the health sector in general for policy intervention, one has to understand the nature of information asymmetry and how to narrow down the information gap to reduce the possibilities of market failure or increase market efficiency. By its very nature, health service is little known to the service taker and most known to the service provider when it comes to experts' opinions or service provisioning. Therefore, the demand we see here is often "supplier-induced", for example, as the doctors prescribe and recommend the patients strictly place their demand for tests and related health services. In other words, patients' demand curve for health services is not very similar to that of general goods and services observed in any economic transaction; instead, it can be shifted by the suppliers themselves. Quite obviously, a possible "moral hazard" problem might emerge, and overpricing or over-testing evidence will not be uncommon, as it is already documented in the literature (Lam et al. 2020; Mullainathan and Obermeyer 2019). Such over-testing may complicate interpretations and increase errors in statistical inferences drawn based on these tests. Undoubtedly, it increases financial hardship and out-of-pocket expenses, leading to possible catastrophic health shocks in many cases. This is a moral hazard problem where the returns of doctors, medical practitioners, and health experts emerge at the expense of the patient's health service purchase expenses. Therefore, the health sector in any country, be it advanced or developing, needs stringent regulation and public intervention in terms of quality (monitoring) and quantitative (expenditure).

Second, looking into the adverse selection problem, which essentially says in Akerlof's (Akerlof 1970) terminology in the second-hand car market that bad cars drive away good cars from the market, it is pretty predictable that health insurance services will find it difficult to be viable in poor and unequal economies. This is so because, in an economy where people who can pay (say, type-1) for health services such as hospitalisation care, etc., will not be as willing to pay for the insurance as those who cannot (type-2) afford to pay that. If the population concentration is high among type-2 in any country or region, the insurance provider will find the business viable if the premium is high. However, type-2 people may not find the health insurance product affordable. This is precisely why the private health insurance market fails, and public intervention is needed. This is visible in developing countries, where poverty inequality is a big concern, and the South Asia region is no exception. In such regions, private health insurance takes much time to take off and penetrate the market without public sector participation. In the countries of the South Asian region, we can see active initiatives and government involvement to help health insurance take off and make it financially viable.

As discussed above, any analysis of the demand side of the health sector would be incomplete without understanding the economic fundamentals behind market failures. While we discuss the health sector from its demand side in the South Asian region, we will divide the analysis into three parts: (i) role of health insurance designed by the government, private sector or in PPP mode, in spearheading health service demand, (ii) income and other factors driving the demand, (iii) role of regulation in driving and shaping the demand, and (iv) any other public initiatives, innovations, designs, comprehensive policy package such as Universal Health Coverage, that push the health service demand. We will provide a comparative description of the demand for the health sector from these three crucial perspectives and its evolution over time, specifically in the pre-and post-COVID timelines. Demand-side financing (DSF) can be consumer-led, such as tax rebates, cash transfers, and vouchers, or producer-led, such as referral vouchers and capitation payments. The DSF, to increase access to health services among the underserved and poor, has recently been the focus of health sector intervention in most developing countries, including the SA countries. Figure 6.1 depicts how DSF and supply-side financing of health sector subsidy works and the superiority of DSF.

The World Bank document discusses the core features of DSF, which involve the rationale for the choice of service covered. Merit goods have positive externalities, and market failure would occur if no intervention is made, such as preventive care for cancer screening, immunisation, etc., and choice of providers.

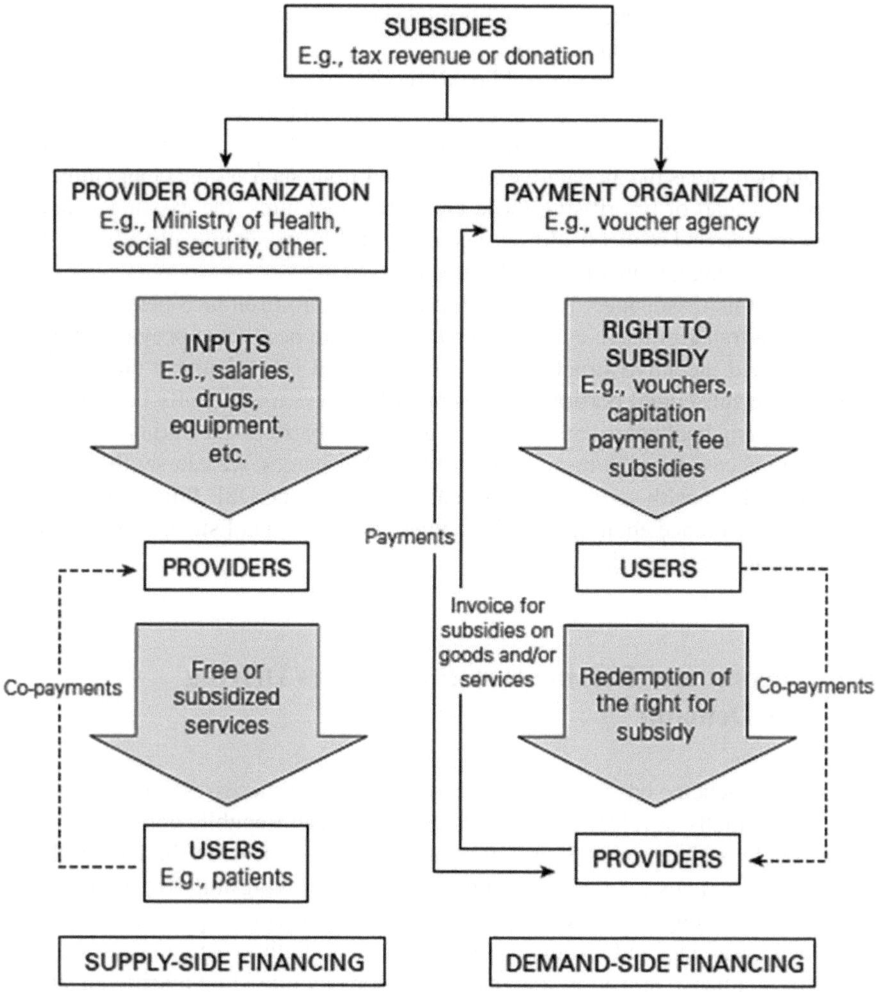

Fig. 6.1 Exploring the dynamics of demand and supply side financing in health care services: a closer look at the impact and opportunities. *Source*: World Bank (2005)

6.4 The Insurance Sector in the South Asian Region: Role of Public Initiatives

In India, various insurance programmes such as Social Health Insurance (SHI), the Rashtriya Swasthya Bima Yojana (RSBY), and the Employee State Insurance Scheme (ESIS) play a crucial role in providing healthcare coverage. However, these programmes generally fall outside the Demand-Side Financing (DSF) scope due to their reliance on specific identification requirements, such as the Below Poverty Line (BPL) card or health cards denoting these schemes' membership. Their primary aim is to enhance access to hospital services for marginalised populations, specifically those living in poverty.

This focus on providing general health service coverage can contradict a fundamental principle of DSF, which seeks to stimulate demand for "merit goods" in the healthcare sector. Merit goods, by nature, offer significant positive externalities, particularly in areas like preventive care for conditions such as cancer and infectious diseases. Instead of prioritising these preventive measures, the existing insurance frameworks target broader health service accessibility, which may not align with the goals of fostering a more effective healthcare system.

Despite this dissonance, it is essential to delve into insurance penetration as it can spark a transformative cycle that engages private healthcare providers through well-designed incentive structures. This engagement is particularly vital in South Asia, where substantial portions of the population have traditionally been excluded from accessing healthcare services due to economic barriers. By initially improving healthcare access through these public insurance schemes, we can set the stage for more inclusive health service delivery and strengthen the DSF framework. Hence, discussing insurance about the DSF becomes crucial for a holistic understanding of healthcare dynamics in the region.

6.5 Income and Income-Boosting Factors Driving the Demand

The voucher scheme has a rich history, though its recent successes have drawn more attention. Initially developed in Taiwan and the Korean Republic during the 1960s, these vouchers aimed to improve access to essential services. In the United States, similar programmes emerged to support Spanish-speaking migrant workers who often faced challenges in accessing health services, particularly preventive care, due to limited awareness and resources. Initially, these initiatives were designed as welfare programmes to assist low-income populations by providing nutritional supplements, educational resources, and health access. In various African nations, as well as in Nicaragua and several other countries, vouchers have proven effective in promoting the proper utilisation of health services and preventing sexually transmitted infections. These vouchers can specifically purchase a limited range of services, such as lab tests or essential health products like medication. One significant outcome of this approach is that competition among service providers increases when patients hold vouchers—assuming the service provider is not exclusively affiliated with a voucher system. This heightened competition can lead to improved efficiency and better quality of care (Johnson et al. 2003; Luft 1984). Furthermore, if vouchers are strategically tied to underutilised health services, they can encourage using crucial preventive measures. These include strategies to combat infectious diseases, mental health support, family planning, immunisation campaigns, and overall preventive healthcare services, which yield substantial social benefits that often outweigh private gains and external costs.

Figure 6.2 illustrates how these vouchers are designed to enhance the accessibility and effectiveness of health services: another innovative approach, Output-based Aid (OBA), merges producer-led and consumer-led incentives. Organisations like the World Bank and the UK's Department for International Development (DFID) significantly design these initiatives. DFID's Global Partnership for Output-based Aid (GPOBA) has effectively implemented these strategies.

Additionally, vouchers and accreditation initiatives represent targeted demand-side financing (DSF) tools, fostering competition among service providers. This competitive nature of vouchers offers a more precise method to drive efficiency and superior service delivery compared to traditional models that often involve public service providers. This practice has gained traction in numerous countries, including India, China, Kenya, Nicaragua, Taiwan, Uganda, and Bangladesh, showcasing the versatility and impact of voucher systems in enhancing healthcare access and quality.

Another type of DSF comprises direct benefit transfer (DBT) and conditional cash transfer (CCT) in India, played essential roles where on condition that the

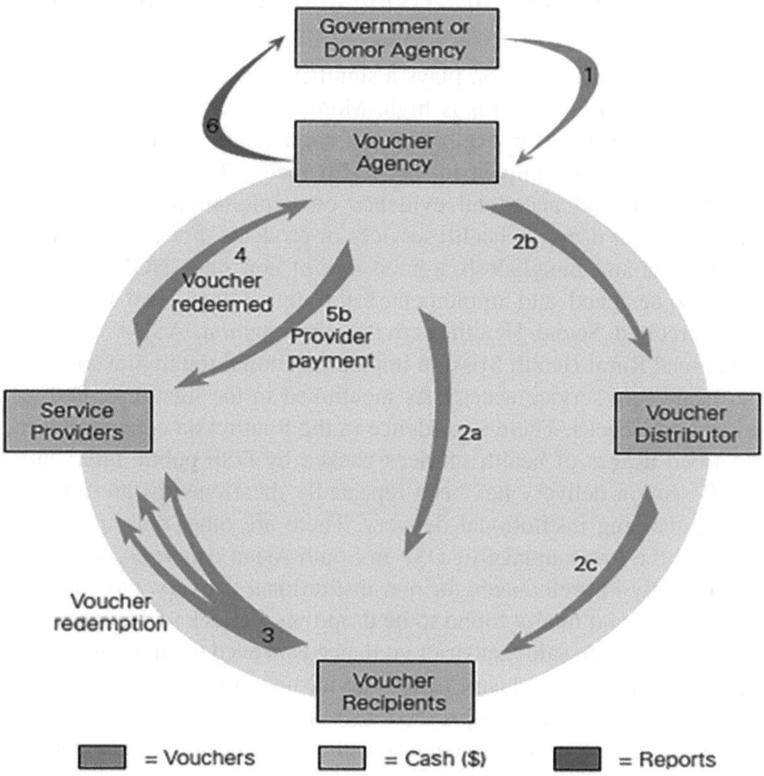

Fig. 6.2 A comprehensive model of health care delivery to citizens. *Source*: World Bank (2005)

mother routinely takes care of the child's immunisation and nutrition, etc., as checked and monitored and by the Anganwadi workers, will get back the cash directly transferred to the bank account or any other benefits she is eligible for. It is argued in favour of DSF that not continuously reducing financial barriers is an effective DSF intervention. Other mechanisms, such as transport facilitation for geographical distance and other means of providing access, can be a better approach towards DSF. The CCT is mainly used in welfare programmes, originally designed and rolled out with grand success in Latin American countries. Here, the government transfers funds conditional upon specific active actions towards health check-ups or private health interventions; Janani *Suvidha Yojana* in India and Nepal's Safe Delivery Incentive Programme are good examples. In Bangladesh, the government launched many such schemes in 33 *upazilas* (districts), which involve cash and in-kind transfers involving transport and other expenses for accessing prenatal check-ups, emergency, and delivery-related healthcare access provided by skilled attendants. This has led to a miraculous drop in maternal mortality rates in 2015 by 75% and helped Bangladesh reach MDG-5.

6.6 Role of Regulation in Driving and Shaping the Demand

We can easily see that regulation plays a significant role in the health sector since the possibility of market failures is high. Monitoring and overseeing pricing and service quality, as well as the exploitation of capitalising knowledge and information asymmetry, can be rampant in the health sector. There is much evidence—casual empiricism and anecdotal evidence on exploitation as a reason behind overconsumption or usage of health services or products. For example, in the DSF schemes in India and Bangladesh, a good mix of non-state, NGO, and public-led initiatives are designed and implemented through village-level health workers' ASHA (Accredited Social Health Activist) participation. ASHA was pivotal in India's National Rural Health Mission implementation through preventive and promotional healthcare service access. As mentioned in the literature, DSF schemes have several drawbacks. There is evidence in the South Asia context that there are overprescribed usages of health services backed by DSF public intervention. For example, C-section delivery has been repeatedly mentioned as an unwanted outcome of regularising institutional delivery. There are other reasons for the challenges behind the lower uptake of DSF in South Asian countries, such as cultural reasons, primarily in preferences for non-institutional delivery, targeting people—often the enrolled and finally found to be drop-outs for lack of motivation and cultural barriers; it is often said that strict vigilance is needed to target the truly need to increase access and build inclusive health service network. Among other constraints is a shortage of trained staff and professionals for properly managing such floating schemes. The lack of proper payments and fiscal constraints are solid reasons for this.

6.7 Comprehensive Policy Package Such as Universal Health Coverage

Many health coverage schemes are in different forms; one example is community health insurance (CHI), which caters to poor and vulnerable people (Gupta et al. 2010). The WHO-OECD, Asia-Pacific report, 2022[9] states: "Life expectancy decreased by 1 year during the COVID-19 pandemic and maternal mortality ratio is still twice the Sustainable Development Goal target in lower-middle and low-income countries in the region…In 2020, the average neonatal mortality rate amongst lower-middle and low-income countries in Asia-Pacific was 15.8 deaths per 1000 live births, almost halving the rate observed in 2000 but still above the SDG target of 12 deaths or less per 1000 live births. Maternal mortality ratio averaged around 140 deaths per 100,000 live births in lower-middle and low-income Asia-Pacific countries and territories in 2019, still two times higher than the SDG target of less than 70 deaths per 100,000 live births". In low- and medium-income Asia-Pacific countries, almost 50% of health expenses are out of pocket.

6.7.1 Shortages and Constraints

Access to the healthcare system is profoundly constrained by income levels and socio-economic factors, which serve as significant obstacles for individuals residing in various developing economies across South Asia. The data showcased in Table 6.3 and depicted in Fig. 6.3 present a compelling narrative of the struggles individuals encounter in their pursuit of medical services.

Particularly striking is the revelation that women aged 15–49 often face systemic exclusion from these critical healthcare benefits, with noticeable disparities evident across different countries in the region. This exclusion not only limits their access to necessary medical care but also highlights broader issues of gender inequality embedded within the healthcare framework.

Logistics presents a significant barrier to accessing healthcare throughout India, impacting both rural and urban populations. In rural areas, the challenges are particularly acute. These communities suffer from a glaring lack of healthcare services, a situation exacerbated by minimal public investment in health infrastructure. Instead, government funding predominantly favours urban regions, leaving rural residents with limited options.

The private healthcare sector, which has been expanding, primarily concentrates on urban areas, further neglecting the needs of rural inhabitants. Compounding this issue is the alarming shortage of qualified healthcare personnel across the country, with rural regions experiencing an even more acute deficit. As a result, individuals in these areas often find themselves travelling extensive distances—sometimes up

[9] https://pesquisa.bvsalud.org/portal/resource/pt/who-364682.

Table 6.3 Women aged 15–49 who reported problems in accessing care due to financial reasons, by socioeconomic characteristics

Country (year)	Lowest income quintile (poorest)	Highest income quintile (richest)	Urban	Rural	Lowest education	Highest education
Bangladesh (2017)	65.3	24.6	37.8	46.2	61.4	19.1
Cambodia (2014)	79.2	41.2	44.5	68.9	74.5	32.1
India (2019–2020)	37.5	8.1	14.4	24.7	29.2	10.2
Indonesia (2017)	27.6	7.4	13.5	16.9	34.1	7.7
Myanmar (2016)	58.9	14.9	26.5	37.1	51.1	12.4
Nepal (2016)	70.7	29.5	49.2	64.4	73.0	26.4
Pakistan (2017)	45.7	11.1	20.0	36.5	41.1	9.4
Papua New Guinea (2017)	84.0	36.8	40.4	66.9	78.5	20.1
Philippines (2017)	63.1	26.1	40.5	49.9	70.5	31.8

Source: DHS surveys, various years

to 100 km—just to reach the nearest healthcare facility. Figure 6.4 depicts Women aged 15–49 who reported problems in accessing care due to distance by socioeconomic characteristics.

When they do manage to access care, many rural healthcare providers are local individuals lacking formal medical training or qualifications. This situation poses serious risks to the quality of care available. Additionally, rampant poverty serves as a formidable obstacle to accessing healthcare services, with nearly 90% of the rural population lacking health insurance. Most residents must bear the financial burden of medical costs themselves, often resorting to out-of-pocket payments or loans to cover expenses. The disparities in health outcomes between rural and urban areas are striking. Rural communities face significant challenges, marked by high rates of infant and maternal mortality, widespread malnutrition, low vaccination rates, and reduced life expectancy.

To tackle these pressing issues, innovative solutions are being implemented. The rise of telemedicine offers a way for individuals in remote areas to consult healthcare providers without the need for long journeys. Women-centric health clinics, often mobile in nature, are being formed to ensure that healthcare reaches underserved populations. Additionally, efforts are underway to expand the availability of mini-hospitals in less densely populated regions. There is also a focus on enhancing the training and accountability of local health providers through formalised programmes, aiming to improve the quality of care in these disadvantaged communities.

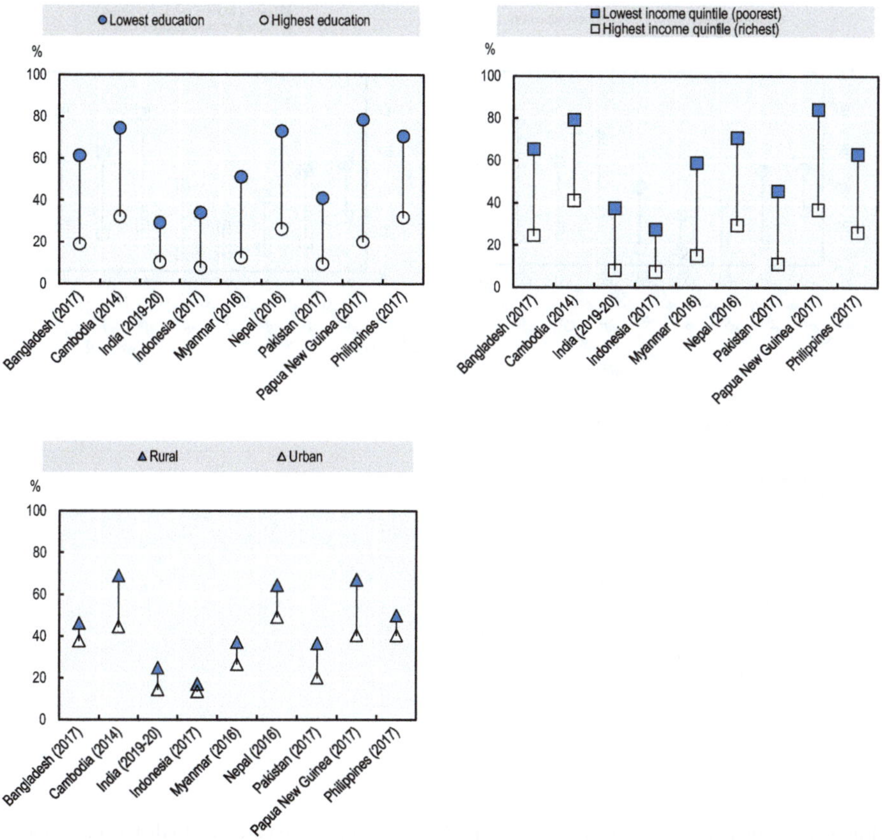

Fig. 6.3 Women aged 15–49 who reported problems in accessing care due to financial reasons, by socioeconomic characteristics

6.8 Exploring the Status and Impact of Insurance Scheme Accessibility

In our previous discussions, we have underscored the vital importance of government involvement in the health insurance sector, particularly within low- and middle-income countries that grapple with significant disparities in healthcare access. To further illustrate this point, we have provided an extensive comparison in Table 6.4, which outlines a variety of Government Schemes alongside compulsory contributory healthcare financing models. This table showcases their respective shares within the broader healthcare financing framework of the Asia-Pacific region, specifically contrasting data from the years 2010 and 2019.

This comparative analysis sheds light on the evolving patterns and trends in healthcare funding mechanisms over this significant time span. It becomes clear that in regions where healthcare access is often starkly unequal, proactive government

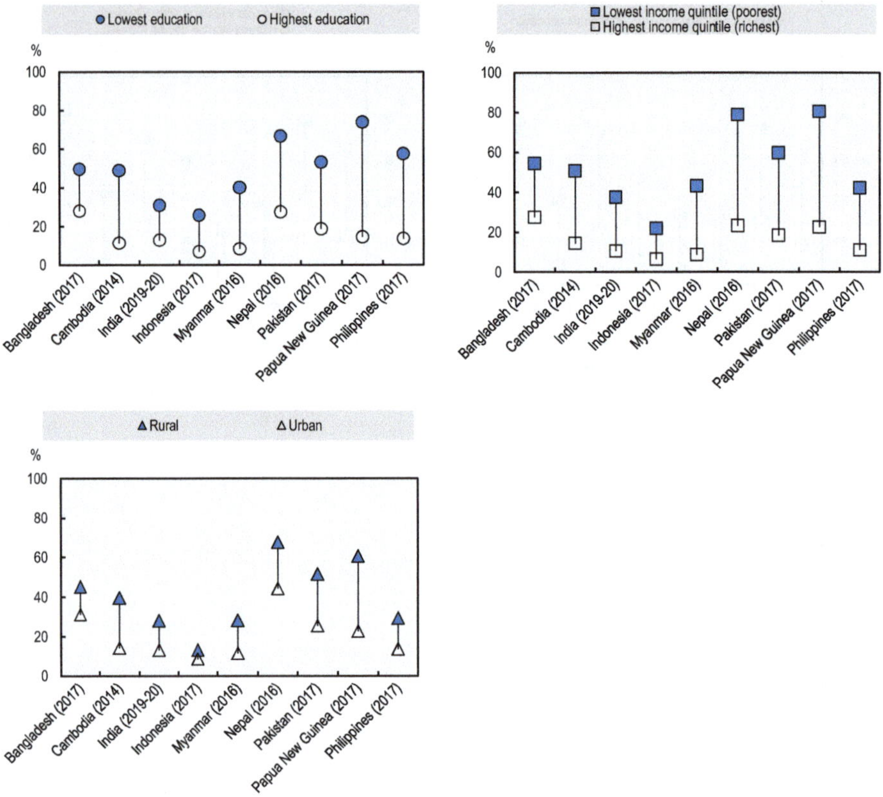

Fig. 6.4 Women aged 15–49 who reported problems in accessing care due to distance, by socio-economic characteristics

intervention is crucial. Such involvement not only promotes a more equitable distribution of healthcare resources but also plays a pivotal role in enhancing the overall health outcomes for the population.

By actively engaging with health insurance systems, governments hold significant potential to enhance healthcare coverage, broaden access to essential medical services, and ultimately contribute to the development of a healthier society. This multifaceted strategy emphasises the vital role that effective governance plays in addressing disparities in healthcare access and fostering the overall well-being of communities.

Interestingly, an examination of health expenditure across different types of services reveals considerable variation among countries in South Asia and the Asia-Pacific region, as illustrated in Fig. 6.5. For instance, certain countries allocate a larger portion of their health spending to curative care, while others prioritise expenditures on medical goods, as seen in places like Nepal and India. In Fiji, preventive healthcare constitutes a remarkable one-fourth of overall health expenditure, signalling a strong emphasis on proactive health measures. In contrast, Sri Lanka dedicates a mere 3% of its health budget to preventive care, highlighting the stark differences in healthcare strategies and priorities within the region.

Table 6.4 Government schemes and compulsory contributory health care financing schemes (as a percentage of total healthcare financing schemes): 2010 and 2019

Countries	2010	2019
Brunei Darussalam	91.7	94.3
Japan	81.9	83.9
New Zealand	81.2	80.3
Papua New Guinea	73	77.8
Thailand	76.2	74.7
OECD	73.2	74.1
Asia Pacific-H	71.1	74.1
Australia	68.6	69.7
Fiji	64	67
Asia Pacific-UM	61.3	62.5
Mongolia	68.6	61.3
Korea	60.9	61
China	51.9	56.1
Lao PDR	33.9	55.9
Singapore	42.4	55.2
Malaysia	53.2	52.3
Indonesia	24.3	49
Sri Lanka	41.6	48.5
Viet Nam	58.1	44.4
Philippines	33.7	41.6
Asia Pacific-LM/L	35.4	41.4
Pakistan	22	33.1
India	25.5	33.1
Cambodia	19.6	28.3
Nepal	26.4	26.5
Bangladesh	21	21
Myanmar	12.8	17.7

Source: WHO Global Health Expenditure Database; OECD Health Statistics 2020

6.9 Progress of Various Demand-Side Interventions in South Asia, Focusing on Innovations, Regulatory Measures, and Price Controls

Globally, countries are grappling with significant fiscal challenges related to health expenses, as highlighted in the IMF's document on health insurance in Asia. A key factor contributing to this issue is the rapid advancement of technology, which has led to the availability of more sophisticated diagnostic tools and treatment facilities. This evolution in healthcare is accompanied by an increasing demand for services, particularly in developing nations, where people are becoming more aware of healthcare options and experiencing improved access due to rising incomes. As a result, out-of-pocket (OOP) expenses for medical care are on the rise, often deterring individuals from seeking necessary and expensive treatments. In situations

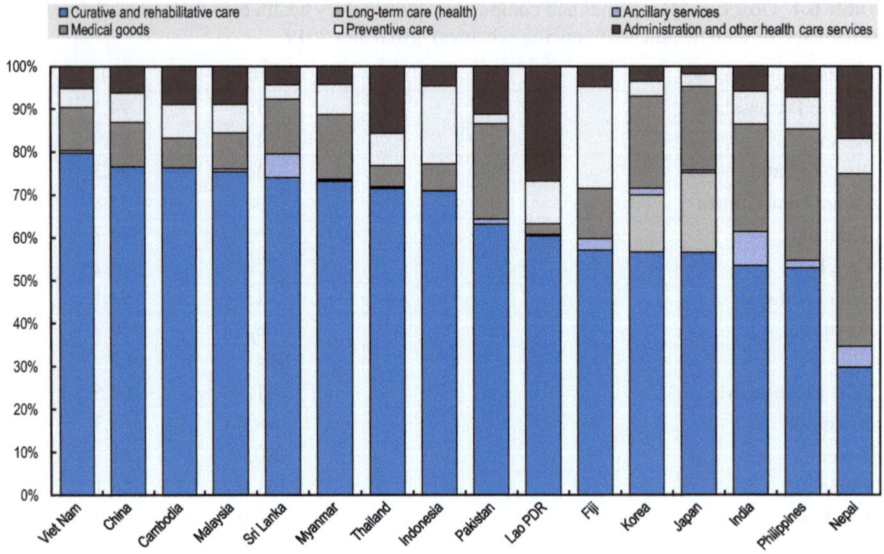

Fig. 6.5 Transforming health expenditure: a closer look at service types: 2019

where governments are financially strained and unable to prioritise health expenditures or offer comprehensive insurance coverage, the intervention of private players becomes crucial. Currently, private insurance markets tend to cater primarily to wealthier populations, leaving many lower- and middle-income individuals without adequate coverage.

In response, governments across numerous low and middle-income countries are working diligently to implement reforms aimed at managing and reducing healthcare spending effectively. This complex challenge necessitates innovative demand-side financing strategies, which focus on making services more accessible to the public. Additionally, it is essential for governments to evaluate whether private healthcare providers demonstrate greater efficiency than their public counterparts and determine if private models should supplement or replace public services. The ultimate goal is to ensure that all citizens have access to high-quality healthcare services that are both sustainable and equitable. Simply expanding coverage is insufficient to resolve the deeper issues present in the healthcare system. A prime illustration of this can be seen in China, where extensive public health insurance has successfully covered millions of people. However, the coverage has significant limitations, as it typically only includes catastrophic diseases and inpatient services. Ideally, an insurance system should encompass outpatient care as well, otherwise, the costs associated with chronic conditions will continue to escalate, leading to prohibitively high OOP expenses. Despite improvements, China still faces a situation where OOP costs, while significantly reduced, remain considerable at 41%.

The IMF report delves into the potential dynamics of healthcare design, especially if private health insurance were to take precedence, illustrated in Fig. 6.6. In many developed nations, private insurance is often viewed as a means to enhance

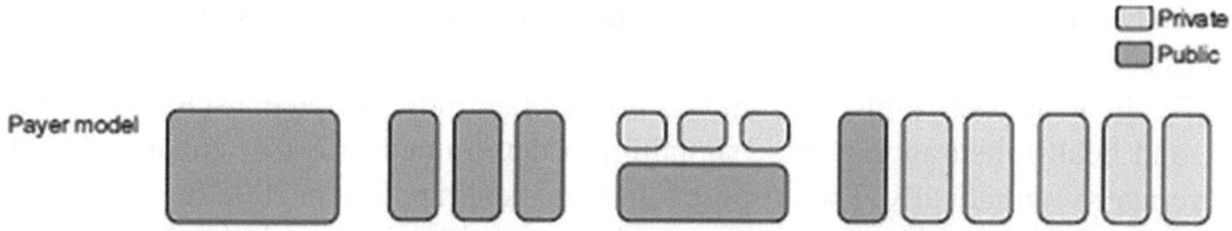

Description (patient view)	▪ Single, state-mandated payer	▪ Multiple state-mandated payers with minimal private sector	▪ State-mandated payer(s) with supplementary private payers	▪ State payers with competing private payers	▪ Multiple private payers only
Country examples	▪ Canada	▪ Thailand ▪ Egypt	▪ China, Taiwan Province of China ▪ Australia ▪ United Kingdom	▪ Germany ▪ Chile ▪ United States	▪ Jamaica ▪ Trinidad and Tobago
Pros	▪ Greatest solidarity ▪ Concentration allows greater bargaining power and maximum risk pool	▪ Enables choice among plans with different benefit design (vs. one state payer) ▪ Easier transitions to other models	▪ Combines a core of mandated provision with optional top-ups ▪ Fosters public-private partnership	▪ Payer of last resort ensures coverage ▪ Likely pushes innovation with competition	▪ Competition drives responsiveness and innovation
Cons	▪ Lack of competition potentially hinders innovation and responsiveness	▪ More complex, more difficult to manage (e.g., harder for patients to navigate) ▪ Creates additional complexity in cross-subsidizing	▪ Overlap of benefit package may result in excess cost, inefficiencies ▪ Potential gaps in key coverage for many people (dental, eye care)	▪ Central state payer tends to be left with higher risks ▪ Duplication of overhead for providers and regulators	▪ Risk selection: to ensure coverage, risk equalization mechanisms needed ▪ Duplication of overhead ▪ More complex

Fig. 6.6 Common healthcare coverage models across the globe. *Source*: McKinsey analysis

the quality of care and broaden the spectrum of available services. Conversely, in numerous developing countries, private insurance is perceived as a vital tool to increase access to healthcare services, particularly for substantial segments of the population who have remained underserved by public insurance frameworks.

6.10 Status and Role of Universal Health Coverage (UHC) as a Demand-Side Intervention

In 2019, the global stage at the United Nations witnessed a momentous occasion when India, alongside 192 other nations, made a historic pledge to advance towards Universal Health Coverage (UHC). This commitment underscored the shared goal of ensuring that all individuals have access to essential health services without facing financial hardship. However, data from the National Sample Survey (NSS) revealed a troubling reality: financial barriers remain a significant obstacle, leaving many individuals with unmet health needs that persist unaddressed.

The vision for UHC in India has deep roots in the country's national agenda, tracing back to the early years following its independence. The National Health Policy of 1983 was a key milestone, reaffirming the country's dedication to the principle of health for all citizens. This foundational policy laid down essential groundwork for subsequent initiatives aimed at expanding access to healthcare services across the nation.

By the year 2000, a pivotal step was taken when India adopted a state-wise family and health insurance policy, signalling a determined effort to enhance health coverage systematically. The proposed national health policy in 2002 further sought to introduce a general health insurance scheme specifically designed to benefit low-income groups. Pilot programmes were launched at the district level, aiming to assess logistics and viability in real-world settings, paving the way for future comprehensive strategies.

In 2003, the Indian Ministry of Finance introduced the Universal Health Insurance Scheme (UHIS). Though initially intended to be inclusive for all citizens, this ambitious programme was soon confined to those living below the poverty line (BPL). Regrettably, despite its good intentions, the UHIS faced significant challenges related to inadequate coverage and sustainability, ultimately leading to its inability to meet its objectives and its subsequent downfall.

In the face of these challenges, a renewed effort emerged with the launch of the Rashtriya Swasthya Bima Yojana (RSBY) in 2008. This scheme aimed to provide a more resilient framework for health insurance tailored to the needs of the under-privileged segments of society. The RSBY represented a significant leap forward in addressing the critical healthcare needs of India's most vulnerable populations, marking a dedicated and ongoing journey towards achieving comprehensive Universal Health Coverage in the country.

References

Akerlof GA (1970) The market for "Lemons": quality uncertainty and the market mechanism. Quart J Econ 84(3):488–500. https://doi.org/10.2307/1879431

Ali (2020). Playing on the employee benefit turf: India vs. South-East Asia. https://www.linkedin.com/pulse/playing-employee-benefit-turf-india-vs-south-east-asia-ali.

Financial Express, The (Dhaka) (2020) Job Loss recovery might put progress of last decade at risk: Study, June 26

Gupta I, Joe W, Rudra S (2010) Demand side financing in health: how far can it address the issue of low utilization in developing countries. World Health Report, p 27

Johnson, R., Rossmiller, G. E., & Sandiford-Rossmiller, F. (2003) Ag econ angst crisis revisited, Australian Journal of Agricultural and Resource Economics, Australian Agricultural and Resource Economics Society, 47(2):261–274, June

Lam JH, Pickles K, Stanaway FF (2020) Why clinicians overtest: development of a thematic framework. BMC Health Serv Res 20:1011. https://doi.org/10.1186/s12913-020-05844-9

Luft HS (1984) On the use of vouchers for Medicare. Milbank Mem Fund Quart Health Soc 62(2):237–250

Mullainathan, S., & Obermeyer, Z. (2019) Diagnosing Physician Error: A Machine Learning Approach to Low-Value Health Care, NBER Working Papers 26168, National Bureau of Economic Research, Inc.

Sakamoto, M., Begum, S., & Ahmed, T. (2020) Vulnerabilities to COVID-19 in Bangladesh and a Reconsideration of Sustainable Development Goals. Sustainability 12(13):5296. https://doi.org/10.3390/su12135296

World Bank (2005) Demand-side Financing for Sexual and Reproductive Health Services in Low and Middle-Income Countries: A Review of the Evidence, Report, Washington DC

Chapter 7
Health Care System in South Asia: Addressing Supply Side Challenges

Abstract This chapter addresses the critical supply side challenges facing healthcare systems in South Asian economies over the last 5 years. It highlights the significant shortages of healthcare professionals, inadequate infrastructure, and the high out-of-pocket expenses that hinder access to essential services. The chapter argues for the development of light-touch regulations that promote innovation while addressing malpractices, emphasising the need for increased public health expenditure and the potential role of experienced nurses in alleviating workforce shortages. It also explores the burgeoning medical tourism sector as a dual-edged sword, revealing disparities in healthcare access and quality across the region. The analysis underscores the importance of effective government interventions and regulatory frameworks to enhance healthcare delivery, particularly in rural areas, and advocates for regional cooperation to improve health outcomes. Ultimately, this chapter calls for a comprehensive approach to reform healthcare systems in South Asia, leveraging trade in services and collaborative efforts to build a resilient and equitable healthcare landscape.

Keywords Healthcare Challenges · Medical Tourism · Supply Side Issues · Regulatory Framework · Health Expenditure

7.1 Introduction

The supply side challenges in the healthcare system within South Asian economies have escalated to a critical juncture. Doctors and support staff often shoulder the burden of alleged shortcomings in government hospitals, leading to public outcry when politicians bring these incidents to light. The significant gaps in the system deny many individuals access to necessary healthcare services, making it an urgent issue that demands immediate attention.

To address these challenges, the potential benefits of developing sophisticated yet light-touch regulations that foster innovation and expansion without inhibiting

A. Banik et al., *Extraordinary Health Hazards and their Socio-Economic Effects in South Asia*, South Asia Economic and Policy Studies,
https://doi.org/10.1007/978-981-95-5729-5_7

progress to reduce malpractices are significant. For instance, price controls can lead to shortages, compromise quality, or result in overcharging in other critical areas, exacerbating rather than alleviating the supply side issues. However, with the proper regulations, these issues can be mitigated, leading to a brighter future for healthcare in South Asia.

There is a prevalent argument that promoting transparency and competition will lower prices across the board while also boosting India's medical tourism sector, which has the potential to create numerous jobs. Additionally, South Asia faces a shortage of doctors, with most practising in urban areas. This significantly contributes to the region's high out-of-pocket healthcare expenses, exceeding 80%. One major factor contributing to this shortage is the underperformance of the Medical Council of India, which controls doctor licensing and regulations. In response to this issue, the government has proposed a bill to dissolve the MCI, liberate medical education from restrictive rules, and introduce an exit exam at the undergraduate level. However, one aspect of the supply side issue that has been overlooked is the potential for experienced nurses to take on greater responsibilities in providing care. The region must leverage its cadre of professional nurses to help mitigate supply shortages. Furthermore, addressing the gaps in rural South Asia is a task that requires immediate and significant government intervention. The primary aim of national health policies should be to gradually increase healthcare expenditure from the current level of 3.5% of the Gross Domestic Product (GDP), a crucial step in improving healthcare services. This increase in spending is not just a necessity, but a vital investment in the future of healthcare in South Asia.

7.2 Debate on Low Public Expenditure on Health in South Asian Countries

It is generally observed that low-income and developing countries underperform in health outcomes primarily due to supply side factors, viz., shortage of doctors, nurses, and health professionals, and on the other hand, due to lack of health equipment and infrastructure. There could be two underlying causes. First, these countries typically have a high population and population density. Hence, a commensurate requirement of a more extensive set of health professionals is needed to cater to the broader needs of this vast population. Second, these countries are poor, so the governments typically have many priorities and fiscal allocations towards developmental expenditures. Precautionary health expenditure preparedness for catastrophic health shocks and increasing OOP may not be among the top priorities of these governments.

According to Banik et al. (2020; 2020), factors such as inadequate health infrastructure and limited access to public health services significantly influence the fatality rates associated with coronavirus disease (COVID-19) across countries,

Table 7.1 Doctors and nurses per 1000 population in the SA countries

Country (Year)	Nurses, per 1000 population	Doctors, per 1000 population
Pakistan (2019)	0.4	1.1
Bangladesh (2020)	0.4	0.7
India (2020)	1.7	0.7
Sri Lanka (2020)	2.1	1.2
Nepal (2020)	2.1	0.9
China (2019)	3.1	2.2
OECD	**9.6**	**3.6**

Source: Compiled from various sources

along with the impact of BCG vaccination (The Economic Times 2020).[1] Recent evidence indicates that developing and certain developed nations suffer from subpar public health infrastructure (The Guardian 2016). Without comprehensive data, the number of hospital beds per thousand people can serve as a valuable proxy for evaluating access to public health. Generally, a higher availability of hospital beds increases the likelihood of saving lives. When hospitals become overwhelmed with patients, it raises a critical question about public access to healthcare services. For example, as of April 2020, South Korea effectively managed the situation, achieving a Case Fatality Rate (CFR) of approximately 2%. The country benefited from a robust number of hospital beds, with 12.3 per 1000 inhabitants, compared to just 2.8, 2.5, 3.2, and 3 beds per 1000 individuals in the USA, the UK, Italy, and Spain, respectively (Table 7.1 and Fig. 7.1). Furthermore, South Korea implemented rapid, large-scale COVID-19 testing and isolated infected individuals efficiently. The nation provided timely medical care and successfully enforced social distancing measures, resulting in an impressive performance without necessitating a lockdown.

Across South Asia (World Bank 2023; WHO 2022), public health expenditure remains alarmingly low, with stark disparities among countries. India, despite being the largest economy in the region, spends only about 2% of its GDP on health, resulting in over half of its population relying on out-of-pocket payments. Bangladesh records the lowest public health investment, with less than 1% of GDP and the highest out-of-pocket burden at nearly 73%, severely impacting low-income families. Pakistan shows marginally better figures but still struggles with inadequate infrastructure. In contrast, Nepal and Sri Lanka allocate slightly more but face systemic issues such as uneven access and limited capacity. Bhutan and the Maldives emerge as exceptions—Bhutan with constitutionally backed healthcare and moderate out-of-pocket costs, and the Maldives leading the region with nearly 9.4% of GDP invested in health and the lowest cost burden on citizens. These comparisons highlight a pressing need for South Asian nations, particularly the larger ones, to elevate health spending to match their development ambitions and reduce health inequities.

[1] https://economictimes.indiatimes.com/industry/healthcare/biotech/healthcare/nations-without-bcg-vaccination-saw-higher-cases/articleshow/74956201.cms?from=mdr

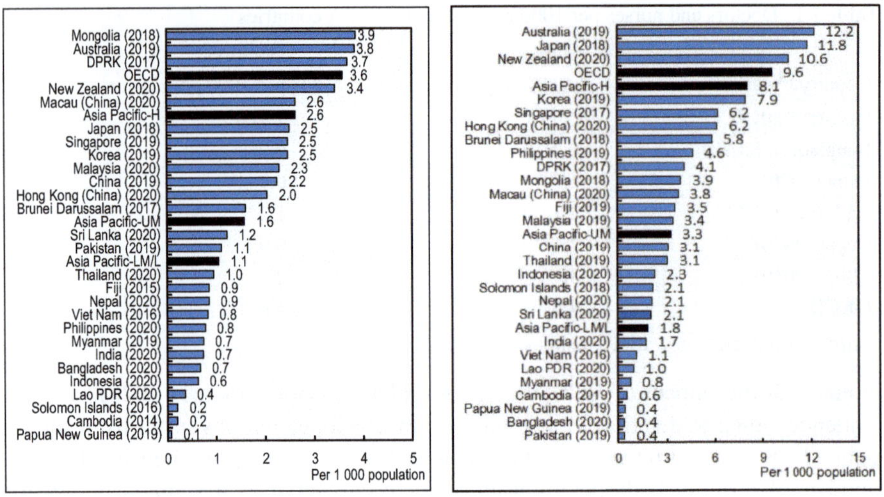

Fig. 7.1 Doctors and nurses per 1000 population in SA and global comparison. *Source*: Global Health Observatory (2020/2022), WHO (https://www.who.int/data/gho). *Note*: We used the data for all non-OECD countries, OECDstat for OECD countries, and OECD average

7.3 Medical Tourism

The healthcare landscape in South Asia reveals significant disparities, often illustrated by the burgeoning growth of medical tourism. This phenomenon highlights the simultaneous existence of supply constraints and a shortage of health infrastructure, particularly in India, where certain regions have flourished as destinations for medical tourists. In contrast, others grapple with persistent unmet demand for healthcare services. This mismatch between supply and demand and regional inequalities in health infrastructure calls for comprehensive policy initiatives addressing these critical issues.

On a positive note, the potential for regional cooperation among South Asian nations offers a promising avenue for advancing health sector development. Medical tourists are increasingly seeking affordable and high-quality treatment that rivals what is available in more developed countries. Notable destinations in Southeast Asia, such as Chennai in India, Langkawi in Malaysia, Phuket in Thailand, and Jakarta in Indonesia, have garnered attention for their healthcare offerings (Chandran et al. 2020). Among these, Singapore shines brightly as a leader in medical tourism, renowned for its cutting-edge technology and modern facilities. The successful establishment of public-private partnership (PPP) has enabled Singapore to cultivate a robust medical tourism network.

In South Asia, India distinguishes itself by providing exceptional medical services tailored to foreign patients, particularly those from nearby regions. In 2017 alone, over 370,000 individuals travelled to India specifically for medical treatments, utilising medical visas for this purpose (Medhekar et al. 2019). Government initiatives, including introducing e-visas and visa-on-arrival options, have propelled India to hold impressive rankings as the fifth most popular medical tourism destination worldwide and second in Asia (MTI 2016). Furthermore, the Indian government has taken proactive measures, such as reducing taxes on imported medical equipment and allowing 100% Foreign Direct Investment (FDI) in medical tourism, both for goods and services.

The range of medical procedures available to tourists in India is diverse. It encompasses cosmetic enhancements, weight-loss surgeries, cardiac procedures, orthopaedic surgeries, transplants, ophthalmologic treatments, wellness programmes, and alternative medicine. Patients are presented with various treatment options, blending traditional and contemporary medical practices. These include allopathy, homoeopathy, Ayurveda, Unani, and yoga (Medhekar et al. 2019).

Despite India's strong positioning in the medical tourism sector, it faces stiff competition from Southeast Asian countries like Thailand, which has developed a reputable cadre of medical practitioners proficient in sophisticated medical technologies. However, it is essential to note that public hospitals in India often lack the necessary resources to capitalise on the growing medical tourism market fully. In contrast, the private healthcare sector features state-of-the-art facilities and skilled professionals, positioning them as key players in attracting international patients seeking quality care.

7.4 The Challenges of Supply Shortages and Fatalities in Healthcare

Health system vulnerabilities in Asia-Pacific countries are particularly acute, especially in lower-income settings where healthcare capacity is frequently limited (Walker et al. 2020). The role of healthcare workers, including doctors, nurses, and other medical professionals, is crucial in confronting the ongoing global crisis triggered by the coronavirus pandemic. Their contributions, which include direct patient care and initiatives in public health preparedness and response, are vital.

The COVID-19 pandemic has highlighted and exacerbated existing shortages in the healthcare workforce, especially regarding the availability of physicians and registered nurses across various countries and territories within the Asia-Pacific region. In countries like Australia, New Zealand, and Japan, the number of medical professionals is substantially higher compared to other nations, giving them a greater capacity to tackle the challenges of the COVID-19 epidemic effectively. However, low-income countries such as Papua New Guinea, the Lao People's Democratic Republic, and Cambodia face significant healthcare personnel shortages, severely limiting their ability to respond to an outbreak effectively and highlighting the disparity in the healthcare workforce between high-income and low-income countries (Fig. 7.2).

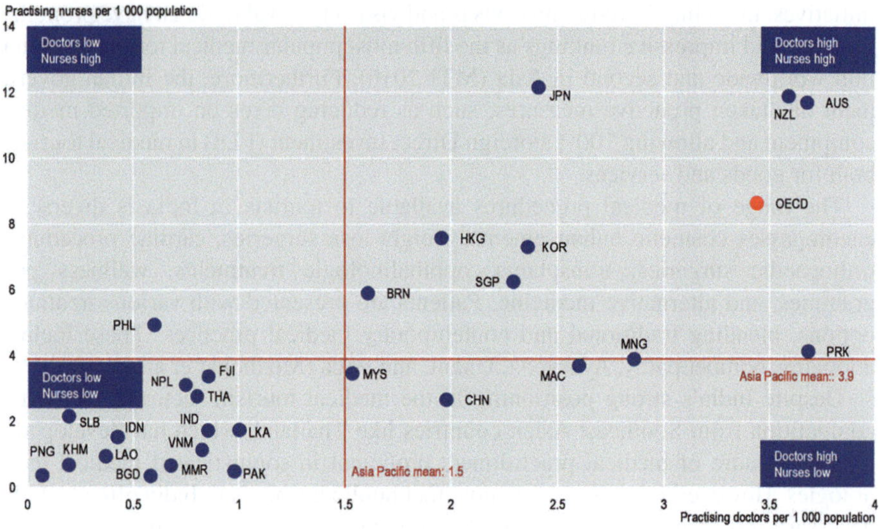

Fig. 7.2 Health service professionals in numbers and global comparison. *Source*: WHO Global Health Observatory, 2020/2022 (https://economictimes.indiatimes.com/industry/healthcare/biotech/healthcare/nations-without-bcg-vaccination-saw-higher-cases/articleshow/74956201.cms?from=mdr) and and OECD Health Statistics, 2020 (https://www.oecd.org/en/data/datasets/oecd-health-statistics.html). *Note*: In this figure, the red labels correspond to the lines, and the intersection of the two lines represents the mean for the Asia-Pacific countries. The OECD dot indicates the mean for all OECD countries (OECD 2020)

7.4.1 Regional Shortages of Healthcare Facilities

A pressing issue currently afflicting healthcare systems throughout the region is the alarming shortage of Intensive Care Unit (ICU) beds and vital critical care resources. This crisis is particularly severe in various Asian and Pacific countries that fall into upper-middle, lower-middle, and lower-income economies. Within this context, the average number of hospital beds available per 1000 population ranges from 2.7 to 3 beds, contrasting with the average of 4.6 beds per 1000 individuals in countries within the Organisation for Economic Co-operation and Development (OECD). The comparison with high-income nations and territories in the Asia-Pacific region is even more striking, where the average rises to approximately 5.4 beds per 1000 people.

These statistics reveal significant heterogeneity among the nations surveyed. For instance, Japan, the Republic of Korea, and the Democratic People's Republic of Korea all demonstrate a robust healthcare infrastructure, each providing more than ten hospital beds for every 1000 people. Conversely, countries like India, Bangladesh, Pakistan, and Cambodia are grappling with a critical scarcity of healthcare resources, each having less than one bed per 1000 people. This dramatic disparity is a poignant illustration of the substantial inequalities in allocating and distributing hospital treatment resources across different countries and regions.

Hospital bed availability becomes vitally important as the globe continues to deal with the COVID-19 pandemic's issues. However, the most pressing concern lies in the capacity of ICUs. The rationale for this concern is clear: a significant proportion of patients who contract COVID-19 develop severe symptoms that demand urgent and specialised treatment in an ICU environment.

Analysis of the latest public data indicates that ICU capacity within the Asia-Pacific region presented a spectrum of availability even before the emergence of the pandemic. It is essential to note that while definitions of "intensive care unit" can vary, the data illustrate a stark range in ICU capacity across the region. For example, Brunei Darussalam reports the highest ICU bed availability, boasting 13.5 beds per 100,000 people. In contrast, countries such as Myanmar and Bangladesh face critical shortages, with fewer than one ICU bed per 100,000 people in each nation.

Moreover, the differences in ICU capabilities reveal more profound economic disparities. As evidenced by data depicted in Fig. 7.3, countries and territories in the Asia-Pacific region classified as upper-middle-income and high-income exhibit, on average, ICU capacities that are three times greater than those of lower-middle-income nations. Additionally, the comparative data underscores that the ICU capabilities of upper-middle or high-income nations are double those of countries within lower-income categories. This substantial gap highlights the healthcare challenges in less affluent nations and emphasises the need for targeted interventions to bolster critical care infrastructure where it is most deficient.

7.5 Not Just a Supply Shortage But a Quality Deficiency as Well

We discuss the supply shortage and its importance in determining health outcomes, health sector disaster management, critical care efficiency, and other related areas. However, there is limited discussion on the quality aspect of it, especially about the public health clinic network where governments spend a lot in their health sector budget allocation, as captured by indicators such as health service providers' absenteeism, quality time they spend on patient care and diagnosis, does that vary across rural and urban regions, in regions having poor connectivity with the urban localities with healthcare infrastructure and amenities. As we discuss the demand side factors and possible policy interventions, we find that health has many public good characteristics, and market failures might emerge due to moral hazard, adverse selection, and free-riding factors. Suitable policy interventions and efficient mechanism designs can mitigate the underlying reasons behind market failures. Two major quality issues emerge in the context of typical health service provisioning in low- and low-middle-income countries. First, health professionals' poor service delivery is measured in both the quality and quantity of time spent on diagnosis and treatment, as observed in public health centres and certain localities, particularly in rural areas. Also, absenteeism among health service professionals (Chaudhury and

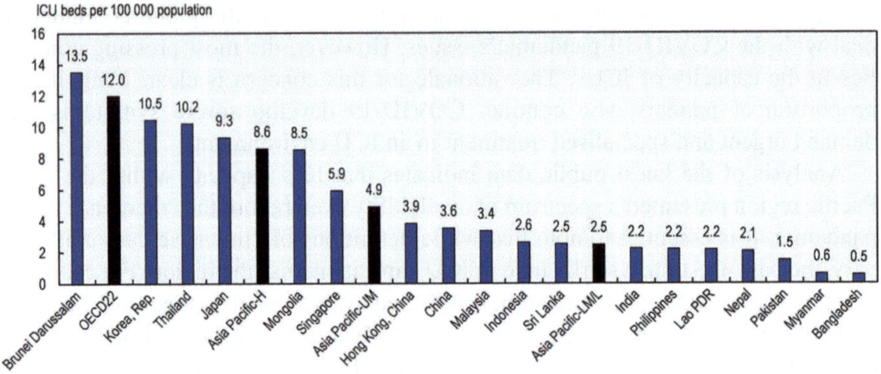

Fig. 7.3 Health infrastructure (ICU beds) in population comparison. *Source*: Phua et al. (2020). The figure for Japan is based on official data from the Ministry of Health, Labour and Welfare. *Note*: Paediatric and neonatal ICU beds are excluded. High-care units/beds are excluded, too (OECD 2020)

Hammer 2004; Chaudhury et al. 2006) is a significant issue, as discussed and debated on several occasions. The *second significant issue requiring special attention is the monetary incentive design for health professionals in public healthcare units, which directly affects the provision of poor-quality services* as a choice, a typical moral hazard problem. Hammer (2013) finds that the quality of care in public primary care units is often deficient, primarily due to a lack of conscientious effort (Das and Hammer 2005, 2007a, 2007b; Das and Gertler 2007; Das et al. 2008).

According to Hammer (2013), working for the government often involves the following responsibilities and activities: One element that should be considered is paying healthcare providers a predetermined remuneration. It has been determined that an individual's level of conscientiousness or presence does not have any bearing on their income, ability to advance in their profession, or any other type of compensation. Even though the providers must retain their dedication to their work, there is no way to ensure that such devotion is maintained. Second, the absence of supervision is an important concern. The responsibility of supervising a vast network of facilities, many of which are located in isolated areas, presents several significant challenges. One of the primary problems that has been found is the lack of efficient accountability procedures, which leads to the limited impact that citizens' complaints have on the behaviour of medical professionals. The migration of a physician to another village is typically a community's priority when meeting its healthcare needs. There is a substantial gap in social standing between those who offer medical care and those who receive it, namely, patients. When running a private practice, one of the most important things to remember is the significant opportunity costs associated with time allocation. The district of Rahim Yar Khan, located in the Punjab province of Pakistan, is a useful example in this case study. The idea of arranging itinerant physicians to visit numerous clinics every week, with a commensurate increase in compensation, looks to have the potential to be successful. It is not yet clear whether or not this phenomenon will continue for an extended period. Implementing a system in which individual communities can compensate visiting medical personnel upon their arrival is one such alternative that might be considered. This strategy ensures that individuals' incentives, particularly regarding attendance, align with their preferences, as payment is an effective method for fostering responsibility. Specifically, this strategy ensures that individuals' incentives align with their desires. Additional research is necessary to investigate the many different delivery modes. On the other hand, the problem of reconciling the failure of the market with the possibility of failure on the part of the government is more difficult to navigate compared to hospitals. If the public does not participate, the private sector may be able to contribute some of the missing resources to make up for the shortage. It is projected that no commercial organisations will fill the subsequent gap left by the public sector's withdrawal of funding for catastrophic care or pure public goods provided by the health industry. This is even though the possibility of this happening exists. A crucial choice that governments must make is determining whether it is more practical to address the incentive problem in publicly provided medical care or to ensure the operational efficiency of hospitals and the provision of clean water. This is an important decision because it might substantially impact the provision of medical care. In addition, it is essential to recognise that we can lack the financial resources necessary to meet the costs associated with all three of the available choices. The body of academic research frequently fails to comprehensively investigate the factors contributing to the chronically poor quality of health services in particular regions and localities. Because of this, the question arises as to whether the level of expertise or quality possessed by health professionals has a significant influence on the creation of such a problem. Alternatively, could a guaranteed fixed payment in the form of a salary, regardless of how well they perform or how much effort they put forth, be the root cause of health professionals' moral hazard problem? This problem manifests in reduced effort in providing services, such as spending less time per patient for diagnosis or treatment. The repercussions for public policy would change depending on the particulars of this scenario. If the reasons only pertain to the design of the policies and the incentive mechanisms, then the method of policy intervention will inevitably differ from case to case. The Nordic countries, although having a respectable level of healthcare sector quality and public participation, have chosen to create payment systems for public health professionals that are related to their efforts. Some examples of these payment systems include fees and capitation based on the number of people enrolled under a doctor. The potential for moral hazards will hopefully be reduced with this strategy. Therefore, it is essential to recognise that the correlation between spending money and higher health expenditure does not automatically result in greater health outcomes. This is something that needs to be acknowledged. Instead, the secret to success lies in identifying and implementing an efficient incentive design for payment structures that maximise the benefits of service quality optimisation, ultimately producing better results.

7.6 Is Regulation the Key to Responsibility?

As previously discussed, healthcare services exhibit significant public characteristics, and market failures are evident within this sector. Effective policy interventions and regulatory oversight are essential to address these market failures and mitigate inefficient outcomes. However, in low-income and developing economies, regulation tends to be minimal and often ineffective. Consequently, economic inefficiencies manifest across various indicators, including pricing and the delivery of quality services, while malpractices proliferate. This situation further diminishes the quality of healthcare provision. Although empirical evidence is scarce, there is ample anecdotal evidence to support these observations.

Conversely, overly stringent regulatory constraints can impede optimal resource allocation within the healthcare sector. In India, for example, the Economic Survey (2019–2020, Chapter 4[2]) points out that the regulation of drug prices through the Drug Prices Control Order (DPCO) of 2013 has resulted in higher prices for regulated pharmaceuticals compared to similar drugs that remain unregulated. The analysis reveals that price increases are particularly significant for higher-priced formulations in contrast to lower-cost alternatives, as well as for drugs dispensed in hospitals rather than in retail settings. This outcome stands in stark contrast to the primary aim of the DPCO, which is to enhance the affordability of medications.

According to Section 3 of the Essential Commodities Act (ECA) of 1955, a regulatory framework known as the DPCO was established to oversee and regulate the prices at which pharmaceutical products are sold. The DPCO includes various provisions, such as identifying the pharmaceuticals subject to price regulation and outlining the methodology for determining the maximum price limit. Both elements fall within the scope of price regulation. The National List of Essential Medicines (NLEM) serves as a comprehensive inventory of pharmaceutical medications that are subject to these price control regulations. The DPCO 2013 encompasses 680 scheduled drug formulations, which are categorised into 27 different therapeutic classes, with regulations governing the pricing of these pharmaceutical formulations.

In addition to maintaining compliance with the DPCO, the National Pharmaceutical Pricing Authority (NPPA) has been responsible for establishing and adjusting the prices of pharmaceutical products. This work falls under the purview of the National Pharmaceutical Pricing Authority. The Drug Price Control Order, or DPCO, in India has been revised several times by the government since its inception in 1983, with the most recent update in 2013. Before 2013, the DPCO used a pricing strategy based on the drug's cost to establish a price ceiling for pharmaceutical products. Under this system, the maximum price of a medication was determined by multiplying the amount of money that manufacturers had to spend on advertising and distribution. The phrase "Maximum Allowable Post-Manufacturing Expenses" (or simply "MAPE") is a term that is used to define a specific factor that has been

[2] https://www.indiabudget.gov.in/budget2020-21/economicsurvey/doc/echapter.pdf

established at a rate of 50% for imported formulations entering India and at 100% for formulations that are created domestically in India.

India reached a critical milestone in its pricing strategy in 2013 when it transitioned from a pricing approach based on costs to a pricing approach based on market factors. The government establishes ceiling prices using the market-based pricing method. These upper restrictions on prices are referred to as ceiling prices. The markup that is legally allowed for retailers to apply to the reference price is represented by these prices, which are the maximum allowed. The reference price is determined by calculating the arithmetic mean of the selling prices of all brands with a market share of at least 1%. IMS Health, a well-regarded market research company, is the origin of the market data exploited for this project. All formulations described in the NLEM were subject to having their maximum permissible markups restricted to a maximum of sixteen per cent after the regulatory authority enforced the restriction.

The NPPA and the DPCO are acronyms for the same organisation. The National List of Necessary Medicines, often known as the NLEM, is a collection of medicines that have been determined to be necessary and of the utmost importance for meeting the needs of India's healthcare system. The Ministry of Health and Family Welfare is responsible for creating this list. The appropriateness of a drug can be evaluated based on several criteria, such as the prevalence of the disease among the population, the safety and efficiency of the pharmacological intervention, and the current cost-effectiveness of the treatment.

In their 2022 report on health regulation, the WHO (2022) explains the existing regulatory framework in South Asian countries, analyses its loopholes, and suggests a path towards achieving the Sustainable Development Goals (SDGs).

7.7 Government Regulation and Policy Interventions in South Asia

In the face of the unprecedented challenges brought on by COVID-19, governments recognised the urgent need for action and responded quickly to support their citizens. The measures they implemented, outlined in Table 7.2, reflect a deep understanding of the struggles faced by individuals and communities during this difficult time. Let us take a closer look at these efforts.

To combat COVID-19, governments in the Asia-Pacific region and beyond have assembled comprehensive response packages. As of July 2020, the set of economic measures in China added up to USD 2161 billion, which is 16% of GDP. The health industry was one of the first to get these extra funds. As shown in Fig. 7.4, the amount of money that the central governments of Asia and the Pacific countries with similar data promised to spend on health system reactions to COVID-19 spread from about 1.1% of GDP in Hong Kong and China to about 0.01% of GDP in Myanmar and Papua New Guinea. For example, to deal with the significant effects

Table 7.2 Examples of containment and mitigation policies in Asia-Pacific countries and territories

Policy	Country examples	Selected examples
Social distancing or physical measures		
Travel restrictions	Australia; Cambodia; Fiji; Hong Kong; China; India; Japan; Lao PDR; Macau, China; Malaysia; Mongolia; Myanmar; Nepal; Pakistan; Papua New Guinea; Philippines; Solomon Islands; Thailand; Viet Nam	**Fiji** closed international airports and placed restrictions on domestic travel on 16 March. Domestic travel resumed in May. **The Solomon Islands closed its borders on 25 March; they will remain** closed until at least 21 January 2021. **Mongolia** imposed a travel ban from high-risk countries, beginning on 27 January with China. From 27 March, all foreign arrivals into **Cambodia** must obtain a visa, a health certificate, and a deposit of USD 2000 to cover potential health care costs.
Banning public gatherings	Australia; Fiji; Hong Kong, China; Mongolia; Myanmar	**Australia** banned public gatherings of more than two people from 29 March until 8 May. **Hong Kong, China,** prohibited public gatherings of more than four people from 27 March until late August.
Mobility restrictions	China; Fiji; India; Indonesia; Nepal; Pakistan; Papua New Guinea; the Philippines; Sri Lanka; Viet Nam	In early January, **China** implemented large-scale mobility restrictions at the national level, which were gradually eased starting mid-February. **India** announced a nationwide lockdown on 24 March, extending localised lockdowns in containment zones. A partial lockdown was introduced in Indonesia in mid-late March, with authority delegated to subnational governments. It was relaxed in June and reimposed on 14 September. **Vietnam** imposed a nationwide lockdown from 1 April to 15 April. Targeted lockdowns were introduced in July following new cases in selected areas of the country. Lockdowns from 15 March to 30 April for Metro Manila (**the Philippines**).

(continued)

Table 7.2 (continued)

Policy	Country examples	Selected examples
School closures	China; Fiji; India; Indonesia; Japan; Lao PDR; Macau, China; Malaysia; Mongolia; Myanmar; New Zealand; Pakistan; Philippines; Solomon Islands; Thailand; Viet Nam	In **Indonesia**, schools in most affected areas were closed at the end of March. Schools in low-risk areas began opening in July. In mid-March, **the Lao PDR** closed all schools. Schools reopened 2 months later with new social distancing measures. **Mongolia** closed all schools, universities, and educational institutions from 27 January to 1 September. Live classroom lessons are broadcast on TV.
Workplace closures	Bangladesh; Macau, China; New Zealand; Papua New Guinea;	On 21 January, Macau, China, introduced a temporary mandatory remote work arrangement for civil servants. On 24 March, **Papua New Guinea** imposed work-from-home requirements.
Closure of non-essential services	Australia; China; New Zealand; Solomon Islands; Viet Nam	On 25 March**, New Zealand implemented the closure of all non-essential businesses, and** re-opening began in late April. The government in the **Solomon Islands** temporarily reduced public services to essential services only from 25 March until 8 May.
Improved personal and environmental hygiene		
Use of masks in public places	Australia; Hong Kong, China; New Zealand; Pakistan; Viet Nam	Victoria, **Australia,** mandated wearing masks in public places on 11 October. **Hong Kong, China,** required mask-wearing in all public places from 23 July, including on public transport. From **16 March,** Vietnam made wearing face masks compulsory for people in public.
Testing, tracking, and tracing of infected individuals, with confinement of infected persons		
Contact tracing apps	Australia; Brunei Darussalam, China; India; Japan; Malaysia; Singapore; Vietnam	**Australia** launched a contact tracing application, "COVIDSafe", on 26 April. **India** launched the Aarogya Setu (Health Bridge) app in April. **Japan** launched its Contact-Confirming Application on 19 June. **Malaysia** launched its contact tracing application, MySejahtera, on 17 April.

(continued)

Table 7.2 (continued)

Policy	Country examples	Selected examples
Large-scale testing and quarantine policies	China; Hong Kong, China	In May, China tested the whole city of Wuhan, which has almost 11 million residents. Over 5 days, the nine-million metropolis of Qingdao underwent a mass-screening programme in October. From 1 to 14 September, the government of **Hong Kong, China,** offered optional one-off viral testing services to all residents; around 1.8 million individuals took part in the testing campaign.

Source: WHO (2020a). Compiled the authors of the reports from the IMF Policy Tracker and national sources (https://www.oecd.org/en/publications/health-at-a-glance-asia-pacific-2020_26b007cd-en/full-report.html)
Note: "Not all measures were implemented nationwide"

of COVID-19 in Australia, the federal government put more than 14% of GDP into fiscal and balance sheet steps. These steps include spending more than AUD 9.4 billion on health care. For instance, AUD 1.4 billion will be allocated to ensure Medicare, AUD 3.4 billion will be spent on emergency response, including the purchase of personal protective equipment and health screenings, and AUD 3.6 billion will be allocated to support hospitals in their COVID-19 response. Every Australian state and territory also announced spending plans in response to the COVID-19 pandemic. These plans include health sector actions (OECD 2020; Australian Government 2020).

Following the pandemic, there is a general lack of real-time data on how COVID-19 influences the sources of health finance throughout the Asia-Pacific countries. Driven by a notable increase in borrowing, government expenditures will likely climb as a proportion of GDP in 2020 even if government income drops (Fig. 7.5). Part of this rise in government expenditure has been to support the quick reaction to the epidemic by raising the ability of health systems to control the COVID-19 spread (WHO 2020a, 2020b).[3]

In light of the COVID-19 pandemic, Edejer et al. (2020) conducted a study to estimate the additional costs associated with implementing the core components of a strategic readiness and response plan. One scenario projected that the costs per capita for low-income nations over 4 weeks and 12 weeks under the current conditions would amount to USD 3.3 and USD 9.1, respectively. This represents a considerable financial burden that may exceed the budgetary capacities of some countries.

[3] https://documents1.worldbank.org/curated/en/882021601529585420/pdf/Economic-Impact-of-COVID-19-Implications-for-Health-Financing-in-Asia-and-Pacific.pdf

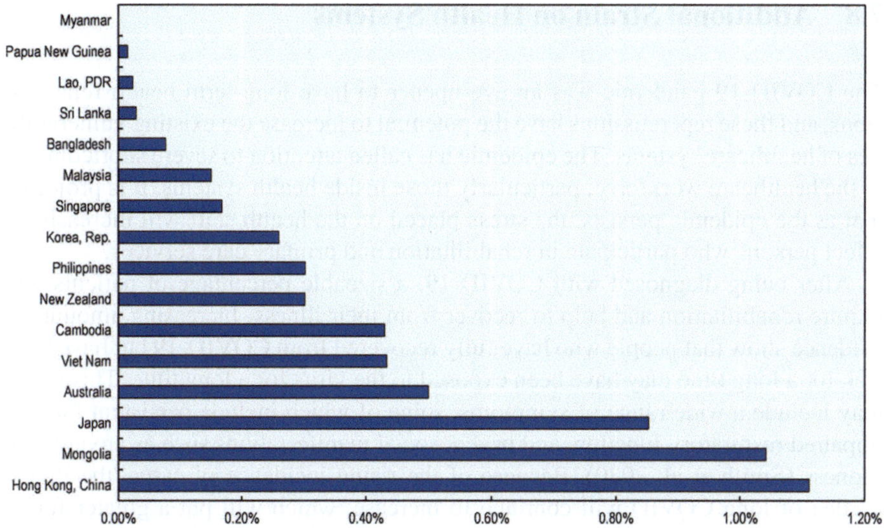

Fig. 7.4 Central Government Budgetary Commitments to Health System in Responses to COVID-19: Asia and Pacific countries. *Source*: Asian Development Bank (2020) and Government country websites (Australia, Japan, the Republic of Korea, and New Zealand)

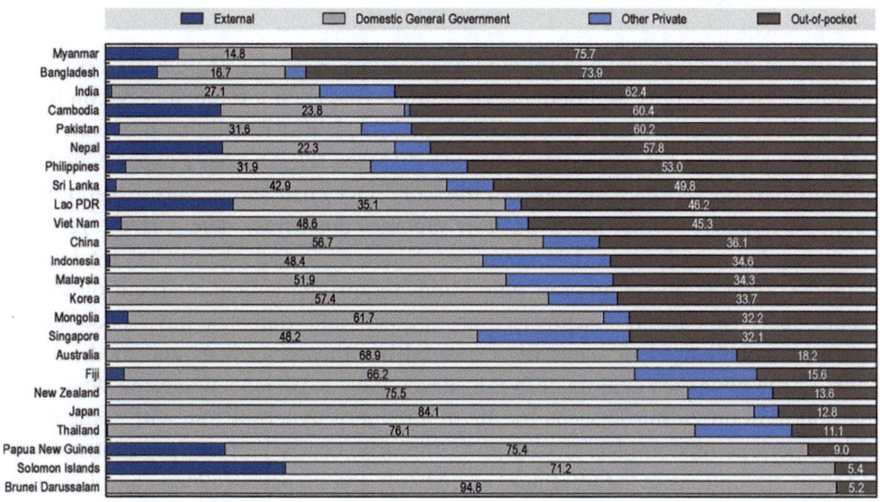

Fig. 7.5 Share of health expenditure: Asia and Pacific countries (2020). *Source*: OECD (2020)

7.8 Additional Strain on Health Systems

The COVID-19 pandemic was an eye-opener to have long-term health repercussions, and these repercussions have the potential to increase the existing vulnerabilities of healthcare systems. The epidemic has called attention to severe shortcomings in the healthcare workforce, particularly those inside health systems. It is projected that as the epidemic persists, the stress placed on the health staff will increasingly affect persons who participate in rehabilitation and primary care services.

After being diagnosed with COVID-19, a sizeable percentage of patients will require rehabilitation and help to recover from their illness. Increasing amounts of evidence show that people who have fully recovered from COVID-19 but have been sick for a long time may have been exposed to the virus for a long time. This group may include a wide range of symptoms, some of which include persistent fatigue, impaired respiratory function, and psychosocial manifestations such as anxiety and sadness (Smith et al. 2020). Because of the rising incidence of cases, the illness burden of long COVID will continue to increase, which will put a greater future demand on healthcare services and infrastructure.

7.9 Emergence of Demand for Mental Health

The global pandemic has precipitated a secondary crisis by profoundly disrupting health services' supply and demand dynamics. Based on a rapid survey conducted by the World Health Organisation (WHO 2020b), it was found that prevention and treatment services for non-communicable diseases (NCDs) have experienced significant disruptions since the onset of the COVID-19 pandemic. This disruption has been particularly pronounced in low-income countries. The survey received responses from 163 out of 194 countries. Since the onset of the COVID-19 pandemic, a considerable number of individuals requiring medical intervention for ailments such as cancer, cardiovascular disease, and diabetes have encountered significant challenges in accessing essential healthcare services and medications. Most of the countries examined in the survey have experienced varying degrees of disruption in providing services for the treatment of hypertension, with some countries experiencing complete disruption. Similarly, nearly half of the countries have reported disruptions in the treatment of diabetes and diabetes-related complications. Furthermore, a significant proportion of countries, approximately 42.5%, have encountered disruptions in cancer treatment, while 31% of countries have faced challenges in providing services for cardiovascular emergencies. Rehabilitation services have experienced disruptions in approximately two-thirds of the countries above. In many countries surveyed, personnel from the Ministry of Health who addressed NCDs were either partially or entirely redeployed to assist in managing the COVID-19 pandemic. The prevalence of public screening programme postponements was also extensive, as reports from over 50% of countries indicated. Screening mammograms conducted in specialised facilities in Australia were temporarily halted between late March and late April/early May 2020 due to the COVID-19 restrictions.

The COVID-19 pandemic and its accompanying measures had a substantial impact on HIV, TB, and malaria care delivery. This disturbance has the potential to raise death rates and reduce life expectancy in low- and middle-income nations (Hogan et al. 2020). In countries strongly affected by HIV, tuberculosis, and malaria, notably in South Asia, the indirect effects of COVID-19 on these three illnesses, which result in extra fatalities, may outweigh the direct effects of the COVID-19 virus itself (The Global Fund 2020).

According to the findings of a survey conducted by the Global Fund, several obstacles have been identified in the realm of HIV prevention. These challenges encompass issues related to HIV testing and case identification for not only HIV but also Tuberculosis (TB) and malaria. Additionally, preventive activities have been disrupted or postponed, while healthcare personnel and laboratory staff have been redeployed to combat the COVID-19 pandemic. The qualitative data analysis from the survey reveals that the primary factors contributing to the cancellation or delay of activities are implementing lockdown measures, restrictions on individual gatherings, and halting transport services.

In 2020, the World Health Organization's Independent Accountability Panel brought attention to the severe effects of the COVID-19 pandemic on pregnant women, infants, young children, and teenagers.[4] The supply of reproductive health commodities was inadequate; there were cases of both fixed and mobile reproductive health clinics being closed, and the provision of sexual and reproductive health services was reduced. The implementation of lockdowns and movement restrictions, coupled with the reassignment of health workers from maternity to COVID-19 units, has resulted in a reduction in the accessibility of critical healthcare services for pregnant women and newborns. Additionally, the disruption of immunisation campaigns has further exacerbated the challenges faced in ensuring the well-being of this vulnerable population.

The COVID-19 pandemic has introduced a level of unpredictability and uncertainty, necessitating the implementation of various containment measures such as lockdowns and physical distancing. These measures and the subsequent economic downturn have negatively affected populations' physical and mental well-being. Furthermore, they have exacerbated existing health disparities, particularly among individuals with pre-existing mental health conditions (Moreno et al. 2020). The prevalence of violence against women and girls, specifically domestic violence, has escalated in tandem with the emergence of the COVID-19 pandemic.[5]

Potential approaches exist to alleviate the consequences of containment strategies. Australia has successfully implemented various supplementary health

---

[4] https://iapewec.org/wp-content/uploads/2020/07/IAP-2020-Report-Executive-Summary-English.pdf

[5] https://www.unwomen.org/en/news/in-focus/in-focus-gender-equality-in-COVID-19-response/violence-against-women-during-COVID-19

measures to alleviate the negative consequences of the COVID-19 pandemic. These measures include adopting telehealth consultations and providing extra financial resources for mental health services.[6]

Different causes can account for the observed variations in death rates. Changes in population density are one of these. Rural-urban composition, the number of tourists from different countries, can play a significant role in this regard. Furthermore, demographic traits are also important. The IMF (2020) highlights variations in containment and mitigation strategies, explicitly focusing on limitations on mobility, the promptness and efficacy of their implementation, and the presence of testing and contact tracing infrastructure, which have also exerted an influence. There is still a significant knowledge gap regarding the potential impact of COVID-19 on health expenditure and the various channels of health financing in Asia-Pacific nations and territories. Nevertheless, it is worth noting that the financial burden associated with the COVID-19 response might exceed the fiscal capabilities of Asia-Pacific nations, particularly those with lower income levels.

The provision of preventive and therapeutic interventions for non-communicable diseases, as well as for HIV, tuberculosis, and malaria, has experienced significant disruptions in the wake of the COVID-19 pandemic. This has the potential to result in a significant increase in mortality rates and years of life lost, particularly in countries with lower economic status. The substantial impact of COVID-19 on "pregnant women, newborns, young children, and adolescents" extends to indirect consequences.

The COVID-19 epidemic has fundamentally affected the health systems and economy of many nations and territories. Ensuring that economic constraints, whether they emerge during or beyond the end of the epidemic, do not reroute already limited resources from essential health services in low- and middle-income countries is of great importance.

7.10 Navigating Regulation and Supply Side Interventions: Charting a Path Forward in a Post-COVID World

Table 7.3 indicates that public health expenditure in South Asian countries is below the global average. The Maldives exhibits a relatively higher proportion of public health expenditure, accounting for 5.2% of its GDP. In contrast, Bangladesh has the lowest allocation, with public health expenditure constituting merely 0.47% of its GDP. According to a recent study conducted by Davies et al. (2020), it has been found that certain cities in South Asia, namely, Karachi in Pakistan and Delhi in India, are facing significant challenges in terms of their capacity to provide

[6] https://www.health.gov.au/sites/default/files/documents/2020/10/budget-2020-21-prioritising-mental-health-and-telehealth-covid-19-pandemic-response-budget-2020-21-prioritising-mental-health-and-telehealth-covid-19-pandemic-response.pdf

Table 7.3 Basic facilities in the health sector and Social Security Coverage in South Asian countries

Countries	Public health exp (% GDP)	Basic sanitation services	Employment with Social Security	Employment without Social Security	Potential job losses (millions)
Afghanistan	0.49	38.75	3.7	96.3	12.37
Bangladesh	0.47	43.78	2.5	97.5	
Bhutan	2.49	65.67	14.00	86.00	
India	0.91	50.48	10.3	89.7	112.8
Maldives	5.21	96.2			
Nepal	1.00	51.28	3.4	96.6	2.27
Pakistan	0.72	54.45	3.9	96.1	11.71
Sri Lanka	1.62	93.41	24.1	75.9	0.92
World	5.8	69.94	41.3	58.7	

Source: ESCAP (2020)

adequate healthcare services in response to the escalating demand caused by the transmission of the coronavirus. These challenges primarily stem from a shortage of intensive care beds, healthcare personnel, and financial resources. Except for Sri Lanka (24%), Bhutan (14%), and India (10%), the prevalence of social security coverage among workers is notably low, as less than 4% of workers possess any form of social security. According to the International Labour Organisation (ILO 2020) and the United Nations Economic and Social Commission for Asia and the Pacific (ESCAP 2020), approximately 140 million workers are projected to experience job displacement.[7]

Table 7.4 shows the health security rankings of South Asian countries. The column labelled "Rank" denotes the relative position of each country regarding global health security, where lower numerical values correspond to higher rankings. The numerical value assigned to each country's health security is represented by the "Score" column, where higher scores indicate more robust health security measures. According to the data presented in the table, India is positioned at the 57th rank with a score of 46.5, whereas Bhutan holds the 85th rank with a score of 40.3. Pakistan is positioned at the 105th rank with a score of 35.5, while Nepal is at the 111th rank with a score of 35.1. Bangladesh, on the other hand, holds the 113th rank with a score of 35.0. Sri Lanka is positioned at the 120th rank with a score of 33.9, while the Maldives holds the 121st rank with a score of 33.8. Among the countries listed, Afghanistan exhibits the lowest ranking, denoted by a position of 130 and a score of 32.3.

In summary, the health sector is grappling with significant challenges that present an opportunity to cultivate a more robust and resilient healthcare system. One major hurdle is the presence of supply side bottlenecks, which impede the development of comprehensive health infrastructure. Additionally, a critical shortage of healthcare professionals—including doctors, nurses, and paramedics—severely

[7] https://www.ncbi.nlm.nih.gov/pmc/articles/PMC8022444/

Table 7.4 Health security ranking and a score of South Asian countries

	Global health security rank and score*	
Countries	Rank	Score
India	57	46.5
Bhutan	85	40.3
Pakistan	105	35.5
Nepal	111	35.1
Bangladesh	113	35.0
Sri Lanka	120	33.9
Maldives	121	33.8
Afghanistan	130	32.3

Source: Rasul et al. (2021)

Notes: *The "higher the score, the better (lower) the rank. The score is 0–100. 100 is the best health security condition. The rank and scores are based on the following criteria: (A) Prevention of the emergence of release of pathogens; (B) Early detection and reporting for epidemic of potential international concern; (C) Rapid response to and mitigation of the spread of an epidemic; (D) Sufficient and robust health system to treat the sick and protect health workers; (E) Commitment to improving national capacity, financing and adherence to norms, and (F) Overall risk environment and country vulnerability to biological threats" (Klimczuk et al. 2022)

hampers the delivery of quality medical care. In South Asia, the exorbitant costs associated with healthcare services create formidable barriers for impoverished communities that strive to obtain essential medical assistance. As a result, many individuals find themselves bearing the financial burden of healthcare expenses, often leading to delayed or neglected treatment, which has troubling repercussions for public health. However, the rising significance of trade in services offers promising avenues for transformative solutions. By creating and strengthening trade agreements that promote the exchange of healthcare services, nations have the potential to unite in enhancing the accessibility and affordability of medical care. India is poised at the forefront of this initiative, leveraging its expanding expertise in health infrastructure to empower neighbouring countries. By providing invaluable resources, training, and investment, India can help bolster these nations' healthcare systems. This spirit of collaboration holds the promise of improved health outcomes for vulnerable populations throughout the region. The next chapter will delve into this inspiring and impactful journey, highlighting the potential for change and the restoration of health equity.

References

ADB (2020) COVID-19 Policy database. Asian Development Bank / ERCD. Available at: https://data.adb.org/dataset/adbcovid-19-policy-database

Australian Government (2020) Economic and fiscal update July 2020. Commonwealth of Australia. Available at: https://budget.gov.au/2020-efu/economic-fiscal-update.htm

Banik A, Bhaumik PK (2020) India: emerging as a major destination of quality healthcare services. In: Trade in health services in South Asia: an examination of the need for regional cooperation. Springer, pp 105–126

Banik A, Nag T, Chowdhury SR, Chatterjee R (2020) Why do COVID-19 fatality rates differ across countries? An explorative cross-country study based on select indicators. Glob Bus Rev 21(3):607–625

Chandran SD, Puteh F, Azmi NA, Suki NM (2020) Exploring the development of the medical tourism industry in the Southeast Asia region. Int J Bus Ecosyst Strat 2(3):28–32

Chaudhury N, Hammer JS (2004) Ghost doctors: absenteeism in rural Bangladeshi health facilities. World Bank Econ Rev 18(3):423–441

Chaudhury N, Hammer J, Kremer M, Muralidharan K, Rogers FH (2006) Missing in action: teacher and health worker absence in developing countries. J Econ Perspect 20(1):91–116

Das J, Gertler PJ (2007) Variations in practice quality in five low-income countries: a conceptual overview. Despite differences among countries, findings from these studies offer important lessons for improving health care around the world. Health Aff 26(Suppl2):w296–w309

Das J, Hammer J (2005) Which doctor? Combining vignettes and item response to measure clinical competence. J Dev Econ 78(2):348–383

Das J, Hammer J (2007a) Money for nothing: the dire straits of medical practice in Delhi, India. J Dev Econ 83(1):1–36

Das J, Hammer J (2007b) Location, location, location: residence, wealth, and the quality of medical care in Delhi, India: quality of care varied by neighbourhood but not necessarily by patients' income level. Health Aff 26(Suppl2):w338–w351

Das J, Hammer J, Leonard K (2008) The quality of medical advice in low-income countries. J Econ Perspect 22(2):93–114

Davies N, Sweeney S, Torres-Rueda S, Bozzani F, Kitson N, Barasa E, Procter SR, Quaife M, CMMID COVID-19 Working Group, Eggo RM, Vassall A (2020) The impact of Coronavirus disease 2019 (COVID-19) on health systems and household resources in Africa and South Asia. MedRxiv, 2020–05. https://doi.org/10.1101/2020.05.06.20092734

Economic Times, The (2020) BCG vaccination policies make a ten times difference in Covid-19 incidence, mortality: New study, April 3

Edejer TTT, Hanssen O, Mirelman A, Verboom P, Lolong G, Watson OJ, Boulanger LL, Soucat A (2020) Projected health-care resource needs for an effective response to COVID-19 in 73 low-income and middle-income countries: a modelling study. Lancet Glob Health 8(11):e1372–e1379

ESCAP (2020) COVID-19 and South Asia: national strategies and subregional cooperation for accelerating inclusive, sustainable and resilient recovery. COVID-19 response. United Nations. Economic and Social Commission for Asia and the Pacific (ESCAP)

Global Health Observatory Report (2020/2022) Summary of the observatory report on access to rights and care 2020, Saint Denis (France)

Hammer JS (2013) Balancing market and government failure in service delivery. Lahore J Econ 18(Special E):1–19. Available at: https://ideas.repec.org/a/lje/journl/v18y2013ispp1-19.html

Hogan AB, Jewell BL, Sherrard-Smith E, Vesga JF, Watson OJ, Whittaker C et al (2020) Potential impact of the COVID-19 pandemic on HIV, tuberculosis, and malaria in low-income and middle-income countries: a modelling study. Lancet Glob Health 8(9):e1132–e1141

ILO (2020) World Social Protection Report, A Flagship Report, Geneva

IMF (2020) Regional economic outlook update: Asia and Pacific: navigating the pandemic: a multispeed recovery in Asia. International Monetary Fund, Washington, DC. Available at: https://www.imf.org/en/Publications/REO/APAC/Issues/2020/10/21/regional-economic-outlook-apd

Klimczuk A, Berde E, Dovie DA, Klimczuk-Kochanska M, Spinelli G (2022) Coronavirus disease (COVID-19): socio-economic systems in the post-pandemic world: design thinking, strategic planning, management, and public policy. Front Commun 7:1034562

Medhekar A, Wong HY, Hall JE (2019) Factors influencing inbound medical travel to India. J Health Organ Manag 33(2):155–172

Moreno C, Wykes T, Galderisi S, Nordentoft M, Crossley N, Jones N, Cannon M, Correll CU, Byrne L, Carr S, Chen EY (2020) How mental health care should change as a consequence of the COVID-19 pandemic. Lancet Psychiatry 7(9):813–824

MTI (2016) Medical tourism index Asian region. Available at: www.medicaltourismindex.com/overview/destination-ranking/

OECD (2020) Health at a glance: Asia/Pacific 2020: measuring progress towards universal health coverage. OECD Publishing, Paris. https://doi.org/10.1787/26b007cd-en

Phua J, Faruq MO, Kulkarni AP, Redjeki IS, Detleuxay K, Mendsaikhan N, Sann KK, Shrestha BR, Hashmi M, Palo JEM, Haniffa R (2020) Critical care bed capacity in Asian countries and regions. Crit Care Med 48(5):654–662

Rasul G, Nepal AK, Hussain A, Maharjan A, Joshi S, Lama A, Gurung P, Ahmad F, Mishra A, Sharma E (2021) Socio-economic implications of COVID-19 pandemic in South Asia: emerging risks and growing challenges. Front Sociol 6:629693

Smith SR, Jenq G, Claflin T, Magnant C, Haig AJ, Hurvitz E (2020) Proposed workflow for rehabilitation in a field hospital setting during the COVID-19 pandemic. Phys Med Rehabil 12(8):823–828

The Global Fund (2020) Mitigating the impact of COVID-19 on countries affected by HIV, tuberculosis and malaria. Global Health Campus, Geneva. Available at: https://www.theglobalfund.org/media/9819/covid19_mitigatingimpact_report_en.pdf

The Guardian (2016) Which country has the world's best healthcare system? Published on 9th February 2016. Available at: https://www.theguardian.com/society/2016/Feb/09/which-country-has-worlds-best-healthcare-system-this-is-the-NHS

Walker PG, Whittaker C, Watson O, Baguelin M, Ainslie KE, Bhatia S, Bhatt S, Boonyasiri A, Boyd O, Cattarino L, Cucunubá Z (2020) The global impact of COVID-19 and strategies for mitigation and suppression, vol 26. Imperial College London, pp 1–19

WHO (2020a) The impact of the COVID-19 outbreak on Asia-Pacific health systems. Available at: https://www.oecd.org/en/publications/health-at-a-glance-asia-pacific-2020_26b007cd-en/full-report.html

WHO (2020b) COVID-19 significantly impacts health services for noncommunicable diseases. World Health Organisation, Geneva. Available at: https://www.who.int/news-room/detail/01-06-2020-covid-19-significantly-impacts-health-services-for-noncommunicable-diseases

WHO (2022) Regulations and laws promoting health and well-being goals (SDG3) in WHO South-East Asian countries. In: Regulations and laws promoting health and well-being goals (SDG3) in the WHO South-East Asian countries

World Bank (2023) South Asia Development Update, October 2023: Toward Faster, Cleaner Growth, Report, Washington DC

Chapter 8
Bridging Healthcare Gaps in South Asia: A Collaborative Journey Towards Healthier Communities

Abstract This chapter examines the evolving landscape of Primary Health Care (PHC) and Universal Health Coverage (UHC) in South Asia, focusing on Bangladesh, India, Nepal, Pakistan, and Sri Lanka. With the region projected to house over 2 billion people by 2025, it faces significant health challenges exacerbated by urbanisation and socio-economic disparities. This chapter critically evaluates the performance of PHC frameworks, emphasising the need for integrated service delivery and community empowerment to enhance health outcomes. It highlights India's Ayushman Bharat initiative, which aims to provide comprehensive health coverage to vulnerable populations through Health and Wellness Centres and the Pradhan Mantri Jan Arogya Yojana (PM-JAY). Despite progress, challenges persist, including inadequate hospital infrastructure and high out-of-pocket expenditures. This chapter also explores the impact of COVID-19 on UHC, revealing that countries with robust health systems and political commitment fared better during the pandemic. Furthermore, it discusses the potential of cross-border healthcare services and medical tourism in India as avenues for improving access to quality care. Ultimately, this chapter advocates for a strengthened regional health system to address shared public health challenges and improve health equity across South Asia.

Keywords South Asia · Universal Health Coverage (UHC) · Primary Health Care (PHC) · Ayushman Bharat · Medical Tourism

8.1 Introduction

The South Asian region (SAR) is a diverse and vibrant area of the world that includes the countries of Afghanistan, Bangladesh, Bhutan, India, the Maldives, Nepal, Pakistan, and Sri Lanka. As we look ahead to January 2025,[1] this region is projected

[1] https://www.worldometers.info/world-population/southern-asia-population/ accessed on January 22, 2025.

A. Banik et al., *Extraordinary Health Hazards and their Socio-Economic Effects in South Asia*, South Asia Economic and Policy Studies,
https://doi.org/10.1007/978-981-95-5729-5_8

to be home to around 2.08 billion people, representing 25.29% of the global population. The SAR faces many challenges that profoundly affect health outcomes, stemming from shifting patterns of disease, rapid urbanisation, and a variety of complex social and economic issues. In response to these pressing challenges, Primary Health Care (PHC)[2] emerges as a highly cost-effective strategy designed to tackle these issues through integrated service delivery, cross-sector collaboration, and community empowerment. Historically, the PHC approach has been a cornerstone of health policy across South Asian countries, aiming to deliver comprehensive health services accessible to all. Despite its foundational role, the region has not yet fully tapped into the extensive potential offered by PHC-oriented health systems, which can significantly improve health outcomes and equity.

This chapter explores the current PHC frameworks within the Universal Health Coverage (UHC)[3] context across five key South Asian nations—Bangladesh, India, Nepal, Pakistan, and Sri Lanka. It provides a comprehensive critical evaluation of PHC performance in these countries, highlighting the factors that facilitate effective implementation and the barriers that impede progress. Additionally, the chapter focuses on UHC in India, advocating for substantial investments in fostering a culture of innovation and collaboration. It underscores the importance of strengthening the continuum of healthcare services across four levels: primary, secondary, tertiary, and quaternary. This strategy is vital for enhancing universal and non-universal healthcare systems, ensuring equitable access to necessary care for a healthier future. Lastly, it examines Cross-Border Health Care Services in India, positioning them as a pathway to quality and affordable medical care.

8.2 Exploring UHC and Performance of South Asian Countries

The health industry is divided into four stages of care: "primary, secondary, tertiary, and quaternary" (Torrey 2024). These tiers are a reflection of the specialised knowledge and skill sets needed by healthcare professionals as well as the increasing complexity of the problems they handle. Usually requiring visits with a primary care physician, primary care is the first point of contact. Referral to a specialist, such as an endocrinologist or oncologist, for specialised treatment is known as secondary care. Tertiary care refers to specialist medical treatment carried out in hospital

[2] It is recognised as the first of the four levels of the health care system.

[3] UHC ensures that all individuals can access essential health services—including promotion, prevention, treatment, rehabilitation, and palliative care—when and where needed, without financial hardship. It emphasises the availability of skilled and fairly distributed health workers, supported with quality-assured medical resources and decent working conditions. UHC aims to prevent people from falling into poverty due to high out-of-pocket healthcare expenses that can deplete savings, force asset sales, or lead to debt, thereby endangering both individual and family futures (UNICEF 2021).

environments, such as cardiac surgery or renal dialysis. Ultimately, quaternary care provides extremely sophisticated treatments, marking an advanced level of expert care.

Health concerns have risen to the top of political agendas in the wake of the COVID-19 pandemic, the worst global health crisis in more than a century. This crisis has presented chances for leaders to overhaul national health systems to reach UHC, therefore facilitating more efficient use of resources at all four levels of healthcare. Countries that have made significant strides towards UHC usually respond to upheavals, crises, or disease outbreaks, revealing weaknesses in their health systems. South Asia has significant variations in demography, economic performance, and health indices both within and across nations (UNICEF 2021). Although every country has different problems, there are also shared problems all over the world. The primary focus should be on health systems' ability to function, which includes ensuring essential medicines and supplies are available, recruiting, training, and retaining healthcare workers; securing efficient and equitable health financing; and finally, refocusing health systems on primary care, with a focus on Non-Communicable Diseases (NCD) prevention services and improving basic public health capabilities (Kumar 2019). Along with the general underperformance of South Asia's health systems, Chapts. 6 and 7 explored the difficulties resulting from the disparity between demand and supply in the healthcare industry. Although many elements outside of the healthcare sector, such as education, nutrition, poverty, gender equality, and security, influence health outcomes, appropriate health services are still essential for maintaining and enhancing public health. Generally, countries with better health care services experienced better health results.

It is possible to track the performance of South Asian countries in achieving UHC and compare their outcomes with those of other countries (WHO 2020; World Bank 2020) during the COVID-19 period. According to the most recent UHC service coverage index, "the average score of South Asia was 53" (UNICEF 2021). All countries in the region have improved their scores since 2017, except for Nepal. Sri Lanka, the Maldives, and Bhutan scored above 50, while India, Nepal, Bangladesh, Pakistan, and Afghanistan scored lower (UNICEF 2021).

The UHC service coverage index determines the average coverage of vital health services in a nation, even when the circumstances of these nations vary substantially. Low levels of financial protection, coupled with high Out-Of-Pocket Expenditures (OOPE) and inadequate quality and availability of essential health services, mainly account for gaps in ineffective health coverage in the region. Low public health investment is closely related to these problems. Common issues that are not specific to South Asia, such as data completeness and quality, present challenges that hinder accurate comparisons between the responses of many nations to the epidemic. Still, responses and results have varied significantly both throughout the region and within each nation.

Lessons on the significance of response capability, a strong social compact, political will, and universal health care systems may be gleaned by studying the results of superior-performing nations. Countries that have effectively reacted to the epidemic, such as Bhutan, the Maldives, and initially Sri Lanka, also have superior performance on UHC measures (UNICEF 2021). They concentrated on prompt, definitive measures, such as swiftly enhancing testing and monitoring capabilities and utilising established health system infrastructures.

South Asia's response to COVID-19 is primarily influenced by the performance of UHC, particularly in public health spending and resource allocation. Low public financing has led to underinvestment in health, particularly among low-income individuals. A strong social contract, commitment to health investment, and a primary care-focused health system can enhance a robust response. UHC is crucial for health security, stability, and sustainability.

8.3 UHC in India[4]

Ayushman Bharat To make universal health care a reality, the National Health Policy 2017 called for the introduction of Ayushman Bharat, the national initiative of the Indian government. The Sustainable Development Goals (SDGs) serve as the basis for this endeavour, which aims to "leave no one behind".

The primary aim of Ayushman Bharat is to replace the existing fragmented and sector-specific approach with a unified, need-based healthcare model. It envisions transforming the healthcare system by strengthening prevention, health promotion, and ambulatory care across all levels—primary, secondary, and tertiary. Ayushman Bharat uses a continuity of care method, which is made up of two factors that work together:

- Health and Wellness Centres (HWCs).
- Pradhan Mantri Jan Arogya Yojana (PM-JAY).

8.3.1 Health and Wellness Centres (HWCs)

By converting current Sub-Centers and Primary Health Centres, the Indian government declared in February 2018 the establishment of 150,000 HWCs. The goal of health and wellness centres is to offer a wide range of services to meet the basic medical needs of everyone in the area. By bringing primary healthcare closer to people's homes, these clinics will provide Comprehensive Primary Health Care (CPHC). In addition to providing free diagnostic services and needed medications, they focus on maternity and child health services as well as NCDs. Therefore, the HWCs enhance connectivity, ensure consistency, and create opportunities within society. With an emphasis on health promotion and disease prevention, these centres work to involve and empower individuals and communities, encouraging them to

[4] For details, visit, https://nha.gov.in/PM-JAY, accessed on January 23, 2025.

adopt healthier habits and make lifestyle adjustments that help lower the chances of chronic illnesses and related health problems.

8.3.2 PM-JAY

The second component of the Ayushman Bharat initiative is the Pradhan Mantri Jan Arogya Yojana (PM-JAY), launched by the Prime Minister of India on September 23, 2018, in Ranchi, Jharkhand. This flagship health assurance scheme offers annual health coverage of ₹5 lakhs per family for hospitalisation related to secondary and tertiary care. PM-JAY aims to benefit approximately 55 crore individuals from over 12 crore economically disadvantaged and vulnerable families, representing the bottom 40% of India's population.[5] Eligibility for the scheme is determined based on deprivation and occupational criteria outlined in the 2011 Socio-Economic Caste Census (SECC), covering both rural and urban households. Initially introduced as the National Health Protection Scheme (NHPS), it was later renamed as PM-JAY. Additionally, the scheme extends coverage to families previously enrolled under the Rashtriya Swasthya Bima Yojana (RSBY), even if they are not listed in the SECC 2011[vi]. The funding for PM-JAY is entirely provided by the government, with implementation costs shared between the Central and State governments.

Key Features of PM-JAY[6] It is the world's largest healthcare scheme, fully financed by the government.

- Provides ₹ five lakhs per family per year for secondary and tertiary care hospitalisation.
- Eligible for over 12 crore poor and vulnerable families.
- Offers cashless access to healthcare services at the hospital's point of service.
- Aims to mitigate catastrophic expenditure on medical treatment.
- Covers expenses up to 3 days before and 15 days after hospitalisation.
- No restrictions on family size, age, or gender.
- Covers all pre-existing conditions from day one.
- Benefits are portable nationwide.
- Services include approximately 1929 procedures.
- Public hospitals receive reimbursement for healthcare services equivalent to private hospitals.

Benefit Cover Under PM-JAY The PM-JAY scheme in India offers cashless coverage of up to INR 5,00,000 per eligible family per annum for specified secondary and tertiary care conditions, addressing the fragmented system of government-funded health insurance schemes in India, which typically have annual caps ranging from

[5] https://www.nha.gov.in/PM-JAY

[6] https://www.nha.gov.in/PM-JAY

INR 30,000 to INR 3,00,000 per family. The scheme covers all costs linked to the following parts of treatment[7]:

- "Medical examination, treatment, and consultation
- Pre-hospitalisation costs
- Medications and medical consumables
- Non-intensive and intensive care services
- Diagnostic and laboratory investigations
- Medical implantation services (when necessary)
- Accommodation benefits
- Food services
- Complications arising during treatment
- Post-hospitalisation follow-up care for up to 15 days"

The benefits of INR 5,00,000 are provided on a family floater basis, meaning they can be utilised by one or all family members. While RSBY had a family cap of five members, PM-JAY has been designed without limitations on family size or age of members. Additionally, pre-existing conditions are covered from the very first day, allowing any eligible individual with a medical condition before enrolment in PM-JAY to receive treatment for those conditions immediately upon joining the scheme.

8.3.3 *Reflections on Impact and Assessment so Far*

In an intriguing development, the health insurance scheme's demand side expanded to encompass the target population, resulting in a significant achievement: within 5 years, approximately 56% of all eligible beneficiaries were successfully enrolled. However, a contrasting challenge arises on the supply side; evidence from studies across multiple states reveals a concerning shortage of empanelled hospitals available for registered beneficiaries. This disparity has led to high out-of-pocket healthcare expenditures, creating a financial burden for many families. According to the National Health Authority (NHA), the autonomous organisation under the Ministry of Health and Family Welfare responsible for implementing the PM-JAY scheme, more than 253 million health cards have been issued, as recorded on the NHA dashboard as of 5 October 2022.[8]

Additionally, it is noteworthy that HWCs have evolved significantly beyond the traditional functions of PHCs. Their remit has broadened to encompass critical issues such as NCDs and mental health, marking a transformative shift in focus from mere healthcare to a more holistic approach to overall health. This paradigm

[7] https://abdm.gov.in:8081/uploads/RFE_for_AV_IEC_Div_V9_62245b9ecb.pdf

[8] https://www.google.com/url?q=https://www.indiaspend.com/data-viz/three-charts-on-ayushman-bharats-achievements-and-shortfalls-878004&source=gmail&ust=1737705989038000&usg=AOvVaw04NKObj6m5bDZ_2KPDOgp- accessed on January 23, 2025.

includes preventive measures, timely intervention, and health education, reflecting a commitment to comprehensive well-being. Staffing structures have also been revamped to support this holistic model. Many existing primary health and sub-centres have been transformed into HWCs to enhance service delivery, offering a thorough range of primary healthcare services. As of December 2022, government data indicates that approximately 150,000 HWCs are operational, underscoring the initiative's progress in providing maternal and child health services, diagnostic services, and access to free essential medications per PM-JAY guidelines (Fig. 8.1).

Moreover, as detailed on its dashboard, the PM-JAY scheme has designated 27,252 Empanelled Healthcare Providers (EHCPs), through which beneficiaries can avail themselves of cashless services. Nonetheless, a substantial concern arises regarding the level of active participation; only 19,756 EHCPs were operational in 2022, a figure that falls dramatically short compared to the vast number of individuals eligible for the scheme across various states.

In August 2023, a report by the Comptroller and Auditor General (CAG) revealed discrepancies based on data collected in November 2022.[9] For instance, the latest statistics from the NHA dashboard indicate that Assam has only 349 EHCPs, which equates to just two hospitals for every 100,000 residents. This issue is exacerbated in regions such as the Andaman and Nicobar Islands, Assam, Maharashtra, Jharkhand, Haryana, and Meghalaya, where local EHCPs have been unable to deliver the comprehensive range of services mandated by the scheme (Iqbal 2023), as noted in the CAG report.

The PM-JAY scheme, which emerged from the previous health insurance initiative known as RSBY, explicitly supports the poorest 40% of households. Eligibility for these households is determined through a rigorous selection process based on the socio-economic caste census—an extensive enumeration that ranks rural households in terms of their access to essential resources like health, housing, and education, as well as various occupational criteria (including those reliant on begging, rag-picking, or domestic work in urban settings). Some states, such as Uttarakhand, Karnataka, and Himachal Pradesh, have surpassed the established eligibility criteria,[10] extending healthcare services to additional populations (Fig. 8.2).

Tamil Nadu has the highest number of hospitalisations per 100,000 Ayushman cards issued, with over 179,003 for every 100,000 enrolled individuals (Fig. 8.3). Kerala has the second-highest utilisation rate at 74,280, followed by Rajasthan and Karnataka at 52,168 and 41,089, respectively. Assam has the lowest utilisation at

[9] https://cag.gov.in/uploads/download_audit_report/2023/Report-No.-11-of-2023_PA-on-PMJAY_English-PDF-A-064d22bab2b83b5.38721048.pdf accessed on January 23, 2025.

[10] Dr. Chandrasekhar from HSTP emphasises that this is why certain states are reporting enrollment rates exceeding 100% in the programme. Efforts are underway to consult the NHA for clarification on this issue, and updates will be provided once a response is received. Currently, it is estimated that about half of the eligible population is effectively covered by the health insurance scheme. https://www.google.com/url?q=https://www.indiaspend.com/data-viz/three-charts-on-ayushman-bharats-achievements-and-shortfalls-878004&source=gmail&ust=1737705989038000&usg=AOvVaw04NKObj6m5bDZ_2KPDOgp- accessed on January 23, 2025.

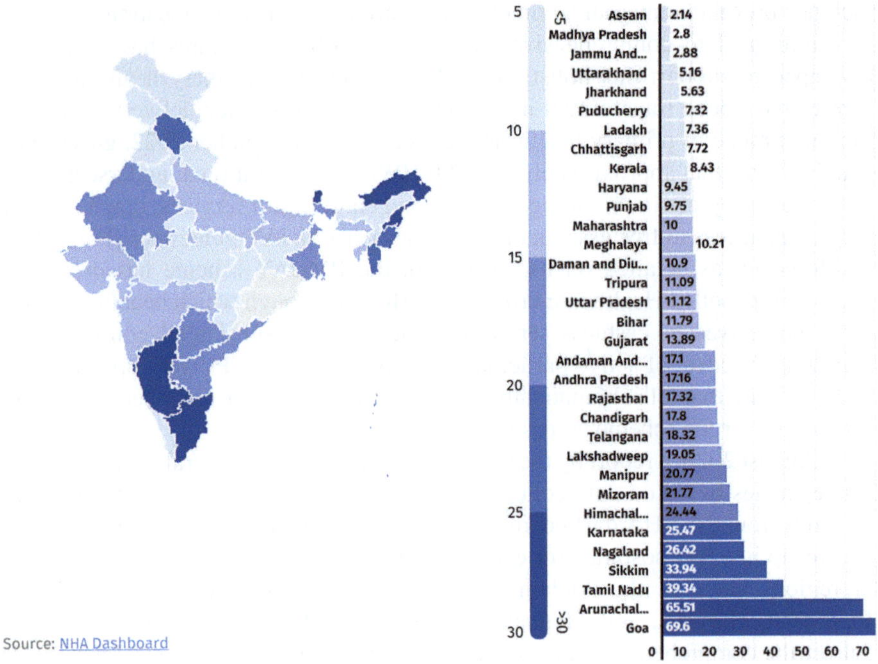

Fig. 8.1 Number of empanelled hospitals per 100,000 people

5292 per 100,000 beneficiaries. Uttar Pradesh has had 2.6 million hospitalisations since the programme's initiation.

The primary objective of the PM-JAY scheme is to mitigate OOPEs on healthcare, yet the results have shown a mixed picture. For instance, a study conducted in Ahmedabad revealed a notable reduction in out-of-pocket expenses among beneficiaries, suggesting a substantial positive impact on alleviating financial burdens associated with medical care (Patel 2025). Similarly, research at a tertiary care hospital in Himachal Pradesh documented a dramatic decrease in out-of-pocket expenditure, plummeting from 76.1% to 30% following hospital admission under the PM-JAY scheme. This was accompanied by a significant drop in Catastrophic Health Expenditure (CHE), which fell from 65.5% to 29% (Kanwal et al. 2024).

It is worth noting that the PM-JAY initiative has successfully extended healthcare access to over 50 crore individuals, with more than 29,972 empanelled hospitals ready to offer necessary services (Arora and Chaturvedi 2024; Sharma et al. 2024). One of the key strengths of this programme is its comprehensive coverage, which includes pre-existing medical conditions, thereby enhancing its relevance and utility for vulnerable populations who often face barriers to healthcare access (Arora and Chaturvedi 2024). However, despite these achievements, a National Council of Applied Economic Research study highlighted some troubling statistics. It found that 87.9% of individuals resorted to dipping into their savings to cover health-related costs. In comparison, 11.3% sought financial assistance from friends

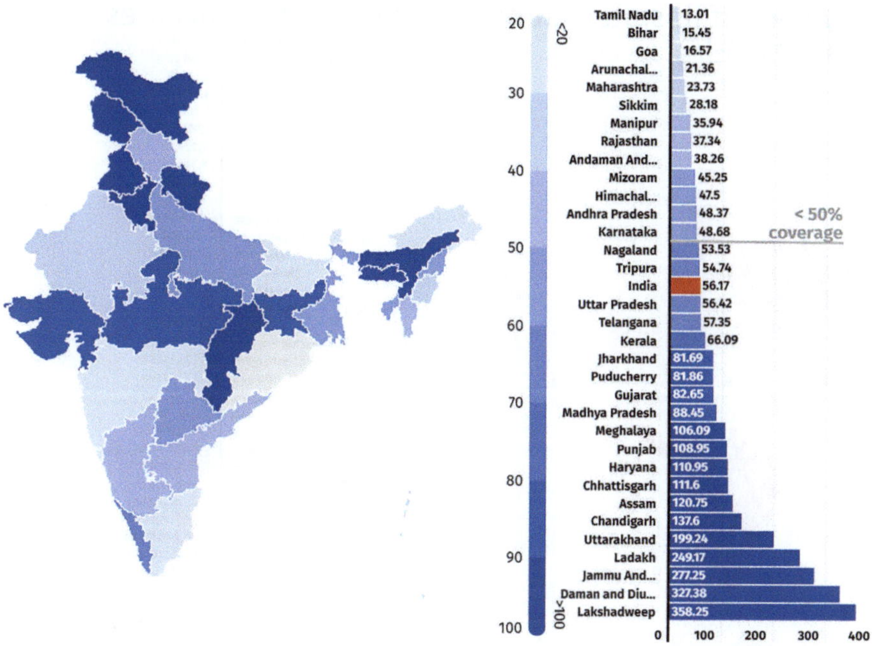

Fig. 8.2 Percentage of eligible beneficiaries who have an Ayushman Card (2022–2023). *Note*: The total does not include the hospitals empanelled in Delhi, West Bengal, and Odisha. Assuming the average family size is 5, and coverage is more than 100% of eligible beneficiaries, experts say the state has covered more people than listed under the SECC. We have also contacted the NHA, asking why some states have over 100% enrolment. Source: NHA Dashboard

and relatives, and a mere 0.3% utilised health insurance. The study surveyed four states: "Odisha, Maharashtra, Punjab, and Uttar Pradesh" (NCAER 2023). Interestingly, another study from 2022 indicated that during the COVID-19 pandemic, enrolment in either public or privately funded health insurance did not lead to a reduction in OOPEs. Furthermore, while having health insurance might have increased the likelihood of seeking healthcare services, it did not effectively shield individuals from financial risks. However, data from the National Family Health Survey (NFHS) 2019–2020 revealed that membership in PM-JAY or any other health insurance plan did not lead to better rates of institutional delivery or lowered OOPE (GoI 2021). Challenges persist, such as a lack of public awareness and infrastructural shortcomings that can impede the programme's effectiveness in certain areas (Sharma et al. 2024). Additionally, it is worth noting that outpatient care, which significantly contributes to health expenditure-induced poverty, is not included under the PM-JAY coverage. This exclusion points to a critical gap in providing comprehensive financial protection for healthcare expenses (Thakur and Faizan 2024). Overall, the Ayushman Bharat initiative has made significant progress in reducing out-of-pocket healthcare costs for many; there remains a pressing need

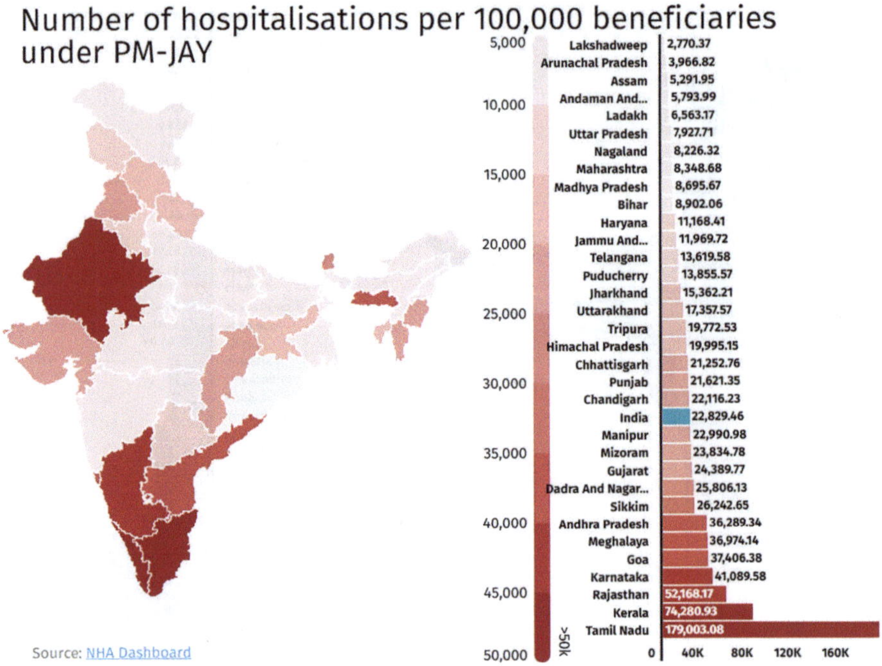

Fig. 8.3 Exploring the impact of PM-JAY utilization across Indian states (2022–2023)

for ongoing efforts to address its existing limitations and ensure expansive coverage, especially regarding outpatient services.

In addition to the Ayushman Bharat scheme, a significant initiative implemented by the central government, various state governments across the country have also introduced their own state-level UHC programmes. These programmes are specifically designed to cater to the healthcare needs of targeted populations within their respective regions, ensuring that essential health services are accessible to those who need them most (see Fig. 8.4).

8.4 Exploring Cross-Border Health Care Services in India: A Gateway to Quality and Affordable Medical Care

Regional integration processes often highlight critical aspects such as trade, economic development, and security. However, the significance of health should not be overlooked, as it intricately connects with these essential domains. In light of this, it is noteworthy that India's Prime Minister Narendra Modi convened a pivotal video conference with members of the South Asian Association for Regional Cooperation (SAARC) on 15 March 2020, in response to the escalating COVID-19 pandemic. This high-level meeting marked the first large-scale gathering of regional

Fig. 8.4 Indicative list of government-sponsored healthcare coverage/insurance schemes: Indian States. *Source*: Health Care Insurance-India Shodhganga; https://shodhganga.inflibnet.ac.in/handle/10603/405148 Accessed on January 23, 2025

leaders since 2014 and was a launching pad for the COVID-19 emergency fund. Initially, this fund was bolstered by an allocation of US$10 million, complemented by voluntary contributions from the SAARC nations that totalled an impressive US$8 million (Adhikari 2022). However, despite this promising start, the subsequent disbursement of the fund has been limited. By December 2020, reports revealed that financial assistance had been provided to several countries: "Indian rupees (INR) 6.12 crore (approximately US $845,000) to Nepal, 3.64 crores (around US $500,000) to Bangladesh, 1.69 crore (about US $233,000) to Bhutan, 1.55 crore (nearly US $213,000) to Sri Lanka, 60.14 lakh (approximately US $83,000) to the Maldives, and 29.3 lakh (around US $40,436) to Afghanistan" (UNICEF 2021). Notably, no funds were allocated to Pakistan (Mishra 2020).

In addition to these collaborative health efforts, India is witnessing remarkable growth in its medical tourism sector, particularly at the secondary, tertiary, and quaternary levels. With its state-of-the-art healthcare facilities and specialised services, India has emerged as a preferred destination for patients from numerous South Asian countries. The medical tourism industry was valued at an impressive 9 billion US$ in 2022, with approximately two million patients travelling from 78 countries each year to seek diverse medical services, including advanced medical treatments, wellness programmes, and In Vitro Fertilization (IVF).

This influx of international patients generates significant revenue—about 6 billion US$ for the industry—and presents a positive trajectory for growth, with projections indicating an escalation to 13 billion US$ by 2026.[11] This anticipated growth is spurred by the Indian government's "Heal in India" initiative, which creates jobs and revenue and cultivates foreign exchange for hospitals. Moreover, it enhances India's soft power, positioning the nation as the Global Healing Centre. As a result, a burgeoning demand for advanced medical equipment and technology fosters continuous improvements within the Indian healthcare system. This creates a beneficial cycle, where increased demand drives quality advancements, generating even greater demand.

Trade in health services, often called Medical Tourism, has garnered significant policy attention in various developing regions, particularly in South Asia (Banik and Bhaumik 2020; Banik et al. 2020). Several factors have contributed to the notable growth of these services in the region. The ease of travel and advancements in information and communication technologies enable patients to access higher-quality treatments at lower costs, particularly in India. This accessibility has further increased the demand for portable health insurance coverage, both public and private, due to patients' mobility. Many medical tourists arriving in India come from Southeast Asia, the Middle East, Africa, and South Asia. Additionally, "patients from Australia, Canada, China, Russia, the United Kingdom, and the United States"[12] play a vital role in this flourishing sector. Notably, Chennai has emerged as

[11] "India eyes to be a huge medical tourism hub in coming years". *Times of India*. Retrieved January 23, 2025

[12] https://en.wikipedia.org/wiki?curid=22310611

the healthcare capital of India, attracting numerous patients with its advanced medical facilities and skilled practitioners.

Research indicates (Banik and Bhaumik 2014) that a significant arbitrage opportunity exists for local professionals and service providers within a specific South Asian economy, attributed to the existing demand-supply gap in healthcare services. The industry encompasses various organisations and groups. Key factors include treatment processes—considering quality, safety, and risk—and system-level implications for both countries of origin and destination. These aspects involve financial considerations and the effects on providers and professionals resulting from cross-border trade in the healthcare sector.

The barriers must be removed to achieve greater economic welfare, as defined by modes 3 and organising "a regional skills council to standardise skills would be essential to take advantage of the arbitrage opportunity. Once these are identified, investments may be encouraged, and the movement of natural persons without barriers such as simplified visa, favourable work permit, dual taxation, among others, may be resolved"—this is a "win-win situation in light of economic welfare gains in the region" (Banik 2020).

In recent years, tech-savvy companies have emerged as key players in the medical tourism sector, developing innovative online platforms that streamline the experience for international patients seeking care. The appeal of pursuing medical treatment in India is substantial, offering a wealth of advantages that attract individuals from around the globe. First, the cost of medical services in India is significantly lower compared to many countries such as Western Nations and East Asian nations, providing an economical alternative without compromising the quality of care. Patients also benefit from access to cutting-edge medical technologies and practices that align with international standards, ensuring they receive world-class treatment. A further advantage lies in the proficiency of healthcare professionals in India; many of them have received training in prestigious institutions located in the United States and the United Kingdom. This global education results in a workforce that not only excels in medical expertise but also minimises language barriers, as a large number of medical staff are fluent in English, making communication seamless for international patients. These factors collectively establish India as a leading destination for medical tourism, adept at addressing a wide array of healthcare needs, from complex surgeries to routine checks. Moreover, the intricate nature of regional integration presents significant potential for the collaborative and multifaceted aspects of public health policy to develop and thrive in a synergistic manner. Incorporating health considerations into regional integration efforts is essential in today's fast-evolving global governance landscape, helping to tackle shared public health challenges that transcend national borders. Within the South Asian context, it is evident that many individuals from neighbouring countries gravitate towards India for medical services due to their affordability, especially in the face of their own economic constraints.

Many experts believe that integrating the healthcare systems of South Asian countries can help tackle future health challenges more effectively. India, for example, has a large pool of trained and skilled health professionals. This gives the country an edge in offering healthcare services across borders, especially through Mode 1 (cross-border supply) and Mode 2 (consumption abroad).[13] Allowing such services to flow freely between countries can increase regional trade in healthcare. Both policymakers and health officials in South Asia could benefit from a more unified system. For Mode 3 (commercial presence), South Asian nations need to ease restrictions on foreign direct investment (FDI) in the health sector. They should also ensure that domestic regulations are transparent. These steps can help attract more FDI in healthcare. Mode 4 (movement of natural persons) is also important for South Asia. Countries such as Bangladesh, Pakistan, Afghanistan, Nepal, and Sri Lanka have a large and varied healthcare workforce. India is powerful in exporting such services. Therefore, South Asian countries should consider easing rules to allow the movement of healthcare professionals. This would also encourage support from developed and other developing nations. However, one major challenge is the low quality of education in some parts of the region. This makes it hard to prepare new workers for the healthcare sector. All four modes of service trade influence how South Asian countries absorb new technologies in healthcare. In February 2019, the Indian government broadened its e-tourism visa framework to make the application and travel process easier for medical tourists. Under this provision, foreign visitors can stay in India for up to 6 months. Furthermore, from 30 August 2019, rules were revised to allow foreign nationals to receive most medical treatments in India without requiring a medical visa, except for organ transplants. In an exciting development announced in August 2023, the Government of India's Ministry of Home Affairs introduced the Ayush Visa category,[14] specifically promoting travel for healthcare purposes.

---

[13] In the context of the World Trade Organization (WTO), "Mode 1, 2, 3, and 4" refer to the four different ways services can be traded internationally, categorised as: Mode 1: Cross-border supply, Mode 2: Consumption abroad, Mode 3: Commercial presence, and Mode 4: Presence of natural persons; essentially describing how a service is delivered from one country to another, whether through physical movement of goods, consumer travel, setting up a business entity abroad, or sending individuals to provide services directly.

[14] The Ayush (AY) visa is a visa category for foreign nationals who want to receive medical treatment in India using Ayush or other traditional Indian systems of medicine. The Ayush visa is available in four sub-categories:

- Ayush Visa (AY-1): For foreign nationals seeking treatment under the Ayush system.
- Ayush Attendant Visa (AY-2): For attendants or family members of patients with an AY-1 visa.
- e-Ayush Visa: An electronic version of the Ayush visa,
- e-Ayush Attendant Visa: An electronic version of the Ayush Attendant visa.

To apply for an Ayush visa, the applicant should submit:

- A medical invitation letter from an accredited Ayush institution.
- A document that explains your medical history and why you need treatment.
- A passport that's valid for at least 180 days.
- A completed application form.

You can apply for an Ayush visa through the regular paper visa option or the e-visa portal.

In conclusion, South Asian countries must take cautious yet progressive steps to eliminate trade restrictions on services, particularly in the health sector. This will ultimately strengthen the region's overall health delivery system, enabling it to confront future extraordinary health challenges effectively.

References

Adhikari M (2022) Promises and perils of regional response to COVID-19 in Asia. Political Settlements Research Programme (PSRP)

Arora PK, Chaturvedi PR (2024) Ayushman Bharat Pradhan Mantri Jan Arogya Yojana: evolution and journey so far. Curr Med Res Practice 14(2):49–52

Banik A (2020) Trade in health Services in South Asia. Springer Singapore

Banik A, Bhaumik PK (2014) Assessing the barriers to trade in services in South Asia. Glob Bus Rev 15(4):795–814

Banik A, Bhaumik PK (2020) India: emerging as major destination of quality healthcare services. In: Trade in health services in South Asia: an examination of the need for regional cooperation. Springer, pp 105–126

Banik A, Nag T, Chowdhury SR, Chatterjee R (2020) Why do COVID-19 fatality rates differ across countries? An explorative cross-country study based on select indicators. Glob Bus Rev 21(3):607–625

Government of India (2021) National Family Health Survey-2019-20 (NFHS 5). Ministry of Health and Family Welfare, New Delhi

Iqbal N (2023) Three charts on Ayushman Bharat's achievements and shortfalls. Indiaspend. Available at: https://www.indiaspend.com/data-viz/three-charts-on-ayushman-bharats-achievements-and-shortfalls-878004

Kanwal S, Kumar D, Chauhan R, Raina SK (2024) Measuring the effect of Ayushman Bharat-Pradhan Mantri Jan Aarogya Yojna (AB-PMJAY) on health expenditure among poor admitted in a tertiary Care Hospital in the Northern State of India. Indian J Community Med 49(2):342–348

Kumar R (2019) Public–private partnerships for universal health coverage? The future of "free health" in Sri Lanka. Glob Health 15(Suppl 1):75

Mishra S (2020) In India's COVID funds for SAARC nations, Nepal gets Lion's share. The Week, 3 December 2020

NCAER (2023) National Data Innovation Centre, Delhi. Available at: https://www.ncaer.org/news/a-remedy-for-health-insurance. Accessed 23 Jan 2025

Patel, M.R. (2025) Financial Toxicity in Diabetes: The State of What We Know. Curr Diab Rep 25, (32) https://doi.org/10.1007/s11892-025-01588-0

Sharma D, Chauhan AS, Guinness L, Mehndiratta A, Dhiman A, Singh M, Prinja S (2024) Understanding the extent of economic evidence usage for informing policy decisions in the context of India's national health insurance scheme: Ayushman Bharat Pradhan Mantri Jan Aarogya Yojana (PM-JAY). BMJ Glob Health 9(6):e015079

Thakur R, Faizan MA (2024) Magnitude of health expenditure induced removable poverty in India: some reflections of Ayushman Bharat. Heliyon 10(1)

Torrey T (2024) Levels of medical care: primary, secondary, tertiary, and quaternary. Verywell Health. Available at: https://www.verywellhealth.com/primary-secondary-tertiary-and-quaternary-care-2615354

UNICEF (2021) Accelerating progress towards universal health coverage in South Asia in the era of COVID-19. Available at: https://www.unicef.org/rosa/media/17021/file/Accelerating%20progress%20towards%20Universal%20Health

WHO (2020) Health Systems | Universal Health Coverage, World Health Organisation. Accessed 24 Jun 2020

World Bank (2020) South Asia economic focus, spring 2020: the cursed blessing of public banks. World Bank, Washington, DC

Chapter 9
Final Thoughts and Policy Insights

Abstract In conclusion, this book provides a comprehensive analysis of the post-pandemic situation in South Asia, highlighting the region's unique challenges and responses. The pandemic has exacerbated existing socio-economic vulnerabilities, with significant repercussions on health systems, economic stability, and educational outcomes. Through a detailed examination of healthcare interventions, vaccination strategies, and economic policies, this book underscores the critical role of digital tools and innovative governance in navigating the crisis. It emphasises the importance of effective policy implementation and regional cooperation to enhance healthcare access and mitigate poverty. The findings reveal that while South Asian countries initially managed to contain the virus's spread, the economic toll has been profound, particularly in nations like India, where lockdowns led to substantial GDP losses. The analysis also points to the urgent need for adaptive mitigation strategies, including universal health insurance schemes and regulatory reforms, to address systemic deficiencies in healthcare delivery. Ultimately, this book advocates for a collaborative approach to healthcare integration, leveraging the region's human capital and fostering sustainable economic growth in the post-pandemic landscape, thereby laying the groundwork for a more resilient future.

Keywords Post-Pandemic challenges · South Asia · Healthcare Infrastructure · Economic Impact · Vaccination Strategies · Policy Insights

The COVID-19 pandemic emerged as a significant global event, leaving a profound and lasting impact on societies and economies worldwide. Its effects have severely affected health systems, economies, and poverty levels. The extent of the pandemic's impact has varied significantly across different nations and regions, influencing the lives of millions based on the unique characteristics of each locale. A key factor contributing to the differences in COVID-19 fatality rates is the varying states of healthcare infrastructure, demographic profiles, and vaccination strategies adopted by countries, including the use of the BCG vaccine. With an estimated 7.08 million

A. Banik et al., *Extraordinary Health Hazards and their Socio-Economic Effects in South Asia*, South Asia Economic and Policy Studies,
https://doi.org/10.1007/978-981-95-5729-5_9

(Mathieu et al. 2020)[1] deaths globally and the deepest economic recession since World War II, the pandemic has had diverse regional repercussions (Raihan and Islam 2024). For instance, South Asia faced a variety of health and economic challenges. India recorded over 534,000 deaths and experienced a sharp economic downturn, while other nations in the region were affected to a lesser degree. The reported death tolls in other countries include Pakistan with 30,656 deaths, Bangladesh with 29,446, Sri Lanka with 16,728, Nepal with 12,031, Afghanistan with 7789, Maldives with 308, and Bhutan with just 21.[2] The relatively short duration of the pandemic, aided by global measures such as lockdowns, social distancing, and rapid vaccine distribution, enabled a quicker economic recovery bolstered by unprecedented counter-cyclical policies.[3]

This book delves deeply into a spectrum of scenarios surrounding the COVID-19 pandemic, meticulously examining various interventions and their effectiveness, with a special emphasis on the economies of South Asia. It presents an in-depth analysis of healthcare systems' demand and supply dynamics across four distinct health service levels in South Asia before and during the pandemic. One of the striking findings revealed by the investigation is that nearly all initiatives employed information technology as a vital tool to amplify their reach and scalability, underscoring the essential role that digital tools played in public health responses during this crisis. Through a thorough examination, the book critiques various health sector interventions. It scrutinises policies related to vaccination campaigns, the enhancement of health infrastructure, and the overall efficacy of these measures in the face of the COVID-19 challenge. This book emphasises that implementing healthcare policies effectively is as important as the policies themselves; the administration and monitoring processes are critical for achieving meaningful outcomes. In addition, it seeks to illuminate the innovative governance strategies that various nations adopted to navigate the unprecedented challenges brought on by the pandemic adeptly.

---

[1] Updated January 21, 2025. As of January 2023, taking into account likely COVID-induced deaths through excess mortality, the 95% confidence interval suggests that the pandemic has caused between 19.1 million and 36 million deaths. See *"The pandemic's true death toll"—The Economist.*

Ritchie, Hannah; Mathieu, Edouard; Rodés-Guirao, Lucas; Appel, Cameron; Giattino, Charlie; Ortiz-Ospina, Esteban; Hasell, Joe; Macdonald, Bobbie; Beltekian, Diana; Roser, Max (5 March 2020). *"Coronavirus Pandemic (COVID-19)". Our World in Data.*

[2] Coronavirus COVID-19 Global Cases by the Center for Systems Science and Engineering (CSSE) at Johns Hopkins University (JHU)". Retrieved 3 December 2023.

[3] Countercyclical policies are economic or financial strategies designed to counteract the natural cyclical fluctuations of the economy. These policies seek to stabilise economic performance by mitigating the effects of economic cycles. For instance, the government may increase spending and lower taxes during a recession to stimulate recovery. Conversely, during periods of economic expansion, the government might raise taxes and cut spending to manage inflation and reduce debt. Examples of countercyclical policies include progressive taxation, which imposes a higher tax rate on income as the economy expands, and infrastructure spending, where the government increases investment in infrastructure in response to potential recession threats. Regarding economic theory, Keynesian economics supports implementing countercyclical policies, while New Classical macroeconomics advocates a laissez-faire fiscal approach.

The book comprises four comprehensive pillars or objectives to structure the discourse. First, it lays a solid foundation by examining the economic and socio-economic landscapes of South Asian countries before the pandemic, which played a significant role in determining their performances throughout the crisis. Second, it provides an overview of the nature and scale of interventions executed in response to the pandemic. Third, it assesses the outcomes from multiple perspectives during and after COVID-19. Lastly, it explores preparations for adaptive mitigation, including designing health insurance schemes to protect these economies from the grave risks of extreme poverty that catastrophic health events can precipitate. Throughout its chapters, this book aspires to present a series of regional snapshots from various perspectives. It integrates discussions on the obstacles within the health service sector, offers insights into the four tiers of the healthcare system, and stresses the urgent need for regional cooperation and integration as essential components for enhancing overall welfare in South Asia.

It has been observed that the COVID-19 pandemic has presented significant challenges to the economies of South Asia, a region marked by a large population, widespread poverty, and inadequate socioeconomic conditions. With more than one-third of the world's poorest individuals living in South Asia, where a substantial majority rely on agriculture in rural areas, the impact of the pandemic has been particularly profound. Before the outbreak, approximately 649 million people in South Asia faced moderate to severe food insecurity, with a staggering 271 million grappling with severe food scarcity. Alarmingly, 16% of children in the region exhibited signs of severe malnutrition, while 36% suffered from stunted growth. The onset of COVID-19 has intensified these challenges, further deteriorating the region's already fragile economic stability.[4]

South Asia is home to bustling megacities such as Delhi, Mumbai, Karachi, and Dhaka, all of which face extraordinarily high population densities. Many residents struggle to access necessities, including adequate hygiene, sanitation, and clean water. For example, nearly 42% of Afghan households are forced to consume contaminated water, while over 50% lack the soap and water essential for proper hand hygiene (Temory 2023). The combination of high population density, poor living conditions, and unfavourable working circumstances significantly hinders efforts to maintain social distancing. Economic constraints burden most of the population, leaving them with limited resources and a fragile ability to cope with the impacts of a pandemic. Additionally, many individuals depend solely on informal or self-employment, which means they do not benefit from social or health safety nets.

In light of these challenges, South Asian countries initially managed to contain the virus's spread and protect lives more effectively than many developed nations. However, this relative success came at a significant economic cost, as prolonged lockdowns severely disrupted economic activities. The study indicates that a 1-month lockdown can result in an astonishing annual GDP loss between 1.5% and

[4] https://en.wikipedia.org/wiki/COVID-19_pandemic_in_South_Asia accessed on January 21, 2025.

2.0%. In India alone, each day of lockdown is estimated to lead to an economic loss of approximately $4.64 billion.

Chapters 4 and 5 examined the economic ramifications of COVID-19 and the challenges faced by South Asia. Various estimates highlight the significant struggles within the region, which have been exacerbated by limited fiscal capacity. As a result, the pandemic led to severe output losses and a notable increase in poverty and unemployment levels across South Asia. Among these nations, India experienced the most profound impact. According to the World Bank,[5] in 2020, the region's output contracted by an estimated 6.7%, mainly reflecting the pandemic's fallout and nationwide lockdowns, particularly in India and Bangladesh. However, economic activity began to recover in the latter half of the year, buoyed by a resurgence in industrial production as initial stringent lockdown measures were relaxed. The pandemic hit India while it was already contending with a deceleration in economic growth; consequently, the output contracted by 9.6% in the fiscal year 2020/2021, primarily due to significant declines in household spending and private investment. The informal sector, which accounts for approximately 80% of employment, also suffered considerable income losses during this period.

In the rest of the region, while the economic impact of COVID-19 has been somewhat less severe, it remains significant in South Asia. Economies heavily reliant on tourism and travel, such as the Maldives, Nepal, and Sri Lanka, have been particularly affected. Bangladesh, one of the fastest-growing emerging markets and developing economies before the pandemic, saw growth slow to an estimated 2% in the financial year 2019/2020. In Pakistan, growth is projected to have contracted by 1.5% during the same period, influenced by localised COVID-19 containment measures and the effects of pre-outbreak monetary and fiscal tightening.

The COVID-19 pandemic caused significant disruptions to development, leading to a substantial decline in human capital for millions of children and young people across South Asia. For example, in Bangladesh, nearly 15 months of school closures resulted in an estimated 26 months' worth of learning loss. In Tamil Nadu, India, students returning to in-person learning exhibited marked deficiencies in their reading and math skills. In Pakistan, children from the poorest households fell further behind in math during the pandemic compared to their wealthier peers, underscoring the widening educational gap.

Additionally, notable declines in cognitive and social-emotional development have been documented across the region. In Bangladesh, toddlers tested in 2022 performed significantly worse than those assessed in 2019. Furthermore, school enrolment in several South Asian countries has not rebounded to pre-pandemic levels. By the end of 2021, preschool enrolment in Pakistan had decreased by over 15% points. Additionally, enrolment among children aged 6–14 in Pakistan dropped by 6% points after schools reopened, resulting in 7.6 million children withdrawing from school entirely. Across South Asia, there has been a dramatic rise in the

[5] https://thedocs.worldbank.org/en/doc/171081599838759959-0050022020/original/GlobalEconomicProspectsJanuary2021RegionalOverviewSAR.pdf. Accessed on January 25, 2025.

number of individuals neither employed nor enrolled in education or training. Moreover, in several countries, evidence of recovery has been scarce even after 18 months.[6]

The immediate shock of the pandemic had a profound impact across the region, leading to significant disruptions, including large-scale migration, decreased outputs from micro, small, and medium enterprises (MSMEs), supply chain constraints, labour shortages, and demand shocks. Nevertheless, despite these considerable challenges, South Asia has adeptly navigated the aftermath, bolstered by comprehensive vaccination campaigns, a youthful population, and proactive policy initiatives to mitigate the pandemic's effects.

During the COVID-19 pandemic, the Government of India implemented various initiatives to address crucial aspects, including trade and economic development, while tackling the challenges posed by the virus in the region. On 15 March 2020, a significant moment occurred when the Prime Minister of India convened a video conference with South Asian Association for Regional Cooperation (SAARC) member states. This meeting represented the first substantial convening of regional leaders since 2014 and catalysed the establishment of the COVID-19 Emergency Fund. Initially, the fund received an allocation of ten million US$, further augmented by voluntary contributions from SAARC countries, totalling eight million US$ (Adhikari 2022).

Despite this encouraging start, the subsequent distribution of the fund has been relatively restrained. By December 2020, reports indicated that financial assistance was disbursed to various countries, including Indian rupees (INR) 6.12 crore (approximately US $845,000) to Nepal, 3.64 crores (around US $500,000) to Bangladesh, 1.69 crores (about US $233,000) to Bhutan, 1.55 crores (nearly US $213,000) to Sri Lanka, 60.14 lakh (approximately US $83,000) to the Maldives, and 29.3 lakhs (around US $40,436) to Afghanistan. Notably, Pakistan did not receive any allocation from the fund (Mishra 2020).

It is important to emphasise the efforts surrounding vaccine development, distribution, and vaccination in India. The country has a strong vaccine production capacity. In January 2021, the Drug Controller General of India authorised two vaccines. The first, Covishield, was developed by Oxford University and AstraZeneca and is produced locally by the Serum Institute of India (SII) (Basu and Srivastava 2022). The second vaccine, Covaxin, was developed and manufactured in India by Bharat Biotech. As a leading global vaccine manufacturer, India was expected to immunise its population and distribute vaccines to other nations in Asia and Africa. India took a humanitarian approach through its "Vaccine Maitri" initiative, delivering millions of doses of its COVID-19 vaccines to South Asian countries and beyond shortly after vaccinating segments of its population.

In line with its "Neighbourhood First" policy, India prioritised vaccine delivery to its immediate neighbours, including Afghanistan, Bhutan, Bangladesh, Nepal,

[6] https://www.worldbank.org/en/news/press-release/2023/02/16/covid-19-s-impact-on-south-asia-s-youth-could-last-generations. Accessed on January 25, 2025.

the Maldives, Sri Lanka, and Myanmar. On January 20, 2021, Bhutan and the Maldives became the first countries to receive 150,000 and 100,000 doses, respectively (Singh et al. 2023). Bangladesh and Nepal received two million and one million doses the following day. By late January, India donated 500,000 doses of the COVID-19 vaccine to Sri Lanka, marking the beginning of that country's vaccine rollout. Despite China's attempts to expand its influence in the region, Sri Lanka and Bangladesh chose Indian vaccines over Chinese alternatives.

On 22 January, Myanmar received 1.5 million doses as part of India's vaccine diplomacy. Approximately one-fourth of India's total COVID-19 vaccine supply has been allocated to South Asian countries. This highlights that these geographical neighbours are a top priority and account for 29.44% of India's global vaccine distribution. On 8 February 2021, India donated over half a million COVID-19 vaccine doses to Afghanistan, a war-torn nation. The Afghan government described India's vaccine initiative as a "strong sign of generosity and sincere cooperation" (Singh et al. 2023).

In South Asia, the ability to vaccinate the population is significantly shaped by various political, economic, and social factors. The pace of vaccination in the region has highlighted a critical supply shortage, as major vaccine-producing nations prioritised their own needs. Countries such as Bangladesh, Pakistan, and Sri Lanka have encountered challenges from limited expertise, inadequate raw materials, and insufficient infrastructure to bolster their vaccine production capabilities (Rowland et al. 2021). Consequently, these nations heavily rely on vaccine supplies from larger producers like China, Russia, and India. However, after experiencing a devastating second wave of infections, India has struggled to secure vaccines for its citizens, adversely affecting the availability of vaccines for neighbouring countries, including Bangladesh and Sri Lanka (Basu and Srivastava 2022).

The demand side concept in healthcare has emerged as a pivotal strategy for addressing the critical access and utilisation challenges faced by low-income populations in developing countries, particularly in South Asia. The COVID-19 pandemic's economic repercussions have exacerbated these issues, resulting in widespread job losses and the consequent erosion of employer-sponsored health benefits that served as vital safety nets. In response, some South Asian governments have introduced universal health insurance schemes; however, these initiatives have not yielded the anticipated outcomes. They have often failed to adequately mitigate the significant supply side deficiencies, notably in the availability of healthcare professionals and hospital infrastructure.

A substantial segment of the population remains uninsured, primarily due to the prohibitive costs of available health insurance options. This renders them vulnerable to health risks without adequate coverage throughout their lives. This underscores the pressing need to pivot towards innovative demand-side interventions within South Asian economies. Key areas for focus include regulatory measures, access to transportation, sustainable insurance frameworks, and adequate price controls, which are essential for fostering a more equitable healthcare environment.

Moreover, it is important to recognise that healthcare professionals in public hospitals often serve as scapegoats for systemic deficiencies. Allegations of negligence are frequently politicised, overshadowing the underlying issues of supply shortages and systemic inefficiencies. The stark imbalance between healthcare demand and supply frequently culminates in the denial of necessary medical services for many individuals.

To navigate these challenges effectively, it is imperative to establish regulatory frameworks that balance sophistication and minimalism, ensuring they do not impede innovation and growth in the healthcare sector while seeking to prevent malpractice. For instance, while price controls may appear straightforward, they can lead to unintended repercussions, including shortages, compromised quality, or inflated costs in other critical areas. Rather than alleviating supply side challenges, such measures may inadvertently exacerbate the issues they intend to address. A compelling argument posits that promoting transparency and fostering healthy competition within the healthcare market could facilitate significant price reductions. This strategy would enhance the overall quality of care and invigorate India's burgeoning medical tourism industry, creating jobs and stimulating economic growth.

We undertook an in-depth analysis of the Ayushman Bharat initiative, the cornerstone of the Government of India's strategy to achieve Universal Health Coverage (UHC) in alignment with the National Health Policy 2017. Ayushman Bharat signifies a transformative move from a fragmented, sector-based healthcare delivery system toward a more integrated, demand-driven framework. The initiative aims for systemic reform across the healthcare continuum, bridging preventive, promotive, and ambulatory care across primary, secondary, and tertiary settings. Central to this initiative is a continuum of care model encompassing two synergistic components: Health and Wellness Centres (HWCs) and the Pradhan Mantri Jan Arogya Yojana (PM-JAY). This dual strategy aims to improve access, quality, and health outcomes across the demographic spectrum. Expanding the health insurance scheme's demand side has effectively broadened its reach, with approximately 56% of eligible beneficiaries enrolled within a 5-year timeframe. However, this progress exposes a significant supply side challenge. Empirical studies from various states indicate a troubling deficit of empanelled hospitals available to registered beneficiaries. This imbalance has culminated in elevated out-of-pocket healthcare expenditures, imposing a notable financial strain on numerous families.

The integration of the healthcare systems in South Asia carries significant policy implications for addressing emerging health challenges in the region. First, India boasts a robust cadre of trained healthcare professionals, providing a comparative advantage in the cross-border supply of healthcare services through Modes 1 (cross-border supply) and 2 (consumption abroad). Liberalising these sectors for transnational service provision has significant potential to enhance trade flows of healthcare services within South Asia. Such an integrated framework would allow member states and stakeholders in the health sector to harness the synergies offered by regional collaboration. Secondly, to facilitate service trade under Mode 3 (commercial presence), South Asian countries must implement reforms to liberalise foreign direct investment (FDI) and establish clear and transparent domestic regulatory frameworks governing health services. These reforms are likely to attract foreign investors, ultimately stimulating an increase in FDI within the health sector.

Moreover, South Asia plays a vital role as an exporter of healthcare services through Mode 4 (the movement of natural persons). Countries like Bangladesh, Pakistan, Afghanistan, Nepal, and Sri Lanka possess significant labour pools with varied skill sets in healthcare. At the same time, India maintains a comparative advantage in exporting services via this mode. Thus, regional governments must prepare for the potential liberalisation of the movement of natural persons, facilitating the influx of professional expertise from developed nations and other emerging economies.

There are persistent and pressing concerns regarding the educational standards currently prevailing within the region. Many of these standards often fall short of adequately preparing individuals for effective integration into the healthcare workforce, which is crucial for addressing the growing demands of healthcare delivery. The various modes of service provision, ranging from public health initiatives to private healthcare solutions, have significant implications for comprehending how technology spillover can enhance the healthcare sector across South Asia. These implications become particularly pronounced when considering the rapid advancements in medical technology and practices that could be adopted regionally. However, to fully capitalise on these advancements, it is essential to address the existing deficiencies in educational frameworks and training programmes. This is not only vital for ensuring that new entrants into the healthcare field are properly equipped with the necessary skills and knowledge, but also for fostering a robust, responsive healthcare system that can adapt to the evolving needs of the population. In summary, a focused effort to enhance educational standards within the region is imperative. By doing so, the benefits of regional integration can be maximised, ultimately leading to improved healthcare outcomes and a more competent and skilled healthcare workforce ready to meet the challenges of today and tomorrow.

References

Adhikari M (2022) Promises and perils of regional response to Covid-19 in Asia. Political Settlements Research Programme (PSRP)

Basu D, Srivastava P (2022) COVID-19 in South Asia: health, economics and politics. Invest Econ 81(319):117–140

Mathieu E, Ritchie H, Rodés-Guirao L, Appel C, Gavrilov D, Giattino C, Hasell J, Macdonald B, Dattani S, Beltekian D, Ortiz-Ospina E (2020) Excess mortality during the Coronavirus pandemic (COVID-19). *Our world in data*

Mishra S (2020) In India's COVID funds for SAARC nations, Nepal gets lion's share. *The Week*, 3 December 2020

Raihan S, Islam I (2024) COVID-19 and South Asia: an overview. J Asia Pac Econ 29(4):1685–1693

Rowland C, Ruahla E, Berger M (2021) Drug companies defend vaccine monopolies in face of global outcry. *The Washington Post*, *20*. Published on March 20

Singh B, Singh S, Singh B, Chattu VK (2023) India's neighbourhood vaccine diplomacy during the COVID-19 pandemic: humanitarian and geopolitical perspectives. J Asian Afr Stud 58(6):1021–1037

Temory MD (2023) Impact of COVID-19 pandemic on households income and food security in Afghanistan: case study of Kabul, Kandahar, Nangarhar and Balkh. Int J Fish Aquac Res 9(1):14–31

Index

A. Banik et al., *Extraordinary Health Hazards and their Socio-Economic Effects in South Asia*, South Asia Economic and Policy Studies,
https://doi.org/10.1007/978-981-95-5729-5

MIX
Papier aus verantwortungsvollen Quellen
Paper from responsible sources
FSC® C105338

FSC
www.fsc.org

If you have any concerns about our products,
you can contact us on
ProductSafety@springernature.com

In case Publisher is established outside the EU,
the EU authorized representative is:
Springer Nature Customer Service Center GmbH
Europaplatz 3, 69115 Heidelberg, Germany

Printed by Libri Plureos GmbH
in Hamburg, Germany